Theory and Practice

Theory and Practice

by Jürgen Habermas

Translated by John Viertel

Beacon Press   Boston

Theory and Practice is an abridgment by the author of the fourth edition of *Theorie und Praxis* published in 1971 by Suhrkamp Verlag to which he has added "Arbeit und Interaktion" from *Technik und Wissenschaft als "Ideologie"* published by Suhrkamp Verlag

English translation: © 1973 by Beacon Press

German text: Chapters 1, 2, 3, 6, and 7 © 1963 by Hermann Luchterhand Verlag GmbH; Chapter 5 © 1966 by Suhrkamp Verlag; Chapter 6 © 1968 by Suhrkamp Verlag; and Introduction © 1971 by Suhrkamp Verlag

Beacon Press books are published under the auspices of the Unitarian Universalist Association

First published as a Beacon Paperback in 1974

Published simultaneously in Canada by Saunders of Toronto, Ltd.
Printed in the United States of America

9 8 7 6 5 4 3

Library of Congress Cataloging in Publication Data

Habermas, Jürgen.
    Theory and practice.
    Translation of Theorie und Praxis.
    Includes bibliographical references.
    1. Sociology—Addresses, essays, lectures.
2. Political science—Addresses, essays, lectures.
I. Title.
HM33.H313   301'.01   72–6227
ISBN 0–8070–1526–1
ISBN 0–8070–1527–X (pbk.)

Contents

Translator's Note on German Terms

The difficulties which spring from the fact that crucial terms in German have a quite different range of meaning and connotation from any of the available English equivalents will not be unfamiliar to anyone who has occupied himself with German philosophy, social theory, or psychology. The glossary below is intended to recall some of the main problems that arise as a consequence and to explain the usage adopted in this translation.

Anschauung—English translations of Kant have established "intuition" as the equivalent English term, which raises the problem that this English word has connotations quite different from Kant's intention of reference to the processes of sense perception—inner and outer—and their product. In many contexts, such as *Weltanschauung*, simply "view" has seemed preferable, or even, in some cases, "sense perception" or "perceiving."

Anthropologisch, Anthropologie—the philosophical theory of man and *not* the science of anthropology as it has developed largely in the twentieth century.

Bürger, bürgerlich—*Bürger* means "burgher" (townsman) and also "citizen": thus *amerikanischer Staatsbürger* = citizen of the United States. Furthermore, especially in the Marxist tradition, both noun and adjective have taken on the meaning of the English loanword "bourgeois." The meaning range of the adjective is even wider. Thus, *bürgerliches Recht* can mean either "bourgeois law" or "civil law" or both.

Dezision, also *Entscheidung*—*Dezision* generally used in the context of *Dezisionismus,* an existentialist approach stressing the reaching of a decision rather than its content, and associated in Germany with National Socialist ideology. As the emphasis implies arriving at a pure and uncritical commitment, it seemed

preferable, in various contexts, to translate *Dezision* as "commitment."

Entäussern, Entäusserung—generally, to externalize, externalization; but also: *sich entäussern*—self-alienation.

Erlebnis—there are two German words meaning "experience": *Erlebnis* and the more abstract and general *Erfahrung;*
with its root *leben* (live) *Erlebnis* therefore has the connotation
of "life-experience," an experience through which the subject has
lived.

Geisteswissenschaft—the difficulty here is related to the familiar problem of translating *Geist. Geisteswissenschaft,* literally
the mental or spiritual sciences. It has been translated variously
as "humanities," "sciences of man," "social sciences," etc. In
Knowledge and Human Interest as "cultural sciences."

Mündigkeit—literally "majority" in the sense "legally of
age." For Kant mankind's "majority" is the historical goal of
enlightenment (in "What Is Enlightenment?"). To preserve this
developmental connotation I have generally preferred "mature
autonomy."

Naturrecht, Recht—as *Recht* means both "right" and "law"
(in the legal sense), so *Naturrecht* can be translated as either
"natural right" or "natural law." I have generally preferred the
latter, as in the tradition treated the association of "natural law"
with "law of nature" is important. The German term, of course,
does not have this connotation. So too *Rechtszustand* (legal
order), *Rechtspflege* (jurisprudence), *Staatsrecht* (constitutional
law), etc.

Objektivieren—objectivate, objectivation; "to give form in a
symbolic system, that is, to make into a vehicle for communicative
action. The latter may become external to the subject in the sense
that others participate in it, but it is at the same time that in
which the subject exists" (J. J. Shapiro in *Knowledge and Human
Interest,* footnote 23 to chapter 2).

Praxis—the title *Theorie und Praxis* has been rendered
Theory and Practice, as "practice" in this direct juxtaposition to
"theory" clearly gives the meaning of the German word. However,
in English "practice" has a different range of meaning; therefore,
in other contexts "praxis" was preferred, as it seemed to me that

clarity and accessibility would outweigh the danger of using a term the meaning of which is to be explored in the work itself.

Schein has a very large range of meaning—appearance, illusion, shining (as a light); generally "semblance" seemed the preferable translation.

Sozialstaat—literally "social state," but actually the equivalent of "welfare state" in our usage.

Verhalten—behavior, conduct, comportment; the latter two equivalents have been preferred where the connection with a specific approach which "behavior" has acquired was to be avoided.

Vorstellung—usually "representation" in the English rendering of Kantian terminology; I have generally preferred the more ordinary meaning "conception."

Willensbildung—literally "formation of the will," but associated (a) with the concept of the general or public will, and (b) *Bildung* as formation, education, cultivation. "Decision making" thus represents the same process, but with a somewhat different conceptual background.

Zerstreuung—means not only "dispersal" but also "amusement," "diversion."

Further remarks on terminology can be found in Jeremy J. Shapiro's "Translator's Preface" to Habermas, *Toward a Rational Society,* and throughout the notes to *Knowledge and Human Interest* (again translated by Shapiro).

I am very much indebted to Jeremy J. Shapiro for numerous suggestions and emendations which greatly improved the clarity and accuracy of the translation. I also want to express my gratitude to Lois M. Randall, whose patience, competence, and good taste contributed so much in the editing of the text.

John Viertel

Introduction:

Some Difficulties in the Attempt to Link Theory and Praxis

In the preface to the first German edition I held out the prospect of a systematic investigation into the relationship between theory and praxis. I have not progressed much beyond this announcement of intent but this does not mean that since that time I have neglected this theme. On the contrary, my published work since then shows that the problem has in no way relaxed its hold on me. This new edition of *Theory and Practice* [fourth German edition] presents a welcome opportunity for me to ascertain in a retrospective view (of necessity a somewhat hasty one), where the studies I have undertaken up to this point have led me.

"Theory and Praxis"

The investigations collected in this volume, in which the orientation has been predominantly historical, were to develop the idea of a theory of society conceived with a practical intention, and to delimit its status with respect to theories of different origins. Historical materialism aims at achieving an explanation of social evolution which is so comprehensive that it embraces the interrelationships of the theory's own origins and application. The theory specifies the conditions under which reflection on the history of our species by members of this species themselves has become objectively possible; and at the same time it names those to whom this theory is addressed, who then with its aid can gain enlightenment about their emancipatory role in the process of history. The theory occupies itself with reflection on the inter-relationships of its origin and with anticipation of those of its application, and thus sees itself as a necessary catalytic moment within the social complex of life which it analyzes; and this com-plex it analyzes as integral interconnections of compulsions, from the viewpoint of the possible sublation—resolution and abolition —of all this.

The theory thus encompasses a dual relationship between theory and praxis. On the one hand, it investigates the constitu-tive historical complex of the constellation of self-interests, to which the theory still belongs across and beyond its acts of in-sight. On the other hand, it studies the historical interconnec-tions of action, in which the theory, as action-oriented, can in-tervene. In the one case, we have a social praxis, which, as societal synthesis, makes insight possible; in the other case, a political praxis which consciously aims at overthrowing the existing sys-tem of institutions. Because of its reflection on its own origins, critique is to be distinguished from science as well as from philos-ophy. For the sciences focus away from their constitutive contexts and confront the domain of their subject matter with an objec-tivistic posture; while, obversely, philosophy has been only too conscious of its origins as something that had ontological primacy. By anticipating the context of its own application, critique dif-fers from what Horkheimer has called "traditional theory." Cri-tique understands that its claims to validity can be verified only in the successful process of enlightenment, and that means: in the practical discourse of those concerned. Critique renounces the contemplative claims of theories constructed in monologic form, and in addition, discerns that all philosophy up till now, in spite of all its claims, also only presumes to have such a contemplative character.[1]

To be sure, these assertions are not systematically developed in this volume, but only treated in connection with the history of the problem, in which the Aristotelian distinction between *praxis* and *techne* serves as the connecting thread. As opposed to the classical doctrine of Natural Law,[2] modern social philosophy can assert its claims to a competitive status: to be taken seriously from a scientific viewpoint, only at the cost of a separation from that connection with experience which practical philosophy maintains. Social philosophy, having taken on monologic form, is no longer capable of essentially relating to praxis, but merely to goal-directed purposive action guided by social-technical recommendations. Within this framework historical materialism can be understood as a theory of society conceived with a practical intent, which avoids the complementary weaknesses both of traditional politics and of modern social philosophy; it thus unites the claim to a scientific character with a theoretical structure referring to praxis. In later investigations I have sought to clarify further three aspects of the relation between theory and praxis: (1) the empirical aspect of the relationship between science, politics, and public opinion in advanced capitalistic social systems; (2) the epistemological aspect of the relation between knowledge and interest; (3) the methodological aspect of a social theory which aims at being capable of assuming the role of a critique.

The public sphere

Technical questions are posed with a view to the rationally goal-directed organization of means and the rational selection of instrumental alternatives, once the goals (values and maxims) are given. Practical questions, on the other hand, are posed with a view to the acceptance or rejection of norms, especially norms for action, the claims to validity of which we can support or oppose with reasons. Theories which in their structure can serve the clarification of practical questions are designed to enter into communicative action. Interpretations which can be gained within the framework of such theories cannot, of course, be directly effective for the orientation of action; rather, they find their legitimate value within the therapeutic context of the reflexive formation of volition.[3] Therefore they can only be translated into processes of enlightenment which are rich in political consequences, when the institutional preconditions for practical discourse among the general public are fulfilled. As long as this is not the case, the restrictive compulsions, that is, the inhibitions to communication which have their origin in the structures of the system, themselves become a problem to be clarified theoretically. With a view to our own social system, this question can be rendered more precise under three headings:

(1) In my introduction to *Student und Politik*[4] and in the studies on *Strukturwandel der Oeffentlichkeit* ["Structural Change of the Public Sphere"] [5] I have analyzed the historical interconnection between the development of capitalism and the rise and dissolution of the liberal public. On the one hand, the fiction of a discursive formation of the will that dissolves political rule was institutionalized for the first time within the political system of the bourgeois constitutional state; on the other hand, the incompatibility of the imperatives that rule the capitalistic economic system with a democratic process for forming the public will has become manifest. The principle of publicity, which initially, on the basis of a public constituted by cultivated, reasoning private persons, capable of enjoying art, asserted, in the medium of the bourgeois press, an unambiguously critical function vis-à-vis the secretiveness which was the praxis of the absolutist state. And for this principle a foundation was secured in the procedures of the constitutional organs; but subsequently it has been transformed in its function for demonstrative and manipulative ends. The ever more densely strung communications network of the electronic mass media today is organized in such a manner that it controls the loyalty of a depoliticized population, rather than serving to make the social and state controls in turn subject to a decentralized and uninhibited discursive formation of the public will, channeled in such a way as to be of consequence—and this in spite of the technical potential for liberation which this technology represents.

(2) In the essays on "Technology and Science as Ideology," [6] on "Technical Progress and the Social Life-World," [7] on "Practical Consequences of Technical-Scientific Progress," [8] and on "The Conditions for Revolutionizing Advanced Capitalistic Social Systems," [9] all of which are closely related in theme, I have investigated two tendencies of development which are characteristic of advanced capitalism (disregarding the forms in which centralization manifests itself), with a view to the depoliticization of the public. I refer in the first place to the cumulative growth, on

the part of the state, of interventionist activity which is designed to secure the stability and growth of the economic system; and secondly, the growing interdependence of research, technology, and governmental administration, which has converted the system of the sciences into a primary force of production. State intervention and planned scientific and technological progress can serve to regulate the imbalances and conflicts which result from a process of production governed by the imperatives of capital investment. Of course, it seems to be the case that the capacity for control by the state administration and the productive potentials of science and technology can only be deployed systematically at the cost of producing a conflict, which, for the time being, can be kept latent. This conflict has the following form: on the one hand, the priorities set under economic imperatives cannot be allowed to depend on a general discursive formation of the public will—therefore politics today assumes the appearance of technocracy. On the other hand, the exclusion of consequential practical questions from discussion by the depoliticized public becomes increasingly difficult, as a result of a long-term erosion of the cultural tradition which formerly had regulated conduct, and which, till now, could be presupposed as a tacit boundary condition of the political system. Because of this, a chronic need for legitimation is developing today.

(3) Finally, in the essays on the politics of science and on the reform of higher education (see "On Social Change in Academic Education" and "Democratization of Higher Education—Politicization of Science";[10] further, the collection *Protest Movement and University Reform,*[11] the essay "The Scientization of Politics and Public Opinion," [12] and the introduction to the *Philosophical-political Profiles,*[13] I have examined what consequences result for the system of the sciences itself from the circumstance that science increasingly plays the role of a primary force of production. Their new political significance, which, for example, has led Luhmann to the consideration of whether in the future the primary functional role in the total societal development will accrue to the system of science, represents both a challenge and a problem for the sciences. To begin with, science can study itself: it can investigate empirically and from various points

of view the organization of scientific and technological progress: this is the task of those complex efforts which then lay claim to the title of a "Science of Science." Furthermore, science can analyze reflectively the social context in which it is embedded not only institutionally, but methodologically, and which at the same time determines the utilization of information scientifically produced; this is the task of a substantive critique of science. Finally, the practical utilization of knowledge, its translation into technologies and strategies, on the one hand, and into communicative praxis on the other, can also be prepared scientifically: this is the task of a praxeology which still remains in its very beginnings, and to which the investigation of possible interactions between science and politics would also belong (for example, in the form of political consultation).

The restructuring of the system of higher education which is now under way can be understood as both a part of technological planning *and* at the same time a reaction against it, as an attempt to constitute the system of the sciences as a political entity. An institution of higher learning which is enlightened with respect to the critique of science, and also politically capable of action, could constitute itself as an advocate to urge that among the alternatives of priority for scientific and technological progress, the decision is not made automatically according to the "natural laws" imposed by the military-industrial viewpoint, but is decided, on the basis of a general discursive formation of will, only after weighing politically the practical consequences.[14]

All these investigations of the empirical relationship between science, politics, and public opinion in advanced capitalistic social systems must remain unsatisfactory as long as even the beginnings of a theory of advanced capitalism have not really been worked out. I feel that today the formulation of such a theory must take its departure from three central complexes of problems. (1) Why does the securing of legitimation become one of the most important problems for the system under advanced capitalism? Are conflicts which could be tolerably controlled by state planning displaced into the political system? Must a theory of political crises replace the theory of economic crises? (2) Can the new potentials for conflict and apathy, characterized by withdrawal of motivation and inclination toward protest, which are supported by the subcultures, lead to a refusal to perform assigned functions, of such dimensions as to endanger the entire system? Are groups which render questionable the fulfillment of important functions within the system, possibly merely passively, identical with groups capable of conscious political action in a crisis situation? Is the process of erosion, which can lead to the crumbling of the functionally necessary legitimation of governing authority and of the motivation for carrying out tasks, at the same time a process of politicization which can create potentials of action? (3) Does a wage labor relation which is now extensively mediated politically still result in compulsion for the organization of the working class and the formation of class consciousness? Can strata within the industrial working class be found, which, for structural reasons, are accessible to political enlightenment and which could be won over for noneconomic goals? Have the motives which form political consciousness emigrated from the spheres of productive labor into other spheres of the occupational system?

Up to now we have developed no hypotheses which are sufficiently precise, and are capable of being tested to provide empirical answers to these questions.[15]

Knowledge and interest

In the social philosophical essays on Theory and Praxis I have not treated epistemological questions systematically. Nor is that the context within which the history of these problems is treated in my book *Knowledge and Human Interests* or in my inaugural lecture of the same title,[16] if one were to apply rigid standards. Still, I have carried my historical investigations and exploratory considerations sufficiently far, that the program for a theory of science becomes clearly discernible, a theory which is intended to be capable of grasping systematically the constitutive conditions of science and those of its application.[17] I have let myself be guided by the problem posed by the system of primitive terms (or the "transcendental framework") within which we organize our experience *a priori* and prior to all science, and do so in

such a manner that, of course, the formation of the scientific object domains is also prejudiced by this. In the functional sphere of instrumental action we encounter objects of the type of móving bodies; here we experience things, events, and conditions which are, in principle, capable of being manipulated. In interactions (or at the level of possible intersubjective communication) we encounter objects of the type of speaking and acting subjects; here we experience persons, utterances, and conditions which in principle are structured and to be understood symbolically. The object domains of the empirical-analytic and of the hermeneutic sciences are based on these objectifications of reality, which we undertake daily always from the viewpoint either of technical control or intersubjective communication. This is revealed by a methodological comparison of the fundamental theoretical concepts, the logical construction of the theorems, the relationship of theory to the object domain, the criteria of verification, the testing procedures, and so forth. Striking above all is the difference in the pragmatic function which the information produced by the different sciences can have. Empirical analytic knowledge can assume the form of causal explanations or conditional predictions, which also refer to the observed phenomena; hermeneutic knowledge as a rule has the form of interpretations of traditional complexes of meaning. There is a systematic relationship between the logical structure of a science and the pragmatic structure of the possible applications of the information generated within its framework.

This differentiated relevance to action of the two categories of science just mentioned, I have traced back to the condition that in the constitution of scientific object domains we merely extend the everyday procedure of objectifying reality under the viewpoints either of technical control or of intersubjective communication. These two viewpoints express anthropologically[18] deep-seated interests, which direct our knowledge and which have a quasi-transcendental status. These interests of knowledge are of significance neither for the psychology nor for the sociology of knowledge, nor for the critique of ideology in any narrower sense; for they are invariant. Nor, on the other hand, can they be traced

back to the biological heritage of a concrete motivational potential; for they are abstract. Rather, they result from the imperatives of a sociocultural life-form dependent on labor and language. Therefore the technical and practical interests of knowledge are not regulators of cognition which have to be eliminated
for the sake of the objectivity of knowledge; instead, they themselves determine the aspect under which reality is objectified, and
can thus be made accessible to experience to begin with. They are
the conditions which are necessary in order that subjects capable
of speech and action may have experience which can lay a claim
to objectivity. Of course, the expression "interest" is intended to
indicate the unity of the life context in which cognition is embedded: expressions capable of truth have reference to a reality
which is objectified (i.e. simultaneously disclosed and constituted)
as such in two different contexts of action and experience. The
underlying "interest" establishes the unity between this constitutive context in which knowledge is rooted and the structure of the
possible application which this knowledge can have.

The sciences do not incorporate into their methodological
understanding of themselves this basis of interest which serves as
the *a priori* link between the origins and the applications of their
theories. However, the critiques which Marx developed as a
theory of society and Freud as metapsychology are distinguished
precisely by incorporating in their consciousness an interest which
directs knowledge, an interest in emancipation going beyond the
technical and the practical interest of knowledge. By treating
psychoanalysis as an analysis of language aiming at reflection
about oneself, I have sought to show how the relations of power
embodied in systematically distorted communication can be attacked directly by the process of critique, so that in the self-
reflection, which the analytic method has made possible and
provoked, in the end insight can coincide with emancipation
from unrecognized dependencies—that is, knowledge coincides
with the fulfillment of the interest in liberation through knowledge.[19] Therefore the relation of theory to therapy is just as constitutive for Freudian theory as the relation of theory to praxis is
for Marxist theory. This can be shown in detail in the logical

form of general interpretations and in the pragmatic achievements of explanatory understanding (in comparison to causal explanation and hermeneutic understanding).

Methodological problems

From the circumstance that theories of the critical type themselves reflect on their (structural) constitutive context and their (potential) context of application, results a changed relation to empirical practice, as a kind of methodological inner view of the relation of theory to practice. In the investigations which were collected in the anthology *On the Logic of the Social Sciences* (Frankfurt 1970) and also in the essay "Universalitäts-anspruch der Hermeneutik" ["The Claim to Universality of Hermeneutics"] as well as in my discussions with Luhmann,[20] I have sought to trace the most important methodological questions, to be sure, in a rather problematic and not sufficiently explicit form: the questions which arise from the program and the conceptual strategy of a theory of society which has practical aims. If we begin with the distinctive position of the cognitive subject with respect to an object domain which is constructed of the generative performance of subjects capable of speech and action, and which at the same time has gained objective power over these subjects, we can delimit our perspective in terms of four competing approaches:

(1) Confronted with the objectivism of strictly behavioral sciences, critical sociology guards itself against a reduction of intentional action to behavior. When the object domain consists of symbolically structured formations which are generated according to underlying rule systems, then the categorial framework cannot remain indifferent toward that which is specific to ordinary language communication. Access to the data via understanding of meanings must be permitted. From this results the problem of measurement which is typical for the social sciences. In place of controlled observation, which guarantees the anonymity (exchangeability) of the observing subject and thus of the reproducibility of the observation, there arises a participatory relation of the understanding subject to the subject confronting him

[*Gegenueber*] (alter ego). The paradigm is no longer the observation but the dialogue—thus, a communication in which the understanding subject must invest a part of his subjectivity, no matter in what manner this may be controllable, in order to be able to meet confronting subjects at all on the intersubjective level which makes understanding possible. To be sure (as the example of the ground rules for the psychoanalytic dialogue shows) this makes disciplinary constraints more necessary than ever. The fashionable demand for a type of "action research," that is to combine political enlightenment with research, overlooks that the uncontrolled modification of the field is incompatible with the simultaneous gathering of data in that field, a condition which is also valid for the social sciences. All operations which can be traced back to the language game of physical measurement (even those with instruments which can only be constructed with the aid of complicated theories) can be coordinated with sense perceptions ("observations") and a thing-event language in which the observations can be expressed descriptively. On the other hand, there is no corresponding system of basic measuring operations with which we can coordinate, in an analogous manner, the understanding of meanings based on the observation of signs, as well as a language expressive of a person, that is, in which the understood utterances could be expressed descriptively. There we resort to interpretation based on hermeneutic disciplines, that is, we employ hermeneutics instead of a measurement procedure, which hermeneutics is not. It can be assumed that a theory of ordinary language communication would first be required which does not perfect communicative competence but rather explains it, in order to permit a controlled translation of communicative experience into data (just as logic provides a normative basis for the construction of measurement procedures in certain investigations into the psychology of cognitive development, or transformational grammar in the investigation of the psycholinguistics of children's language acquisition).

(2) Confronted with the idealism of the hermeneutics developed for the sciences of the mind,[21] critical sociology guards itself against reducing the meaning complexes objectified within social systems to the contents of cultural tradition. Critical of ideology,

it asks what lies behind the consensus, presented as a fact, that supports the dominant tradition of the time, and does so with a view to the relations of power surreptitiously incorporated in the symbolic structures of the systems of speech and action. The immunizing power of ideologies, which stifle the demands for justification raised by discursive examination, goes back to blockages in communication, independently of the changing semantic contents. These blocks have their origin within the structures of communication themselves, which for certain contents limit the options between verbal and nonverbal forms of expression, between the communicative and the cognitive uses of language, and finally between communicative action and discourse, or even exclude such options entirely; they thus require explanation within the framework of a theory of systematically distorted communication. And if such a theory, in conjunction with a universal pragmatics,[22] could be developed in a satisfactory manner and could be linked convincingly with the precisely rendered fundamental assumptions of historical materialism, then a systematic comprehension of cultural tradition would not be excluded. Perhaps verifiable assumptions about the logic of the development of moral systems, of structures of the world images and corresponding cult practices, could result from a theory of social evolution; this would reveal whether, as it seems, the contingent manifold of traditional meanings, which are organized within the framework of world images, vary systematically according to features understandable in terms of universal pragmatics.[23]

(3) Confronted with the universalism of a comprehensively designed systems theory, critical sociology guards itself against the reduction of all social conflicts to unsolved problems in the regulation of self-governing systems. It is certainly meaningful to conceive social systems as entities which solve objectively posed problems by means of supra-subjective learning processes; however, the reference system of machine cybernetics proves useful only insofar as a solution of problems of control is involved. Among other things, social systems are distinguished from machines (with learning capacity) and from organisms by the fact that subjective learning processes take place and are organized within the framework of ordinary language communication. A

systems concept which is more appropriate to the social sciences (and which is not designed solely for the production of strategies and organizations, that is, for the extension of control capabilities) can therefore not be taken over from general systems theory; it must be developed in relation with a theory of ordinary language communication, which also takes into consideration the relationship of intersubjectivity and the relation between ego and group identity. Ultra-stability—or in Luhmann's formulation, the reduction of the world's complexity by means of increasing system complexity [*Eigenkomplexitaet*]—represents a designation of goals which results unavoidably from a functionalistic conceptual strategy, although especially on the sociocultural level of evolution the problem of continued existence [*Bestandsproblem*] becomes diffuse, and the talk of "survival" metaphorical.

(4) Finally, confronted with the dogmatic heritage of the philosophy of history, critical sociology must guard against overburdening the concepts of the philosophy of reflection [German Idealism]. From the conceptual strategy of transcendental philosophy there results (already in the followers of Kant, and today also among those who wish to develop a Marxist theory of society in conjunction with Husserl's analyses of the "life-world") a peculiar compulsion to conceive the social world as a continuum in the same way as the world of the objects of possible experience. Thus to the objective structures within which socialized individuals encounter each other and act communicatively, large-scale subjects are assigned. The projective generation of higher-order subjects has a long tradition. Marx too did not always make clear that the attributes ascribed to social classes (such as class consciousness, class interest, class action) did not represent a simple transference from the level of individual consciousness to that of a collective. These are rather designations for something that can only be arrived at intersubjectively, in the consultation or the cooperation of individuals living together.

Objections

In this extremely selective and oversimplified retrospective summary I have emphasized three lines of argumentation along which I have pursued the relation of theory and praxis beyond those historical investigations which are collected in this volume. These arguments are certainly unsatisfactory as far as their degree of explication and completeness is concerned; I have always been aware of the fragmentary and provisional character of these considerations. But only a clearly stated position makes discursive attack and defense possible—that is, substantive argument. Yet certainly inaccuracies have crept in, and to a greater degree than I would have liked. Though I have exposed myself to criticism on this level, I will not deal with this here. However, the objections with respect to my construction itself are on another level. At the moment I can see three objections which must be taken seriously (other opponents of my views have not been able to convince me that their arguments carry weight; naturally I cannot exclude the possibility that psychological reasons are responsible for this; I can only hope that this is not the case). Here too I must confine myself to an outline:

(1) The first objection refers to the inadequately clarified status of the interests that direct knowledge. The formula "quasi-transcendental" is a product of an embarrassment which points to more problems than it solves. On the one hand, I have relinquished taking the position of transcendental logic in the strict sense in my attempt to clarify the systematic relations between the logic of scientific investigation and the logic of the contexts in which the corresponding sciences are constituted and applied. I do not assume the synthetic achievements of an intelligible ego nor in general a productive subjectivity. But I do presuppose, as does Peirce,[24] the real interrelationship of communicating (and cooperating) investigators, where each of these subsystems is part of the surrounding social systems, which in turn are the result of the sociocultural evolution of the human race. On the other hand, the logical-methodological complexes cannot simply be reduced to empirical ones; at least not without paying the price of a naturalism which would claim to explain the technical as well as the practical interest of knowledge in the manner of natural history and thus, ultimately, as biological;[25] or at the cost of a historicism which would, at the very least, tie the emancipatory interest of knowledge to fortuitous historical constellations and would thus

relativistically deprive self-reflection of the possibility of a justificatory basis for its claim to validity.[26] In neither of these two cases
could it be made plausible how theories could have any truth at
all—including one's own theories.

(2) The second objection is directed against the assertion
that in the insights produced by self-reflection, knowledge and
the emancipatory interest of knowledge are "one." Even if one
admits that inherent within reason is also partisanship in favor
of reason, still the claim to universality, which reflection as knowledge must make, is not to be reconciled with the particularity
which must adhere to every interest, even that which aims at self-
liberation. Is not a specific content already claimed for reason,
when linked to emancipatory interest, namely that of a substantive rationality—while reason itself, as a consequence of its own
idea, must exclude any specification in terms of particular goals?
Is the element of decision and commitment, on which every praxis
of subjects instructed by critique depends, especially a revolutionary praxis, not suppressed in a dogmatically asserted interest
of reason, and thereby at the same time immunized? In the end
the normative basis for a critical sociology is smuggled in surreptitiously, when one considers that in the interest of the liberation from the objectified self-deception of dogmatic power, two
things are inevitably mingled: on the one hand, the interest in
enlightenment, in the sense of a relentless discursive validation of
claims to validity (and the discursive dissolution of opinions and
norms the validity of which is based on unjustified claims, no
matter to what extent it is actually accepted); on the other hand,
the interest in enlightenment, in the sense of practical change of
established conditions (and the realization of goals which demand
the risks of taking sides, and thus, precisely, the relinquishment
of the neutral role of a participant in discourse).[27]

(3) The third objection is directed against the irresponsibil-
ity of discussions about the relationship of theory and praxis
which fail to deal with questions of the organization of enlightenment and of enlightened praxis. Oskar Negt has formulated this
objection most clearly on the political level. As I do not pose the
question of organization, and thus do not draw the consequences
of knowledge directed toward liberation, I remain confined to a

prepolitical concept of objective partisanship. Instead, an organizational praxis adequate for the requirements of enlightenment
on a mass scale would have to be discussed; Negt himself had in
mind the decentralized activities which were widespread in the
student movement of his time; hence the examples of spontaneous
self-organization "for which enlightenment and revolutionary
overthrow were no longer posed as alternatives." [28]

An analogous objection is directed, on the theoretical level,
against the possibility of carrying the model of psychoanalysis
over into social theory. For I actually did investigate the critically
motivated process of self-reflection in terms of the example of the
psychoanalytic dialogue, in order to clarify in terms of this the
logic underlying the translation of critique into self-liberation.
Now however, therapy is bound by the rules of the art and by
inhibiting institutional conditions, to which the political struggle,
and especially the revolutionary struggle, is not subject. Therefore from the conservative side the misgivings readily arise that a
transferring of the doctor-patient model to political praxis of
large groups would encourage the uncontrolled exercise of force
on the part of self-appointed elites, who close themselves off
against potential opponents with dogmatic claims of privileged
access to true insight. On the other side the misgiving arises that
the same model leads to a rationalistic denial of the militant
element in the confrontation with political opponents, because
the pacifist illusion arises that the critical insight will by itself
destroy the dominating dogmatism of existing institutions.[29]

Action and discourse

We no longer find, in dialectical logic, as in a certain way
Marx still did, the normative basis for a social theory constructed
with practical intent. Of course, the logic of a self-reflection,
which traces back the formative course of an ego's identity
through all involutions of systematically distorted communications and brings this analytically to this ego's awareness, can be
called "dialectical" if it is the task of dialectics, in the sense of the
Hegelian "Phenomenology" (and of a psychoanalysis which is not
conceived in a scientistic manner), to reconstruct that which has

been repressed from the historical traces of repressed dialogues.[30] But what is dialectical is then only the structure of compulsion that dialectical thought explodes by assimilating itself to it. This is Adorno's central insight.[31] Then, however, our problem is merely deferred. For the structure of distorted communication is not ultimate; it has its basis in the logic of undistorted language communication.

In a certain way, mature autonomy [*Mündigkeit*] [32] is the sole idea which we have at our disposal in the sense of the philosophical tradition—as I asserted in my Frankfurt inaugural lecture[33]—for in every speech act the *telos* of reaching an understanding [*Verstaendigung*] is already inherent. "With the very first sentence the intention of a general and voluntary consensus is unmistakably enunciated." [34] Wittgenstein has remarked that the concept of reaching an understanding lies in the concept of language. We can only say in a self-explicative sense that language communication "serves" this reaching of an understanding. Every understanding reached is confirmed in a reasonable consensus, as we say; otherwise it does not represent a "real" understanding. Competent orators know that every consensus attained can in fact be deceptive; but they must always have been in possession of the prior concept of the rational consensus underlying the concept of a deceptive (or merely compulsory) consensus. Reaching an understanding is a normative concept; everyone who speaks a natural language has intuitive knowledge of it and therefore is confident of being able, in principle, to distinguish a true consensus from a false one. In the educated language of philosophical culture [*Bildungssprache*] we call this knowledge *a priori* or innate. This is based on traditional interpretations. But even independently of these interpretations we can attempt to clarify the normative implications that lie in the concept of possible understanding, with which every speaker (and hearer) is naïvely familiar. This attempt I undertake with the outline of a universal pragmatics; of this work till now only the *Vorbereitende Bemerkungen zu einer Theorie der kommunikativen Kompetenz* has been published.[35]

We can proceed from the fact that functioning language games, in which speech acts are exchanged, are based on an underlying consensus. This underlying consensus is formed in the reciprocal recognition of at least four claims to validity which speakers announce to each other: the comprehensibility of the utterance, the truth of its propositional component, the correctness and appropriateness of its performatory component, and the authenticity of the speaking subject. The claim to comprehensibility must be realized in actuality, if and to the extent to which reaching an understanding is to be attained in a communication. The claim to authenticity can only be realized in interaction: in the interaction it will be shown in time, whether the other side is "in truth or honestly" participating or is only pretending to engage in communicative action and is in fact behaving strategically. The case is otherwise with respect to the assertory claim to the truth of utterances and the claim to the correctness of norms for action, or on the other hand, the appropriateness of norms for valuation which we are to follow. These are claims of validity which can be proven only in discourse. The factual recognition of these claims bases itself in every case, even that of error, on the possibility of the discursive validation of the claims made. Discourses are performances, in which we seek to show the grounds for cognitive utterances.

In actions, the factually raised claims to validity, which form the underlying consensus, are assumed naïvely. Discourse, on the other hand, serves the justification of problematic claims to validity of opinions and norms. Thus the system of action and experience refers us in a compelling manner to a form of communication in which the participants do not exchange information, do not direct or carry out action, nor do they have or communicate experiences; instead they search for arguments or offer justifications. Discourse therefore requires the virtualization of constraints on action. This is intended to render inoperative all motives except solely that of a cooperative readiness to arrive at an understanding, and further requires that questions of validity be separated from those of genesis. Discourse thereby renders possible the virtualization of claims to validity; this consists in our announcing with respect to the objects of communicative action (things and events, persons and utterances) a reservation concerning their existence and conceiving of facts as well as of norms from the viewpoint of *possible* existence. To speak as Husserl does, in discourse we bracket the general thesis. Thus facts are transformed into states of affairs which may or may not be the case, and norms are transformed into recommendations and warnings which may be correct or appropriate but also incorrect or inappropriate.

Solely the structure of this peculiarly unreal form of communication guarantees the possibility of attaining a consensus discursively, which can gain recognition as rational. Because truth (in the most broadly conceived traditional sense of rationality) is distinguished from mere certainty by its claim to be absolute, discourse is the condition of the unconditioned. With the aid of a consensus theory of truth, which would have to justify, in the face of competing theories of truth, why a criterion of truth independent of discourse cannot be meaningfully postulated, the structure of discourse would have to be clarified with respect to the unavoidable reciprocal anticipation and presupposition of an ideal situation of discourse [*Sprechsituation*].[36] And correspondingly, the idealization of pure communicative action would have to be reconstructed as the condition under which the authenticity of speaking and acting subjects can be imputed as well as verified. I cannot go into this here. But I have indicated the derivation from the foundations of ordinary language communication to the extent that in the following sections I can present the strategy with which I wish to respond to the above-mentioned objections.

Objectivity of knowledge and interest

I would like to treat the *first two objections* jointly. In the light of the newly introduced system of relations between action and discourse, the following points, which, of course, I can only discuss in terms of a few strategic indications, present themselves to me in a different light than previously.

(1) In the investigations up to this point I have brought out the interrelation between knowledge and interest, without making clear the critical threshold between communication (which remains embedded within the context of action) and discourses (which transcend the compulsions of action). To be sure, the constitution of scientific object domains can be conceived as a contin-

uation of the objectivations which we undertake in the world of social life prior to all science. But the genuine claim to objectivity which is raised with the instauration of science is based on a virtualization of the pressure of experience and decision, and it is only this which permits a discursive testing of *hypothetical* claims to validity and thus the generation of *rationally grounded* knowledge. Against the sciences' objectivistic understanding of themselves, which naïvely relates itself to the facts, an indirect relationship to action can be shown for theoretical knowledge, but not anything like a direct derivation from the imperatives posed by the praxis of life (nor have I ever asserted that there is such a derivation). The opinions which form the input of discourse—and thus the raw material which is subjected to argumentation with the aim of substantiation—do indeed have their origin in the diverse interrelations of experience and action. The logic of these experiential relations is manifested even in discourse itself by the fact that opinions can only be specified, and their derivation made clear, in languages of a specific form and can only be tested by methods of a specific kind (on a high level of generalization): by "observation" and "interviewing" [*Befragung*]. Therefore the discursively substantiated theoretical statements (which survive argumentation) can in turn be relevant only to specific contexts of application: statements about the phenomenal domain of things and events (or the deep structures which manifest themselves in terms of things and events) can only be translated back into orientations for goal-directed rational action (in technologies and strategies); statements about the phenomenal domain of persons and utterances (or about the deep structures of social systems) can only be translated back into orientations for communicative action (in practical knowledge). The interests which direct knowledge preserve the unity of the relevant system of action and experience vis-à-vis discourse; they retain the latent reference of theoretical knowledge to action by way of the transformation of opinions into theoretical statements and their retransformation into knowledge oriented toward action. But by no means do they remove or resolve (sublate) the difference between opinions about objects based on experience related to action, on the one hand, and statements about facts, founded on discourse that is free of experience and unencumbered by action, on the other; just as little do they affect the difference between those claims to validity which are simply recognized as factual and those which have a reasoned justification.

The status of the two "lower" interests, the technical and the practical interest of knowledge, can, to begin with, be clarified aporetically by the fact that they can neither be comprehended like empirical inclinations or attitudes nor be proposed or justified like variable values in relation to norms of action. Instead we "encounter" these deep-seated anthropological interests in the attempt to clarify the "constitution" of the facts about which theoretical statements are possible (that is, the systems of primitive terms which categorize the objects of possible experience, on the one hand, and, on the other, the methods by which action-related primary experiences are selected, extracted from their own system, and utilized for the purpose of the discursive examination of claims to validity, and thus transformed into "data"). The interests of knowledge can be conceived as generalized motives for systems of action, which are guided by means of the communication of statements which can be true. Actions are channeled by the recognition of claims to validity that can be resolved discursively. That is why, on the higher levels of sociocultural development, the fundamental regulators no longer take the form of particular stimuli (or instincts) but precisely that of general cognitive strategies of the action-related organization of experience. As long as these interests of knowledge are identified and analyzed by way of reflection on the logic of inquiry that structures the natural and the humane sciences,[37] they can claim a "transcendental" status; however, as soon as they are understood in terms of an anthropology of knowledge, as results of natural history, they have an "empirical" status. I place "empirical" within quotation marks, because a theory of evolution which is expected to explain emergent properties characteristic of the sociocultural life-form—in other words, to explain the constituents of social systems as part of natural history—cannot, for its part, be developed within the transcendental framework of objectifying sciences. If the theory of evolution is to assume these tasks, it cannot wholly divest itself of the form of a reflection on the prehistory of culture that is dependent on a prior understanding of the sociocultural life-form. For the time being these are speculations, which can only be confirmed by a scientific clarification of the status enjoyed by the contemporary theory of evolution and research in ethology. Till then, at most, they designate a perspective for the formulation of the problems.[38]

(2) As far as the third, the emancipatory, interest of knowledge is concerned, a more distinct delimitation appears, in my view, to offer itself. This interest can only develop to the degree to which repressive force, in the form of the normative exercise of power, presents itself permanently in structures of distorted communication—that is, to the extent that domination is institutionalized. This interest aims at reflection on oneself. As soon as we seek to clarify the structure of this reflection within the reference system of action-discourse, its difference from scientific argumentation becomes clear: the psychoanalytic dialogue is not a discourse, and reflection on oneself does not provide reasoned justification. What is reasoned justification within the context of acts of reflection on oneself bases itself on theoretical knowledge which has been gained independently of the reflection on oneself, namely, the rational reconstruction of rule systems which we have to master if we wish to process experience cognitively or participate in systems of action or carry on discourse. Till now I have not adequately distinguished posterior reconstruction [*Nachkonstruktion*] from reflection on oneself.[39]

Self-reflection brings to consciousness those determinants of a self-formative process of cultivation and spiritual formation [*Bildung*] which ideologically determine a contemporary praxis of action and the conception of the world. Analytic memory thus embraces the particulars, the specific course of self-formation of an individual subject (or of a collective held together by group identity). Rational reconstructions, in contrast, deal with anonymous rule systems, which any subjects whatsoever can comply with, insofar as they have acquired the corresponding competence with respect to these rules. Reconstructions thus do not encompass subjectivity, within the horizon of which alone the experience of reflection is possible. In the philosophical tradition these two legitimate forms of self-knowledge have generally remained undifferentiated and have both been included under the term of reflection. However, a reliable criterion of distinction is available. Self-reflection leads to insight due to the fact that what has previously been unconscious is made conscious in a manner rich in practical consequences: analytic insights intervene in life, if I may borrow this dramatic phrase from Wittgenstein. A successful reconstruction also raises an "unconsciously" functioning rule system to consciousness in a certain manner; it renders explicit the intuitive knowledge that is given with competence with respect to the rules in the form of "know how." But this theoretical knowledge has no practical consequences. By learning logic or linguistics I acquire theoretical knowledge, but in general I do not thereby change my previous practice of reasoning or speaking.

This circumstance finds its explanation in the fact that self-reflection, as can be shown in the model of the psychoanalytic dialogue between doctor and patient, is not a discourse, but effects, at the same time, both more and less than a discourse.[40] The therapeutic "discourse" effects less, as the patient by no means takes up a symmetrical posture vis-à-vis the doctor from the very beginning; the conditions for a participant in discourse are precisely what is not fulfilled by the patient. It is only the successful therapeutic discourse which brings, as its result that which in ordinary discourse must be required from the very outset; the effective equality of opportunities in perceiving the roles within the dialogue, and in general, in the choice and exercise of speech acts, must first be established between partners in a dialogue who are so unequally equipped. On the other hand, the therapeutic discourse effects more than the ordinary one. Because it remains contained in a peculiar way within the system of action and experience, and thus is not a discourse cut free from action or experience, which has as its theme exclusively questions of validity and must import all contents and information from the outside, successful self-reflection results in insight which satisfies not only the conditions of the discursive realization of a claim to truth (or correctness) but in addition satisfies the condition of the realization of a claim to authenticity [*Wahrhaftigkeit*], which normally is not to be attained discursively at all. In the patient's acceptance of the "worked out" interpretations which the doctor suggests to him and his confirming that these are applicable, he at the same time sees through a self-deception. The true interpretation at the same time makes possible the authentic intention of the subject with respect to those utterances, with which he has till then deceived himself (and possibly others). Claims to authenticity as a rule can only be tested within the context of action. That distinctive communication in which the distortions of the communicative structure themselves can be overcome is the only one in which claims to truth can be tested "discursively" together and simultaneously with a claim to authenticity, or be rejected as unjustified.

Reconstructions are, on the other hand, the object of ordinary discourse. To be sure, compared to other discursive objects they are distinguished by being first generated within a reflexive attitude. Cognitive components of the praxis of life, the claims to validity of which have been rendered problematic, are not what is dealt with in reconstructed rule systems; nor is it those scientific theorems, which cumulate in the rational grounds of such claims to validity; rather the reconstruction of rule systems requires an impulse which originates in the discourses themselves. It is precisely that reflection about presuppositions on which we always already rely naïvely in rational speech. Accordingly, this type of knowledge has always claimed the status of a special, of a "pure" knowledge; in logic, mathematics, epistemology, and linguistics today it forms the core of the philosophic disciplines. This type of knowledge is not constitutive for the objectivating sciences; accordingly, it remains untouched by the technical as well as the practical interest. For sciences of the critical type, which, like psychoanalysis, make self-reflection into a method of procedure, reconstruction, of course, appears to have a constitutive significance on the horizontal as well as the vertical level.[41] It is only reliance upon reconstruction which permits the theoretical development of self-reflection. In this way reconstructions therefore attain an indirect relation to the emancipatory interest of knowledge, which enters directly only into the capacity for self-reflection.[42]

On the institutionalization of discourses

Still a *third objection* remains: is the psychoanalytic dialogue not necessarily misleading as a model for discussion between politically organized groups? How can the translation of theory into praxis be appropriately organized? Before I go into this question, I would like to place the relation of theory and praxis in an evolutionary historical perspective.

Within the reference system of action and discourse the normative question concerning the relation of theory and praxis can be given a surprisingly descriptive aspect. On the one hand, the assumption is plausible that the consensus which supports action is based on claims to validity, that are accepted as factual, in various ways. These claims can only be realized discursively. Furthermore, it can be shown that we must presuppose an ideal situation of verbal communication, on both sides, whenever we wish to carry on discourse. Thus for communicative action, discourses are of a fundamental significance. On the other hand, it is only late in history that discourses have lost their sporadic character. Only when certain domains of discourse are *institutionalized* to such an extent that under specifiable conditions a general expectation exists, that discursive conversations will be initiated, can they become a systematically relevant mechanism of learning for a given society.

In the course of social evolution such institutionalizations of partial discourses, specific to certain domains, signify innovative achievements rich in consequences, which a theory of social evolution would have to explain in relation to the unfolding of the forces of production and the expansion of the capacities for control. Dramatic examples are, first, the institutionalization of discourse in which the claims to validity of mythical and religious interpretations of the world could be systematically questioned and tested; as such we understand the beginnings of philosophy in Athens during the Classical period. Second, the institutionalization of discourse in which the claims to validity of technically exploitable profane knowledge transmitted in the domains of professional ethics could be systematically questioned and tested;

as such we understand the beginnings of the modern experimental sciences, which certainly had their precursors in antiquity and at the end of the Middle Ages. And finally, the institutionalization of discourse in which the claims to validity involving practical questions and political decisions were *intended to be* continually questioned and tested; first in England during the seventeenth century, and later on the Continent and in the United States, with precursors in the Italian cities of the Renaissance, a political public sphere came into being and in connection with this, representative forms of government—bourgeois democracy. These are very crude examples and certainly examples only. Today the traditional patterns of socialization, which till now were ensconced as natural in the cultural tradition, are set free by the psychologizing of children's education and the planning of school curricula according to cultural policy, and rendered accessible to general practical discourse by means of a process of "scientization." Much the same is true in literary and artistic production; "affirmative" bourgeois culture, divorced from the praxis of life and claiming the transcendence of beautiful illusion [*des schoenen Scheins*], is undergoing a process of dissolution.

How equivocal such phenomena may be, and how little the phenomenal form of discourse assures the institutionally secured extension of the discursive learning mechanism to new domains of knowledge and the formation of will which are remote from tradition, can be shown in terms of the example of bourgeois democracy. After the bold fiction of the dependence of all politically consequential decision-making processes on the legally secured discursive formation of will on the part of the citizen public was shattered in the course of the nineteenth century by the restrictive conditions of the mode of production, a polarization of forces resulted, if this oversimplification may be permitted. On the one hand, a tendency has set in to reject as illusion the claim that political and practical questions may be clarified discursively, and to deny, positivistically, the truth value of such questions. In the mass democracies of the advanced capitalistic social systems, the bourgeois ideas of freedom and self-determination are being constricted and have yielded to the "realistic" interpretation that political discourse in public, in political parties and organizations, is in any case mere appearance and will remain such under all conceivable circumstances. The compromise of interests obeys the logic of force, and the balance of forces produced by counterforces and is not accessible to rationalization. In the face of this, a tendency had developed which is to be extensively investigated in this volume: the attempt to explain why the ideas of the bourgeois revolution necessarily had to remain false consciousness, why they had to remain ideology, and could only be realized by those who, due to their position in the process of production and the experience produced by their class conditions, would have the disposition to see through bourgeois ideology. Marx is equally critical of the naïve demand to create bourgeois democracy as he is of the undisguised recantation of bourgeois ideals. He shows that democracy cannot be realized as bourgeois democracy. This insight is based on the critique of political economy, which was seen as a critique of ideology. To make this critique practical was the task of the Communists. From this the Communist Party developed. In this type of organization something very peculiar is institutionalized: externally, in the face of the class enemy, strategic action and political struggle; internally, with respect to the mass of the wage laborers, the organization of enlightenment, the discursive inducement of processes of self-reflection. The vanguard of the proletariat must master both: the critique of weapons and the weapons of critique.

At this point, the history of the race, which, in ever new advances, has institutionalized the discursive form of problem-solving unreflected in a "natural" manner, becomes peculiarly reflexive. In order to assert discursive formation of the will as an organizational principle for the social system as a whole with consciousness and will, the political struggle is now to be made dependent on a theory that makes possible the enlightenment of social classes as to their own nature. However, can self-reflection become fully practical in the form of political struggle—and thus be legitimately made the task of an organization engaged in this struggle?

Organization of enlightenment

Just as we can understand "thinking" as the process of discourse-dependent argumentation internalized by a single subject —so self-reflection too can be conceived as the internalization of a "therapeutic discourse." In both cases the withdrawing of communication into the inwardness of a solitary subject by no means revokes the virtually retained intersubjective structure of the dialogue; the thinking subject just as well as the reflecting subject must play at least two roles of the dialogue, if argumentation is not to become merely analytic (and thus in principle reproducible by machines). In the case of (internalized) discourse this is unproblematic. The positions of the partners in discourse are egalitarian and in principle interchangeable; therefore the internal assignment of roles in the dialogue creates no difficulties in thought. But this is not so in the case of (internalized) therapy. The positions of the partners in the psychoanalytic dialogue are asymmetrical; they change in many ways during the course of the communication and only terminate in a symmetrical relation— which holds between participants in discourse from the very outset—at the conclusion of a successful treatment. The self-reflection of a lone subject therefore requires a quite paradoxical achievement: one part of the self must be split off from the other part in such a manner that the subject can be in a position to render aid to itself. The psychoanalytic dialogue only renders visible this internal labor, divided between parts of the subject; thereby, what retained a virtual presence within the solitary subject due to the internalization of an external relation is reconstituted again as such an external relation.

Still, the model of solitary self-reflection also has its justification. For in it is manifested the risk that consists in the possibility of sophistic delusion that only assumes the appearance of self-reflection: in the act of solitary self-reflection the subject can deceive itself. To be sure it also has to pay the price for its deception itself. If, however, on the horizontal level on which two partners confront each other (the one in the role of conferring enlightenment, the other seeking enlightenment about himself), the misleading of the one is not to be exploited by the other, the unity of the life-context must be secured on both sides institutionally, so that *both* suffer equally from resulting errors and the consequences of such errors. This is the model which Hegel developed in his concept of morality which is subject to the causality of destiny.

In the case of psychoanalysis two fundamental and two pragmatic sanctions against misuse in the sense of exploiting deception can be enumerated. For one, the fundamental theorems lay claim to truth and this claim must be defensible in accordance with the usual rules of scientific discourse, otherwise the theory must be relinquished or revised. Secondly, the appropriateness of the interpretation, which is theoretically derived and applied to the particular case, requires confirmation in successful self-reflection; truth must converge with authenticity—in other words, the patient himself is the final authority. Furthermore, psychoanalysts must comply with the requirements of professional ethics and practices of a legally sanctioned association of physicians; within limits violations of professional norms and regulations can be controlled. Finally, in general the patient can maintain a certain distance from his doctor; in spite of transference (and countertransference) the role of the patient is not a total role, but only one among many within a differentiated system of roles. Within certain limits, the patient retains the option to change analysts or to break off the treatment.

But what is the situation with respect to sanctions on the level of interaction between large groups, which is defined by analogous models of systematically distorted communication, and which, under the guidance of processes of enlightenment, is to be changed politically?

G. H. Gadamer and H. J. Giegel quite rightly criticize undifferentiated attempts to transfer a model borrowed from psychoanalysis to large groups: "A critique which confronts the other, or dominant social prejudices generally, with its compulsory character, and, on the other hand, raises the claim to dissolving such complexes of deception communicatively, will find itself—here I am in agreement with Giegel—in a false position. It must ignore fundamental differences. In the case of psychoanalysis, the suffering and the desire for cure of the patient serve as the tenable basis for the therapeutic activity of the doctor, whose assertion of authority and urging for the clarification of repressed motives are not without compulsion.

"In this, the voluntary submission of the one to the other is the supportive basis. In social life, on the other hand, the resistance of the opponent and the resistance against the opponent are the common presupposition for all." [43] Gadamer is referring here to Giegel's assertion:

> The revolutionary struggle is by no means a psychoanalytic treatment on a large scale. The difference between these two forms of emancipatory praxis results from the fact that the patient is aided in freeing himself from the compulsions to which he is subjected, while for the ruling class, the attempt to gain freedom from the social complex of compulsion, in itself, must appear as a threat to the rule which it exercises over the other classes. The confrontation here presents itself in a much sharper form than in the case of psychoanalysis. The oppressed class not only doubts the ability of the ruling class to conduct the dialogue, but also has good reasons for assuming that each attempt on its part to enter into a dialogue with the ruling class will only serve as an opportunity for the latter to strengthen the security of its domination. [44]

If we confine ourselves to the Marxist example of the organized class struggle which Giegel invokes, then it is evident that the strategic confrontation between classes and the interaction between doctor and patient are not the same thing. This model can only be used for normatively structuring the relationship between the Communist Party and the masses who let themselves be enlightened by the Party concerning their own situation. Still for Marx the theory is the same in both cases. I can apply theories such as psychoanalysis (and the Marxist critique of ideology) in order to guide processes of reflection and to dissolve barriers to communication; the authenticity of the recipient in his relations with himself and with others is an indicator of the truth of the interpretation which the analyst (or the Party intellectual) has suggested. But I can also use this same theory to derive an explanatory hypothesis, without having (or taking) the opportunity of initiating communication with those actually concerned, and thus confirm my interpretation by their processes of reflection. In this case I must remain satisfied with the usual procedures of scientific discourse: for example, whether the patterns of behavior and the patterns of communication identified as pathological are repeated under specified conditions or change under other conditions, which permit one to assume that a process of reflection has taken place. Then, to be sure, that genuine confirmation of the critique remains unattainable, a confirmation which can only be gained in communication of the type of therapeutic "discourse," that is, precisely in successful processes of education [*Bildung*] voluntarily agreed to by the recipients themselves. We must distinguish between the level of theoretical discourse and the organization of processes of enlightenment in which the theory is applied. This organization can (initially) be confined to the groups distinguished by their situation of interest, toward which the enlightenment is directed.

Of course, critique does not bear this mode of employment stamped on its forehead—not even the critique of political economy. Thus Marx by no means excludes situations in which confidence in the opponent's capability to carry on a dialogue is not in principle unjustified and in which the weapon of critique will have greater effect than the critique of the weapons. These are situations in which the initiatives of radical reformism, which seeks to persuade not only within the group, but also externally, are more promising than the revolutionary struggle. Again, in other situations, it becomes difficult in general to distinguish the groups at which active work of enlightenment can be directed from the opponents held captive by ideology; then all that remains is the diffuse dissemination of insights individually gained in the style of the eighteenth-century Enlightenment. It is thus, for example, that Adorno evaluated his own critique. In the face of various sectarian enterprises, one might point out today that in advanced capitalism changing the structure of the general system of education [*Bildungssystem*] might possibly be more important for the organization of enlightenment than the ineffectual training of cadres or the building of impotent parties. With this I only wish to state that these are empirical questions which must not be prejudged. There can be no meaningful theory which per se, and regardless of the circumstances, obligates one to militancy. In any event, we can distinguish theories according to whether or not in their structure they point toward possible emancipation.

Historical remarks on the question of organization

The mediation of theory and praxis can only be clarified if to begin with we distinguish three functions, which are measured in terms of different criteria: the formation and extension of critical theorems, which can stand up to scientific discourse; the organization of processes of enlightenment, in which such theorems are applied and can be tested in a unique manner by the initiation of processes of reflection carried on within certain groups toward which these processes have been directed; and the selection of appropriate strategies, the solution of tactical questions, and the conduct of the political struggle. On the first level, the aim is true statements, on the second, authentic insights, and on the third, prudent decisions. Because in the tradition of the European working-class movement all three tasks at once were assigned to the party organization, the specific differences have become obscured. The theory serves primarily to enlighten those to whom it is addressed about the position they occupy in an antagonistic social system and about the interests of which they must become conscious in this situation as being objectively theirs. Only to the degree that organized enlightenment and consultation lead to those groups toward which this is directed actually recognizing themselves in the interpretations offered, do the analytically proposed interpretations actually become consciousness, and does the objectively attributed situation of interests actually become the real interest of a group capable of action. Marx, who viewed the industrial proletariat as the sole group toward which he directed his analysis, called this constituting the mass of proletarians as "a class for itself." [45] Of course, Marx specified the objective conditions under which the communists, already theoretically enlightened, were to organize the process of enlightenment for the mass of the workers. The economic compulsion for forming "workers' coalitions" and the socialization of labor within the factory system produced a common situation in which the workers would naturally be forced to learn to defend their common interests; the "real subsumption of wage labor under capital" produced the equally real basis on which the participants could be made conscious of the political significance of their economic struggles.

The organization of action must be distinguished from this process of enlightenment. While the theory legitimizes the work of enlightenment, as well as providing its own refutation when communication fails, and can, in any case, be corrected, it can by no means legitimize *a fortiori* the risky decisions of strategic action. Decisions for the political struggle cannot at the outset be justified theoretically and then be carried out organizationally. The sole possible justification at this level is consensus, aimed at in practical discourse, among the participants, who, in the consciousness of their common interests and their knowledge of the circumstances, of the predictable consequences and secondary consequences, are the only ones who can know what risks they are willing to undergo, and with what expectations. There can be no theory which at the outset can assure a world-historical mission in return for the potential sacrifices. The sole advantage which Marx could have been permitted to assure to a proletariat acting in solidarity would have been that a class, which with the aid of a true critique constitutes itself as a class, is only then at all in a position to make clear to itself in practical discourse how it is to act politically in a rational manner—while the members of bourgeois parties and of the ruling class as such are ensnared in ideology and incapable of rationally clarifying practical questions; thus they can only act and react under compulsion.

Those three functions which I have distinguished cannot be fulfilled according to one and the same principle: a theory can only be formulated under the precondition that those engaged in scientific work have the freedom to conduct theoretical discourse; processes of enlightenment (if they are to avoid exploitation and deception) can only be organized under the precondition

that those who carry out the active work of enlightenment commit themselves wholly to the proper precautions and assure scope
for communications on the model of therapeutic "discourses";
finally, a political struggle can only be legitimately conducted
under the precondition that all decisions of consequence will
depend on the practical discourse of the participants—here too,
and especially here, there is no privileged access to truth. An
organization which tries to master all three of these tasks according to the same principle will not be able to fulfill any of them
correctly. And even if this organization is successful according
to the usual criteria of merciless history, as Lenin's Party was,
it exacts the same price for its success which ambivalent victories
have always exacted till now in the unbroken continuity of a
history subject to "natural" uncontrolled causality.

In his famous article "Methodisches zur Organizationsfrage"
("Toward a Methodology for the Problem of Organization,"
September 1922), Georg Lukács developed the most consistent
formulation of a theory of the Party, one which solves the problem of the mediation of theory and praxis solely with a view to
the imperatives of the conduct of the political struggle. This is
the meaning of the thesis: "The organization is the form of the
mediation between theory and praxis." [46] *To begin with,* Lukács
subjects theory to the requirements of strategic action:

> Only posing the question with an organizational orientation
> makes it possible to actually criticize the theory from the
> viewpoint of praxis. If the theory is juxtaposed to an action
> without mediation, without it becoming clear how its effect
> on the latter is intended, thus, without making clear the
> organizational links between them, then the theory itself
> can only be criticized with respect to its immanent theoreti-
> cal contradictions, and so forth.[47]

That the truth of a theory can be tested independently of whether
it is useful for certain discourses which are preparatory to action is immaterial for Lukács. Theoretical statements are to be
selected from the point of view of organizational questions.
Therefore any scope for scientific discourse within the Party is

also prohibited. To permit it would only further opportunism: "While for pure theory the most diverse views and directions can live side by side peaceably, while their oppositions assume the form merely of discussions which can take place placidly within the framework of one and the same organization without threatening to disrupt it, the same questions, when they are given an organizational orientation, present themselves in the sharpest manner as directions which are mutually exclusive. Every 'theoretical' direction or divergence of views must immediately be transformed into an organizational issue if it is not to remain mere theory, an abstract opinion, if it really has the intention of showing the path to its realization." [48] Lukács does not want to tolerate any indecision concerning the validity of hypotheses. Theoretical deviations are therefore to be immediately subjected to sanctions on the organizational level.[49] *Secondly,* just like theory, the enlightenment of the proletariat is also subordinated unhesitatingly to the purposes of the Party leadership. To be sure, like Marx, Lukács sees the task of the Party to consist in inducing the mass of the wage workers to attain "self-knowledge . . . as the knowledge of their objective situation at a certain stage of the historical development," with the aid of a correct theory. But he by no means conceives of the efforts of the Communist Party to develop proletarian class consciousness as a process of enlightenment, "in which all that is involved is rendering the unconscious conscious, the latent actual, and so forth; in a better formulation: in which this process of becoming conscious does not represent a terrible ideological crisis for the proletariat itself." [50] Like Lenin, Lukács is convinced that the proletariat is still powerfully ensnared in the forms of thinking and feeling of capitalism, that the subjective development lags behind the economic crises. However, if "from the absence of a clear and persistent will to revolution within the proletariat" one is not to conclude "the absence of an objective revolutionary situation," [51] if the "conflict between individual consciousness and class consciousness in every single proletarian is by no means accidental," [52] then the Party as the embodiment of class consciousness must act representatively for the masses, and not allow itself to be made dependent on their spontaneity. The Party takes the first conscious step; it steers a still backward proletariat into a struggle, and only during the course of that struggle will it constitute itself as a class. In the Party the still backward class may see a consciousness, anticipated but as yet inaccessible to it, at least as a fetish: "The organizational independence of the Party is necessary, so that the proletariat can directly perceive its own class consciousness as a historical figure [*Gestalt*]." [53]

But with that, *ultimately,* the theory is also withdrawn from confirmation by the agreement of those whom it is to aid in the attainment of self-reflection. If the Party, rendered organizationally independent, must exercise "the uninterrupted *tactical* consideration of the state of consciousness of the broadest and most backward masses," then "here the function of the correct theory for the organizational problem of the Communist Party can be seen. The Party is to represent the highest objective form of proletarian action. However, for that, correct theoretical insight is the absolute precondition." [54] The further theoretical development, of which Lukács speaks at another place, is to be directed by the compulsive choice exercised by the organizational questions; but as far as the masses, which are mediatized, are concerned, the theory is an unassailable objective authority.

Organizational questions are not primary things. Between them and an objective philosophy of history Lukács has established a direct relationship. Stalinist praxis has furnished the fatal proof that a Party organization which proceeds instrumentally and a Marxism which has degenerated into a science of apologetics complement each other only too well. [55]

During the last few years Oskar Negt has undertaken some unorthodox considerations on the question of organization. [56] But if I understand him correctly, he himself still remains captive within the tradition in which the formation of theory and the organization of enlightenment have not been separated from the compulsions of strategic action with sufficient rigor. The autonomy of theory and enlightenment, however, is required for the sake of the independence of political action. No theory and no enlightenment can relieve us of the risks of taking a partisan position and of the unintended consequences involved in this. Attempts at emancipation, which at the same time are attempts to realize the Utopian contents of the cultural tradition, can, under certain circumstances be rendered plausible as *practical* necessities, taking into consideration the conflicts generated by the system (which have to be explained theoretically) and the avoidable repressions and suffering. But such attempts are also tests; they test the limits within which human nature can be changed and above all, the limits of the historically variable structure of motivation, limits about which we possess no theoretical knowledge, and in my view, cannot in principle possess any. If in testing "practical hypotheses" of this kind, we, the subjects involved, are ourselves included in the design of the experiment, then no barrier between experimenter and subjects can be erected. Instead, all the participants must have the opportunity to know what they are doing—thus, they must form a common will discursively.

There are situations in the face of which such considerations are either scurrilous or simply ridiculous; in such situations we must act as best we can—but then without appealing to a theory, whose capacity for justification does not extend that far.

A remark on the objectivating application of reflexive theories

The status of a theory designed for enlightenment entails the distinctive characteristic that its claim to truth must be tested on various levels. The first step of corroboration is scientific discourse; there the claim to truth of theoretically derived hypotheses is supported or refuted in the usual form of scientific argumentation. Naturally a theory which does not survive discursive examination must be rejected, and, of course, the claim to validity of reflexive theories can only be confirmed tentatively. But it can only be realized in the successful processes of enlightenment, which lead to the acceptance by those concerned, free of any compulsion, of the theoretically derivable interpretations. To be sure, processes of enlightenment, too, merely support the theory's claim to truth, without validating it, as long as *all* those potentially involved, to whom the theoretical interpretation has reference, have not had the chance of accepting or rejecting the interpretation offered *under suitable circumstances*. From this results a reservation with respect to the application of reflexive theories under the conditions of a political struggle. I return once again to the doubts raised by Gadamer and Giegel.

The groups which look upon themselves as theoretically enlightened (and which Marx in his time identified as the avant-garde of the Communists or also of the Party) must choose, with a view to their opponents, in each instance between enlighten-ment and struggle, thus between maintaining and breaking off communication. Even struggle, strategic action in the narrower sense, must, of course, remain coupled to discourse within the avant-garde and the groups to which they direct their appeal. In these practical discourses, which directly serve the organiza-tion of the struggle, and not enlightenment, the opponent who has been excluded by the breaking off of communication (and also the potential allies) can only be involved virtually. In rela-tion to this, the interesting task is posed of explaining the op-ponent's temporary incapacity for communication: in other words, thus explaining the ideological compulsion which is sup-posed to result necessarily from his being bound to particular interests. This requires an objectivating application of the theory. For in explanations of this kind, critical of ideology, we presuppose counterfactually an uninterrupted natural (and in the sense indi-cated above, dialectical) relation between the opponents. We abstract from the condition that our own group must claim, with the help of the same theory, to have understood the natural interrelationship, and thereby already have transcended it. Here we see that a reflexive theory can only be applied without con-tradiction under the conditions of enlightenment and not those of strategic action. This difference is explicable as a consequence of the retrospective posture of reflection.

When and insofar as it is successful, the organization of enlightenment initiates processes of reflection. The theoretical interpretations in terms of which the subjects come to know them-selves and their situation are retrospective: they bring to con-sciousness a process of formation [*Bildungsprozess*]. Thus the theory that creates consciousness can bring about the conditions under which the systematic distortions of communication are dissolved and a practical discourse can then be conducted; but it does not contain any information which prejudges the future action of those concerned. The psychoanalyst does not have the right, either, to make proposals for prospective action; the patient must draw his own conclusions as far as his actions are concerned. The retrospective posture of reflection has the result that the enlightenment it offers does enable us to extricate ourselves from a (dialectical) interrelationship of distorted communication. But to the extent to which the theory brings us enlightenment about our captivity within this interrelationship, it also disrupts the latter. Therefore the demand to act dialectically with insight is senseless. It is based on a category mistake. We only act within an interrelationship of systematically distorted communication as long as this interrelation perpetuates itself because it has not been understood in its falseness by us or anyone else. Therefore theory cannot have the same function for the organization of action, of the political struggle, as it has for the organization of enlightenment. The practical consequences of self-reflection are changes in attitude which result from insight into the causalities *in the past,* and indeed result of themselves. In contrast, strategic action oriented toward the future, which is prepared for in the internal discussions of groups, who (as the avant-garde) presuppose for themselves already successfully completed processes of enlightenment, cannot be justified in the same manner by reflective knowledge.

The declaration, critical of ideology, of the temporary incapacity for dialogue on the part of the strategic opponent is also subject to the hypothetical proviso that discourse, which is impossible under the given circumstances, will alone be able to decide the truth of the theory, once this discourse is held among all the participants. Of course, the objective application of a reflexive theory under the conditions of strategic action is not illegitimate in every respect. It can serve to interpret hypothetically the constellations of the struggle, from the viewpoint that every victory sought would not merely (as is usual) lead to the assertion of one particular interest against another, but instead would be a step toward the intended goal, which would make universal enlightenment, and by virtue of it, the uninhibited discursive formation of will, possible for all participants (and thus no longer merely those affected). Seen from that anticipated goal, such interpretations are retrospective. Therefore, for strategic action and for the maxims by which the decisions in the discourse that prepares for this action are justified, these interpretations open up a perspective. But the objectivating interpretations themselves cannot claim a justificatory function; for they must comprehend counterfactually one's own action, which now is only being planned (and the reactions of the opponent), as a moment of a collective process of education or consciousness formation which is not yet concluded. In contrast, the certainty of self-reflection is based on the remembered process of self-formation, which in precisely that act of remembering, is relegated to the past.

That the strategic action of those who have decided to engage in struggle, and that means to take risks, can be interpreted hypothetically as a retrospection which is possible only in anticipation, but at the same time not *compellingly justified* on this level with the aid of a reflexive theory, has its good reason: the vindicating superiority of those who do the enlightening over those who are to be enlightened is theoretically unavoidable, but at the same time it is fictive and requires self-correction: in a process of enlightenment there can only be participants.

I

The Classical Doctrine of Politics in Relation to Social Philosophy

In Aristotle's opus the *Politics* is part of the practical philosophy. Its tradition reaches even into the nineteenth century,[1] till it is finally broken off conclusively by the critique of Historicism.[2] And its course dries up even more completely, the more its currents are diverted into the channels of the specific sciences. Thus, since the end of the eighteenth century, the newly emerging social sciences and the disciplines of jurisprudence have drawn off the waters of classical politics. This process of separation from the body of practical philosophy has ended, for the time, with the establishment of political science on the model of the modern experimental sciences, having little more than the name in common with the old politics. Wherever we still encounter the latter, it seems hopelessly old-fashioned to us. Its justification was contested as long ago as the beginning of the modern period within the framework of philosophy itself; when, in the middle of the seventeenth century, Hobbes occupied himself with "the matter, forme and power of a commonwealth," he was no longer doing politics in the manner of Aristotle, but rather social philosophy. Two hundred years before its final defeat, he resolutely rejected the classical tradition. He completed the revolution in approach, in the whole manner of thinking, which had been initiated in political philosophy by Machiavelli on one side, by Thomas More on the other. The old politics has become alien to all of us, especially in three respects:

(1) Politics was understood to be the doctrine of the good and just life; it was the continuation of ethics. Aristotle saw no opposition between the constitution formulated in the *nomoi* and the ethos of civil life; conversely, the ethical character of action was not separable from custom and law. Only the *politeia* makes the citizen capable of the good life; and he is altogether a *zoon politikon*, in the sense that he is dependent on the city, the *polis*, for the realization of his human nature.[3] In Kant, in contrast, the ethical conduct of the individual who is free only inwardly is clearly distinguished from the legality of his external actions. And just as morality is separated from legality, so the two in turn are separated from politics, which is accorded a most dubious role as the technical expertise in a utilitarian doctrine of prudence.

(2) The old doctrine of politics referred exclusively to *praxis*, in the narrow sense of the Greeks. This had nothing to do with *techne*, the skillful production of artifacts and the expert mastery of objectified tasks.[4] In the final instance, politics was always directed toward the formation and cultivation of character; it proceeded pedagogically and not technically. For Hobbes, on the other hand, the maxim promulgated by Bacon, of *scientia propter potentiam*, is self-evident: mankind owes its greatest advances to technology, and above all to the political technique, for the correct establishment of the state.

(3) Aristotle emphasizes that politics, and practical philosophy in general, cannot be compared in its claim to knowledge with a rigorous science, with the apodictic *episteme*. For its subject matter, the Just and the Excellent, in its context of a variable and contingent praxis, lacks ontological constancy as well as logical necessity. The capacity of practical philosophy is *phronesis*, a prudent understanding of the situation, and on this the tradition of classical politics has continued to base itself, by way of the *prudentia* of Cicero, down to Burke's "prudence." Hobbes, on the other hand, wishes to make politics serve to secure knowledge of the essential nature of justice itself, namely of the laws and compacts. This assertion already complies with the ideal of knowledge originating in Hobbes's time, the ideal of the new science, which implies that we only know an object to the extent that we ourselves can produce it.[5]

Vico's reckoning of gains and losses in his comparison of the modern and the classical method of study

Hobbes commences the twenty-ninth chapter of *Leviathan* with the confident assertion: "Though nothing can be immortal, which mortals make: yet, if men had the use of reason they pretend to, their Commonwealths might be secured, at least, from perishing by internal diseases. . . . Therefore when they come to be dissolved, not by external violence, but intestine disorder, the fault is not in men, as they are the *Matter,* but as they are the *Makers,* and orderers of them." In this the three aforementioned aspects of the distinction between the modern and the classical approach are implicit. First, the claim of scientifically grounded social philosophy aims at establishing once and for all the conditions for the correct order of the state and society as such. Its assertions are to be valid independently of place, time, and circumstances, and are to permit an enduring foundation for communal life, regardless of the historical situation. Second, the translation of knowledge into practice, the application, is a technical problem. With a knowledge of the general conditions for a correct order of the state and of society, practical prudent action of human beings toward each other is no longer required, but what is required instead is the correctly calculated generation of rules, relationships, and institutions. Third, human behavior is therefore to be now considered only as the material for science. The engineers of the correct order can disregard the categories of ethical social intercourse and confine themselves to the construction of conditions under which human beings, just like objects within nature, will necessarily behave in a calculable manner. This separation of politics from morality replaces instruction in leading a good and just life with making possible a life of well-being within a correctly instituted order.

To be sure, "order" thereby changes its meaning, just as does the "domain" which is being ordered—the subject matter of political science itself is changed. The order of virtuous conduct is changed into the regulation of social intercourse. The displacement of the scientific object corresponds to the change in method-

ological approach which has just been indicated. Politics becomes
the philosophy of the social, so that today scientific politics can,
with justification, be counted among the social sciences.

Since the clarification, which Max Weber brought about, in
the so-called value-judgment controversy, and the precise definition of a positivistic "logic of investigation," [6] the social sciences
have been separated completely from the normative elements that
were the heritage of classical politics, a heritage now quite forgotten—that, in any case, was how the matter presented itself to
these sciences' understanding of themselves in the philosophy of
science. But social philosophy already had been forced to conceal
its normative implications from itself; it was no longer permitted
to admit to those elements of moral doctrine still adhering to it;
the normative determinations were submerged in equivocation
about "nature"—human nature and that of human institutions.
In social philosophy both are still current issues: its descent from
classical politics and its determined rejection of the latter's principles. But it would be much more difficult to work this out
systematically in terms of the antinomies contained in the critical
epistemology which formulates the modern social sciences' understanding of themselves. Therefore, it is more appropriate to
attempt a historical explication of the problem: how is knowledge
of the social interrelationships of life with a view to political action possible? How, within a political situation, can we obtain
clarification of what is practically necessary and at the same time
objectively possible? This question can be translated back into
our historical context: how can the promise of practical politics—
namely, of providing practical orientation about what is right
and just in a given situation—be redeemed without relinquishing,
on the one hand, the rigor of scientific knowledge, which modern
social philosophy demands in contrast to the practical philosophy
of classicism? And on the other, how can the promise of social
philosophy, to furnish an analysis of the interrelationships of
social life, be redeemed without relinquishing the practical orientation of classical politics?

On the road toward science, social philosophy has lost what
politics formerly was capable of providing as prudence. This loss

of hermeneutic power in the theoretical penetration of situations which were to be mastered practically was recognized as early as Vico, who, from the viewpoint of the humanistic rhetorical tradition, presented the new philosophy inaugurated by Galileo, Descartes, and Hobbes with a reckoning of profits and losses:

> But now to speak of prudence in civic life, as human affairs are governed by chance and choice, both of which are highly uncertain, . . . therefore those who solely have truth in view only with difficulty understand the paths which these affairs take and, with still greater difficulty, their goals. . . . Thus because one has to judge what is to be done in life according to the weight of these things and their encumbrances, which are called circumstances, and many of them may possibly be strange and incoherent, and some of them frequently wrong and at times even opposed to the goal, the actions of men cannot be measured with the straight ruler of the understanding, which is rigid. . . . The imprudent *scholars,* who go directly from the universally true to the singular, rupture the interconnections of life. The *wise men,* however, who attain the eternal truth by the uneven and insecure paths of practice, make a detour, as it is not possible to attain this by a direct road; and the thoughts which *these* conceive promise to remain useful for a long time, at least insofar as nature permits.[7]

Vico retains the Aristotelian distinction between science and prudence, *episteme* and *phronesis*: while science aims at "eternal truths," making statements about what is always and necessarily so, practical prudence is only concerned with the "probable." Vico shows how this latter procedure, precisely because it makes lesser theoretical claims, brings greater certainty in practice. He points to rhetoric, which employs primarily the capacity of *phronesis* and the art of "topics": "Of the orators we demand above all that they be capable, under the pressures of negotiations which permit no delays or postponement . . . of rendering immediate aid. However, when one places any doubtful proposition before our critical intellects, they will reply: let me meditate a while on this." [8]

This points to a dialectical relation that has only become fully clear with the development of the social sciences of our day: to the degree to which politics is scientifically rationalized, and praxis is instructed theoretically by technical recommendation, there is a growth of that residual complex of problems, in the face of which the analysis of the experimental sciences must confess its incompetence. On the basis of a division of labor between the empirical sciences and the setting of norms not subject to scientific verification, there is a growing scope for pure decision: to a growing degree the genuine area of praxis is withdrawn altogether from the discipline of methodical investigation.[9] In his polemics against the social philosophy of his time, Vico anticipated a tendency which has fully asserted itself only today. Uncertainty with respect to action grows greater, the more rigorous the criteria for scientific verification selected for this domain. Vico therefore rejects the presumption of modern philosophy to "carry the method of scientific judgment over into the practice of prudence." [10] The founding of practical philosophy as a science, which Bacon[11] had demanded and Hobbes first promised to attain, appears misguided to Vico. But here he fails to see that the new methodical approach also discloses a new object, the complex of interrelationships of social life. To be sure, "scientific" objectivation (only much later will it become permissible to say: the rigorous objectivation of experimental science) detaches the social to such an extent from the praxis of life that the application of the insights derived from social philosophy cannot itself be scientifically controlled.

Both parties thus are right for their part. If it should prove possible to clarify these disparate and apparently contradictory claims, or even to reconcile them, then the "reconciliation of the classical and the modern method," to which Vico devoted his work,[12] could become the methodological foundation of a New Science, or another *Scienza Nuova*. We shall trace the development from classical politics to modern social philosophy from the *dual* viewpoint of a change in methodological approach on the one hand and the disclosure of a new scientific object on the other.

The Thomist reception of Aristotelian Politics: the zoon politikon *as* animal sociale

How did the transformation of classical politics into modern social philosophy, which took place in the interval between Aristotle and Hobbes, come about? Aristotle is of the conviction that a *polis* which is truly worthy of the name and is not merely called such, must be concerned for the virtue of its citizens[13]—"for otherwise the community of the city would become a mere association," a *koinonia symmachia.* In Roman Law the latter is called *societas,* meaning an alliance between states as well as a commercial association between citizens—still used today in the sense of "society" or "company." Aristotle invents the fiction of such a private legal system of contracts, entered into for the purpose of securing and regulating a livelihood for all, to show what a *polis* is *not*: if citizens pursuing their own affairs, for the purpose of an orderly commerce through exchange and to provide for the case of warlike involvements, found a legal community, this in itself is *not* to be confused with a state. For, as he argues, though their intercourse takes place within a common locale, still they do so as though they were separated: each of them regards his own house as a city. A *polis,* on the other hand, is defined by its contrast to the *oikos,* the household. Against this, Hobbes deals precisely with the natural law construction of such a commerce of bourgeois private individuals, regulated by private law and protected by the sovereignty of the state. The connecting link between the two authors is, in a peculiar way, the social philosophy of Thomas Aquinas.

On the one hand, Thomas remains completely within the Aristotelian tradition: even if a state may be founded for the sake of survival, and has permanent existence, its existence still is only for the sake of the good life. "For were human beings to unite solely for the sake of mere survival, then beasts and slaves would be part of the *civitas* too; if, again, they were to unite only to gain goods and wealth, then all who are interested in the same manner in economic commerce would have to belong to the *civitas*." [14] A community can only be called a state when it renders its citizens capable of virtuous actions and thereby of the good life.

On the other hand, Thomas no longer understands this community as a genuinely political one: surreptitiously the *civitas* has become a *societas*. Nowhere is the involuntary remoteness from the old politics made visible so clearly as in the literal translation of the *zoon politikon: homo naturaliter est animal sociale.*[15] And another passage says: *naturale autem est homine ut sit animal sociale et politicum.*[16] Significantly, in Thomas the distinction, so decisively presented by his *Philosophus,* between the economic controlling power of the master of the *oikos* and the power of political rule in the public sphere is absent: for the despotic power over the *oikos* was wholly autocratic—*monarchia;* in the *polis,* however, it was the rule over free and equal men— *politie.*[17] However, the *princeps,* whose power Thomas was investigating, rules as a monarch, that is, in principle in the same manner as the *pater familias,* as *dominus. Dominium* now means domination, mastery pure and simple. The opposition of *polis* and *oikos* has been reduced to the common denominator of *societas;* and this is interpreted by analogy to the patriarchically organized domestic and family life, thus actually apolitically by Aristotle's criteria. The order of the *polis* was actualized in the participation of the citizens in administration, legislation, justice, and consultation; the *ordo* retained by Thomas sacrifices the political substance of the citizen's politically oriented will and consciousness as formed in public discussion: *bonum autem et salus consociatae multitudinis est ut eius unitas conservetur, quae dicitur pax.* The criterion of the well-founded *ordo* is no longer the freedom of the citizens, but tranquillity and peace—*pax;* an interpretation of that New Testament concept from a "police" viewpoint rather than from a political one. The central question of the old Politics, concerning the *quality* of governance, has been dropped. The *thema probandum* that Thomist "politics" focuses on—so justly called *social philosophy*—is instead the domestic and family order as extended to the state; it is the status hierarchy of the working citizens. The *ordo civitatis* now embraces labor, rehabilitated by Christianity, which for the Greeks was of a purely apolitical magnitude.[18]

Thus Thomas transforms Aristotelian Politics into a philosophy of the social order, but he does preserve the tradition insofar as he retains the interconnectedness of Ethics and Politics which is so clearly defined in Aristotle. On the one hand, the *ordo civitatis* can no longer be anchored in the *praxis* and *lexis* of free citizens, in public political life; but still, on the other hand, extended to the *ordo societatis,* it is to be capable of serving as the foundation of a moral law concretized in the ethics of hierarchic social˙rank, a code differentiated in terms of status and office, which guarantees universally accessible and immutably certain knowledge of a specific model of conduct. As is well known, Thomas finds his solution for this construction of the *social* order onto-theologically, in an order of *virtue*: the *lex naturae* is the basis of the order of the *civitas* as *societas* both ontologically in terms of the coherence of the cosmos and at the same time in terms of the correspondence of this cosmic lawfulness with the commandments of the Decalogue.

In the subsequent centuries this *lex naturae,* developed from Christianized Stoic Natural Law, becomes subject to the critique of the nominalists. The ontological seal stamped on Thomist social doctrine is shattered, because the social relations under which alone it can maintain credibility are themselves shattered. We shall simply leave this as evident. In any case, the question of the "wherefore" and "to what end?" of human social life, which can no longer be answered by the *ordo societatis,* now yields to another question: how and by which means can the *civitas* be ordered and made tractable? The breaking of the bond once provided by the order of virtue constructed in accordance with Natural Law allows the two elements which are torn apart in the real world also to diverge theoretically: the *dominium* of the princes becomes sovereign and the *societas* privatized under the administration of territorial states. In the same year in which Niccolo Machiavelli wrote his *Principe,* Thomas More was also working on his *Utopia.* The one was familiar, as diplomat, with the relations between the states of the Italian pentarchy; the other, as jurist, was initially the representative of the London burghers in Parliament, then minister and chancellor at the court of Henry VIII, dealing with the internal tasks of an absolutist state administration.

On the narrow social basis of the city-state Machiavelli could

still disregard the organization of the society and concentrate his
attention exclusively on the technique of maintaining and acquiring power. A state of war, universal and in principle irremovable,
is recognized from now on as the fundamental presupposition of
politics. The state is a state in the fullest sense under the conditions of conflict. Politics is the art, practiced internally as well as
externally, of the permanent strategies for asserting one's own
power, an art that can be studied and learned. The power of the
patriarchal households of Christian princes has congealed into the
abstract self-assertion of the sovereign (*suprema potestas*) and at
the same time detached itself from the essential social functions
of the domestic order expanded into a state. It is precisely with
these latter functions that Thomas More deals. On the strategically favorable basis of an island state, he could neglect the
techniques of self-assertion against external foes and actually deny
that essence of the political which is derived from the state of war.
Instead, the *ordo societatis* posed for him empirically the task of
organizing society by the techniques of a legal order.

Salus publica and bonum commune can no longer be determined teleologically. They have become unspecified gaps [*Leer-
stellen*] which Machiavelli can fill, on the basis of an analysis of
the prince's interests, with *raison d'état,* while More, on the other
hand, fills them, on the basis of an analysis of the interests of the
laboring citizens, with an economic order of immanent rationality.

*The break with the tradition: the modern concepts of the
political and the social in the* realpolitikally *demystified
world and the world of the Utopian design. Machiavelli and
More.*

The perspective now has changed in a specific manner: the
political conduct in which Machiavelli is interested and the social
order with which More is concerned are no longer explicated with
a view to the virtuous life of the citizens. The modern thinkers no
longer ask, as the Ancients did, about the moral conditions of the
good and exemplary life, but about the actual conditions of survival. The assertion of physical life, elementary survival, is directly
at issue. This practical necessity requiring technical solutions

marks the beginnings of modern social philosophy. In distinction to the ethical necessity of classical politics, it requires no theoretical foundation for the virtues and the laws in an ontology of human nature. If the theoretically based point of departure of the Ancients was how human beings could comply practically with the natural order, then the practically assigned point of departure of the Moderns is how human beings could technically master the threatening evils of nature. To be sure, beyond the securing of mere survival, social philosophy is also concerned with the betterment, the easing, and the raising of life to a higher level. Still, this is fundamentally different from the moral perfection of life. The pragmatic forms of heightening the agreeableness and strength of life retain their reference to the positive, to the mere maintenance of life. They still remain the comparative inflections of survival, of surviving the elementary dangers to life: the physical threat posed by the enemy or by hunger.

When it comes to these natural evils, social philosophy has not proved very inventive. Throughout the centuries it has only presented variations of the two chief ones which Machiavelli and More took for their point of departure: violent death at the hand of one's neighbor and death by starvation. Machiavelli asks: how can the reproduction of life be made secure politically? More asks: how can it be made secure socially and economically? For only by means of a successful technique for the acquisition and maintenance of power can men be freed from the fear of attacks on their life by others; and from the no less oppressive insecurity that attends the preservation of life amidst hunger and misery they can only be freed by the correct organization of the social order. Depending on which danger appears to be more basic, the self-preservation of life requires either the primacy of mobilized weapons or that of the organized means of subsistence.

To be sure, with the expansion of these two forms of reproduction of life, which are technically investigated here, a characteristic difference between them emerges. While the abolition of hunger opens up a vista on the possibly limitless enhancement of pleasant existence, the extension of the power which removes the fear of violent death, with the removal of the one evil produces another: the danger of enslavement. Therefore those social philosophers who define natural evil politically cannot assume the Utopian character of those who define it economically. Even when they do not wish to forgo a counter-Utopian form of enhancing life, they still fall prey to irrationality: even in Machiavelli *virtu* assumes the sense of a barbaric vitality, the transfigured guise of political power per se. In addition to the two "natural" evils, the threat of hunger and of human enemies, an "artificial" evil, the domination of man by man, becomes a third point of departure for social philosophical investigation: here the intention is to help secure dignity and peace for the oppressed and humiliated, just as Machiavelli promises power and security to those suffering from aggression and anxiety and More promises prosperity and happiness to the toil-worn and overburdened.[19]

As against the old politics, Machiavelli and More each establish a new field of investigation, because they extricate the structure of domination from its ethical context. From the time of Aristotle the issue was legislation to give citizens the possibility and the power to lead the good life; the positive value of the system of authority must prove itself in terms of the virtue of the citizens and of the freedom realized in the laws of the *polis*. Since Aristotle, Politics recognizes good and debased constitutions, and knows that constitution which is absolutely or relatively the best. Machiavelli and More undercut this way of posing the problem: Machiavelli, with the assertion, that in the face of a political substance which remains the same, always entailing relations of domination by a political minority over the mass of the private citizens, the normative orders merely represent historically changing superstructures. The comparative historian "will find that a small section of the populace desire to be free in order to obtain authority over others, but that the vast bulk of those who demand freedom, desire but to live in security. For in all states, whatever their form of government, the real rulers do not amount to more than forty or fifty citizens. . . ."[20] From the vicissitudes of institutions Machiavelli isolates the underlying structure of a relationship of repression which always remains the same. It is determined by the inevitability of aggression and defense, of threats and of self-assertion, of conquest and defeat, revolt and repression, power and impotence. This tension follows naturally, as it were, from the potential or actual reciprocal applications of force; it gives the new concept of the political its meaning.

Thomas More invalidates the traditional way of posing the problem of the constitution by making an analogous point. The substance of the relationship of domination which, underlying the changing normative orders, always remains the same, is conceived by him not in terms of a basic human condition which cannot be abolished, but in terms of the compulsion toward exploitation which is established together with private property:

> And so, when I examine and consider all the flourishing republics in the world today, believe me, nothing comes to mind except the conspiracy of the rich, who seek their own advantage under the name and title of the republic. They also devise and think up all sorts of ways and means to hold onto their ill-gotten gains with no fear of losing them, and then hire the labor of all the poor at the lowest price and abuse them. When once the rich have decreed that all these devices are to be observed in the public name (in other words, in the name of the poor too), they then become laws.[21]

This concept of the state as an institution of economic compulsion points to the basic situation of bourgeois society in which private subjects compete for the acquisition of scarce goods. "For elsewhere [other than in Utopia] everyone knows that however prosperous the republic may be, he will starve of hunger if he does not make some private provision for himself. And so he is forced to believe that he ought to take account of himself rather than the people, that is, others."[22]

From the possibility of overcoming this egoism of self-interest and the risks to life that are connected with it his new concept of the social derives its meaning. More states this concept naïvely: "What greater riches can there be than a life in happiness and peace, with all cares removed, without being worried about one's own daily bread. . . ."[23]

The normative sense of the laws is, to be sure, emptied of its moral substance by the reduction to underlying structures, be they those of political domination or those of economic exploitation; but the normative sense as such is not suspended. These laws still show their instrumental efficacy with respect to the practical tasks of the sustenance and enhancement of life. The normative sense of the laws recommended by Machiavelli is confirmed in preserving the readiness to die and to kill; for only by the force of arms can the natural evil represented by the threat of the enemy be overcome. The normative sense of the laws recommended by More is confirmed in the compulsion to work; for only thus can the natural evil of hunger be overcome.

Aristotle in principle recognized no separation between a politically enacted constitution and the ethos of civic life within the *polis*. Machiavelli and More, each in his own way, carried out the divorce of politics from ethics. The supreme maxim of the New Politics states: "The sole aim of the Prince must be to secure his life and his power. All means which he employs towards this end will be justified." Private virtue is divorced from political virtue; the practical prudence of private persons now obligated to the good—that is, the obedient—life is divorced from the technical prudence of the politician: "A Prince . . . cannot observe all those rules of conduct in respect whereof men are accounted good, being often forced, in order to preserve his Princedom, to act in opposition to good faith, charity, humanity, and religion." [24] More, on the other hand, emphasizes the social heteronomy of private virtue. He retains the humanistic heritage of the morality founded in Natural Law; but he deals primarily with the social preconditions which must be fulfilled before the mass of the citizens can realize the Stoic ideal of leisure. Virtue and happiness as such are here conceived in the traditional manner; but what is modern is the thesis that the technically appropriate organization to meet the necessities of life, the correct institutional reproduction of society, is prior to the good life, without these in themselves representing the content and the goal of moral action.

Just like the techniques for securing power in Machiavelli, so in More the organization of the social order is morally neutral. Both deal not with practical questions, but with technical ones. They construct models, that is, they investigate the fields, which they themselves have newly opened up, under artificial conditions.

Here even before experimental methods were introduced in the natural sciences, methodical abstraction from the multiplicity of empirical conditions was initially tried out. Surprisingly, even in this respect Machiavelli and More are on the same plane to occupy the same level if one assigns the same heuristic significance to the former's "realpolitical" demystification as to the latter's Utopian construction.

As a goal of political technique Machiavelli assumes the assertion of princely power externally as well as the unity and obedience of the citizens internally.[25] He isolates the operations directed toward the attainment of this goal from all social presuppositions. Political action is absolved from traditional and moral bonds and one also cannot count on these in the opponent (recognized as valid is the maxim: "All human beings are ungrateful, fickle, hypocritical, cowardly and selfish"); furthermore, political action cannot rely on established institutions and acquired legitimation for support; instead it must always begin, as it were, afresh (Machiavelli assumes that power is gained by alien force or accident: "He whom fortune alone has elevated from private status to the throne, while he may achieve this with little difficulty, will have all the more in maintaining his position"). The design of Machiavelli's experiment is hardly less fictive than that of More's: absolute freedom in the rational choice of means for the purpose of maintaining power in the exceptional state of latent civil war, of potential revolt, or the actual threat of a competing foe. Under these conditions of *necessità,* Politics is the art of regulating *fortuna,* "so that she will not be capable of showing at each turn of the course, what she is capable of." Cesare Borgia furnished the historical example.[26] The case of the conjunctural state, the foundations of which must still be laid, is a case that is as if created for the analysis of this art. Machiavelli's book of recipes for the technically correct calculus of power laid the foundations for the tradition of the *arcana imperii* which was so influential under the absolutism of the subsequent centuries. As is well known, it instructs the princes in how the *vis dominationis* can be asserted in typical situations by means of mobilizing alliances, soldiers, and monies in the tactically correct manner.

Instead of such empirical rules for a political technique,

More offers an example of a social organization that is conceivable under empirical conditions. As the goal of such an organization he presupposes the welfare of free citizens. His experimental design to a great extent isolates the reproduction of social life from political intervention in the sense of Machiavelli: wars are discounted and the functions of public power reduced to a minimum; furthermore, private ownership of the means of production and of consumers' goods is abolished. The two assumptions permit a model in which social institutions can be reduced to their instrumental significance, just as the means of domination can under the exceptional fictive conditions assumed by Machiavelli. The example of an order based on communal property uncovers the motives of social conflicts. More analyzes how, together with removing the concern for securing the sustenance of life, the causes for a whole series of criminal offenses, the possibility of differentiating social prestige in terms of wealth, and the necessity for legalizing exploitation are also removed. "On top of this, from the daily wage of the poor, the rich wear something away every day, not merely by private fraud but even by public laws." [27] Wealth, prestige, and power lose their appearance of being naturally given. The historical interconnection between social stratification and political domination, on the one hand, and the organization of social labor, on the other, becomes transparent.

> *The change in the methodological approach: from practical knowledge to the pragmatic art of techniques of power and of social organization*

Even an interpretation which is guided by the aim of placing in the foreground the "modern" traits to be found in *The Prince* and in *Utopia,* in order to contrast them with the background of traditional Politics—to be sure, not without a degree of stylization—still should not seek to obscure the frontier which separates Machiavelli and More from Thomas Hobbes, the founder of social philosophy as a science. What is involved here is a limitation in the subject matter as well as in the method.

The attempts to investigate each of the diverging elements of Thomist social philosophy—*dominium* and *societas*—separately

in terms of their purely technical aspect remained abstract. Machiavelli ignored the historical task of accounting for the development of a sphere of bourgeois civil society; More ignored the
political state of affairs resulting from the competition of sovereign states. Hobbes is free of the complementary blindness of
each of his predecessors, because for him the systematic task of
constructing sovereignty on the basis of Natural Law is different
than it was for Machiavelli in sixteenth-century Florence; in
seventeenth-century England Hobbes can only see the regent's
suprema potestas in its functional interrelationship with a *societas*
in the process of burgeois emancipation. A contractual constituting of princely sovereignty is now the order of the day as
political self-assertion, in its content, has become dependent on
the primary needs of the social sphere. Hobbes already justifies
the external assertion of the state's sovereignty as due to the
regent's supreme authority with respect to internal affairs; for he
is to guarantee the commerce, conducted on the basis of contract,
between bourgeois private persons:[28] the social contract and the
contract of political rule coincide. The sovereign bears the sword
of war as the sovereign to whom the sword of justice—competence
in jurisprudence and penal execution—has been entrusted. He
exercises *political* power in Machiavelli's sense because the universal political condition of a *bellum omnium in omnes* (the war
of all against all) is to be eliminated and the untamed political
struggle to be pacified and neutralized for the sake of a rational
organization of society—precisely the Utopian purpose of Thomas
More.

Hobbes overcomes the methodological weakness of his predecessors still more decisively: Machiavelli and More made no
claims to be doing politics and social philosophy as a science—
neither as a *scientia* in the traditional sense of practical philosophy nor as science in the modern sense of that empirical analytic
procedure which was only proclaimed a century after Machiavelli
and More by Bacon (and even he was not able to attain what he
had anticipated). Machiavelli and More stand at the midway
point; methodologically they have broken with the presuppositions of the tradition and have substituted a technical approach
for the practical perspective; but lacking Descartes' rigorous

method of knowledge or the successful method of investigation of Galileo, to a degree they still treated their material pragmatically. Machiavelli arrived at recommendations with respect to techniques; More offered a proposal for social organization.

When More's report of the *Nova Insula Utopia* appeared in 1517 under the title *De optimo Reipublicae statu,* his humanistic readers must have expected a new formulation of the traditional body of political doctrine. But precisely that comparison with the Platonic model, which More himself invokes, shows how misleading the title is: the work does not analyze the essential nature of justice; instead it imitates the contemporary reports of voyagers. Because, according to the conception of the Greeks, justice can only be realized within the order of life attained in the *polis*, they explain the essential nature of justice in terms of the essential nature of the state, and that means the perfected constitution of the governance of free citizens. More, on the other hand, no longer appeals to an essential order, to conditions which must necessarily be recognized, of which he wishes to give an example from experience; More's state is not an ideal in the Kantian sense. Rather, he invents a "fiction" in the manner in the literary sense, where the imagination of something actually existing presents to us objects and persons as though they had been empirically observed—just as contingent and as underivable as the testimony of the senses presents them to us in their reality. In the same manner More creates the illusion of reality within the framework of an invented voyage of discovery, thus the kind of experience which the Ancients called *historia*. "But if you had been in Utopia with me and seen in person their habits and practices, as I did (for I lived there more than five years and would never have wanted to leave except to tell of that new world), then you would openly admit that *this was the only place* where you had seen a people properly governed." [29] This, "the only place" and nowhere else, reveals the dual meaning of the Utopian work and the claim based on it: to fictitiously depict social relations in such a realistic manner that they can be *imagined* as existing under empirical conditions, though of course not to be thought as already actually existing.

More has pragmatically attained the conviction "that wherever there are private possessions, where everything is measured by money, there a state can scarcely ever be justly and successfully managed." [30] Instead of attempting scientifically to test this hypothesis, considered as an experiential principle, More invents the model of a constitution based on correspondingly changed conditions. If this fiction can be endowed with the character of an example from experience with sufficient credibility, which means without contradicting previous experience, then the proof has been rendered that such a social state can be conceived as existing under empirical conditions. Thus the technical prescription according to which the existing state is to be transformed into the desired one—in this case the change in property relations—can be verified indirectly by its correspondence to all previous experience. In principle the same factors are determining for this procedure as for the wholly different procedure of Machiavelli: namely, the technical viewpoint of an analysis based entirely on the pragmatics of experience.

Machiavelli reduces the practical knowledge of politics to a technical skill. For the Ancients, too, the politicians entrusted with the direction of the state were to combine their prudence with certain capabilities, say, the mastery of economics or of military strategy. With Machiavelli, however, only the "mechanical" workmanlike skill of the strategist remains for politics. And he is talking about the art of war in the literal sense,[31] as well as that skill which is cultivated when politics is developed solely from a strategic point of view. It then becomes an "art" without precedent in the canon of the traditional arts—Machiavelli's own distinctive discovery. This art of governing men [*Menschenfuehrung*], as we would say today, is also a technical skill in its way, but it has—and this was inconceivable for the Ancients—human behavior rather than nature as the material on which it operates. The behavior and conduct of human beings themselves, especially their impulses toward self-assertion and subjection, are the materials which the princely artisan is to shape. Machiavelli still attains his psychological insights in the casuistic manner of the historian; but the technical purpose is clearly enunciated: to deal with Politics as the science of domination in order to establish a *regnum hominis,* man's control over history, now mastered too:

Prudent men are wont to say—and this is not rashly and
without good ground—that he who would foresee what has
to be, should reflect on what has been, for everything that
happens in the world at any time has a genuine resemblance
to what happened in ancient times. This is due to the fact
[that the agents who bring such things about are men, and]
that men always have, and always have had, the same pas-
sions, whence it naturally comes about that the same effects
are produced.[32]

To this Horkheimer, looking ahead, comments: "It is the great-
ness of Machiavelli . . . to have recognized the possibility of a science of politics, corresponding in its principles to modern physics
and psychology and to have enunciated its fundamental traits
simply and definitely."[33] This interpretation anticipates the development that only took place after Machiavelli, insofar as for
him the skill of acquiring and preserving power does indeed result from a transferring of workmanlike *techne* to a domain of
praxis till then reserved for *phronesis;* but this still completely
lacks the scientific precision of *calculated technique.* The claim
to a foundation of politics on the principles contained in the
Galilean ideal of science, can, strictly speaking, only be made
within the framework of a mechanistic picture of the world.

To be sure, the guiding cognitive interest of *The Prince* and
the *Utopia* had already suggested "acting in the mode of producing."[34] Machiavelli and More had broken through the barrier,
inviolable in classical philosophy, between *praxis* and *poiesis,* had
sought the relative certainty of workmanlike-technical knowledge
in a field till then reserved for the uncertainty and nontransfer-
able character of practical prudence. However, this initiative
could not be carried out radically until technical knowledge itself was secured theoretically and not merely pragmatically. In
order to attain this, another barrier had to fall: the superior
valuation in the Greco-Christian tradition of the *vita contem-
plativa* over the *vita activa,* the shutting off of theory from *praxis.*
For the Ancients the capacity for goal-directed activity, skill,
techne, was knowledge that always pointed toward theory as the

supreme aim and the highest goal, just as was the prudence of reasonable action, *phronesis;* but they could never themselves be derived from theory or justified in terms of theory. They remained "lower" cognitive faculties precisely for the sake of this self-sufficiency of contemplation. The sphere of action, of doing, the life-world [*Lebenswelt*] of human beings and citizens concerned for their preservation or for their communal life was, in the strict sense, theory-free. This only changed when the modern scientific investigation of nature set about to pursue theory with the attitude of the technician.

This does not mean that the purpose with which modern science pursues knowledge, especially in its initial period, is subjectively directed toward producing insights which can be applied technically. Still, from the days of Galileo on, the intention of research itself is objectively to attain the skill of *"making"* the processes of nature oneself in the same way as they are produced by nature. Theory is measured by its capacity for artificially reproducing natural processes. In contrast to *episteme,* it is designed for "application" in its very structure. Thereby theory gains a new criterion of its truth (aside from that of logical consistency)—the certainty of the technician: we *know* an object insofar as we can *make* it. Due to investigation carried out with the attitude of the technician, however, the technical comportment itself also changes. The certainty of the technician that is distinctive for modern scientific knowledge is not to be compared with the more relative certainty of the classical artisan, who masters his material by long practice.[35]

It was Hobbes who first studied the "laws of civil life" with the explicit purpose of placing political action from now on on the incomparably more certain basis of that scientifically controlled technics which he had come to know in the mechanics of his time. Thus Hannah Arendt characterized the constructions of rational Natural Law correctly as the attempt to find a theory "by which one can produce, with scientific precision, political institutions which will regulate the affairs of men with the reliability with which a clock regulates the motions of time or creation understood in terms of a clock regulates the processes of nature." [36]

But why does Hobbes utilize for this purpose the instrument of the contract, and why does he found his scientific social philosophy on a legal construction? [37]

Hobbes's foundation of social philosophy as science: the problematic origin of the norms of natural reason in the mechanics of natural desires.

The interconnection of *dominium* and *societas,* the unity of state and society had its foundation in classical Natural Law under the synonymous titles of *res publica* and *societas civilis.* But in the meantime the Reformation had led to a positivization and formalization of the prevailing Thomistic Natural Law,[38] which permitted Althusius to pose the question: "*Quis enim exacte scire poterit, quid sit iustitia, nisi prius quid sit ius cognoverit eiusque species? Ex iure enim iustitia.*" [39] Law became the epitome of positive ordinances, which individuals imposed upon each other by contract; and justice now designated no more than respect for the validity of these contracts (Hobbes drew from this the conclusion: "Even if certain actions which are just in one state are unjust in another, justice, which is the obedience of the law, is the same everywhere").[40] Such formal law corresponded to objective conditions insofar as the two great processes which fundamentally changed the interconnection of *dominium* and *societas* asserted themselves within the territorial states of the sixteenth century: that is, the centralization and at the same time the bureaucratization of power within the modern state apparatus of the sovereign national governments, as well as the expansion of capitalistic trade in commodities and the gradual transformation of the mode of production, till then bound to household production. This new complex of interest of national and territorial economies, oriented toward the market rather than the household [manor], developed under the governance of a supreme authority, which was only beginning to attain full sovereignty. Thus, for the time being at least, this sphere "of civil society," authorized by absolute rule, can be appropriately conceived in terms of the categories of the modern state, precisely the categories of a formal law technically applied to the regulation of social intercourse.

The contract is viewed as an instrument that obligates the state to perform its dual task, legally to employ its monopolized power in the service of peace and order, on the one hand, and on the other, to utilize it for the common welfare—but also to limit its power to these functions.

The power legitimized by Natural Law organizes the threat and the employment of force for the protection of civil society, with the goal of removing the fear of enemies, of hunger, and of servitude.

In Althusius the system of contracts remains wholly fortuitous: he enumerates the existing institutions of civil intercourse and of state power without explaining them. The analytic trick, to conceive of them as though they had originated in contracts, does not lead to a demonstration of necessary relations, but merely to a schematization of accidental ones. Althusius cannot explain why individuals should enter into contracts at all, nor can he explain why they should respect the contracts once in force; and above all why the sovereign power, though it is conceived as originating in such contracts, should then, as constituted force, stand uncontested by the parties to the contract. By establishing the causal connection between these three points, Hobbes transforms Natural Law into a science—for such a science has fulfilled its task when it has found out "the effects of anything . . . from the known generation of the same and conversely the generation from their effect. . . ." [41]

The connection between the causes known in terms of their effects is presented as follows: that the sovereignty of the state power results from the necessity to enforce the validity of the system of contracts; that the contract system itself follows from the necessity of making survival in peace and order possible; and finally, that the common interest in peace and order follows from the necessity of removing the contradictions existing in the state of nature. This state of nature itself, presupposed in the same manner by Machiavelli and the Reformation as the evil nature of man and of the depraved world, must be understood in its lawfulness, in order for the legal construction to be founded in the causal connections of a Natural Law that is now interpreted mechanistically.[42] Hobbes must specify *that* compulsion of nature which of itself necessarily produces an artificial compulsion—precisely, an order of law secured by punitive force. And he believes that he has found this compulsion in the fear of violent death: "For every man is desirous of what is good for him and shuns that which is evil for him, but chiefly the chiefest of natural evils, which is death; and this he does *by a certain impulsion of nature, no less than that whereby a stone moves downward.*" [43] In order to escape the permanent risks of an uncontrolled political situation, with its universal relationships of friendship and enmity, men seek the security of a civil order; and indeed men do "desire, even *nature itself impelling them,* to be freed from this misery." [44] What had remained fortuitous in Althusius is given an inner coherence by Hobbes: the social contract and the contract of government are no longer understood merely as instruments for rationalizing nature devoid of law; instead their rationality, which proceeds from the laws of nature itself, is demonstrated. Justice becomes immanent within the nexus of causality.

In its role as the science of the state of nature, a modern physics of human nature replaces the classical ethics of Natural Law. Under naturalistic presuppositions, the traditional determinants which have been retained are transformed and with a profound irony. For after all, the absolute Natural Law of St. Thomas assumed that in the state of nature the ethics of the Sermon on the Mount had been directly realized: that there was no domination: all are free; there were no social distinctions: all are equal; there was no personal and exclusive property: everything is common to all, all have a right to everything. Verbally, Hobbes accepts these determinates; but tacitly he replaces the subject of Law. In place of the *animal sociale* in the Christian-Aristotelian sense of a *zoon politikon* he sets an *animal politicum* in the sense of Machiavelli, in order then to show quite readily that precisely the assumption of these rights, especially the right of all to everything, as soon as it is applied to a pack of "free" and "equal" wolves, will have as consequence a state in which they mutually tear and devour each other. This subtle playing with venerable attributes reveals the radical rethinking of classical Natural Law, so that it becomes the actual absence of all right and justice for the natural environment, which lacks positive regulation and rational compacts. The conditions under which a community of saints was supposed to live, appear, in a diabolical inversion, as the conditions under which human beasts live in a continual life-and-death struggle.

As though it were a game, Hobbes projects absolute Natural Law onto a relationship among men interpreted in the Machiavellian manner; this produces the appearance that the lawfulness of the state of nature has been formulated normatively. But actually Hobbes employs these rights (the right to freedom and equality, the right of all to everything) in a negative formulation: that there is no political domination, no social inequality, no private property—these are merely descriptive specifications divested of their normative character. For his analysis of the natural state of the human species prior to all sociation is not ethical at all; it is purely physicalistic: it deals solely with the apparatus of sensation, with instinctive reactions, with the animal motion of biological entities, with the physical organization of men and their causally determined modes of reaction.

To be sure, this transition, this cinematic "dissolve," from a normative interpretation of Natural Law to a causal interpretation of natural science applied to the laws of the state of nature calls to mind the origins of the modern concept of Natural Law. The world of phenomena had to have been conceived sociocosmically as a state—a *civitas*—governed by unchanging laws, before the empirically ascertained invariants of natural processes could become identified with "causal laws." [45] This prior transference of juridical categories to nature as a whole may have facilitated the equivocal usage of the term "Law of Nature," which Hobbes could not avoid employing in his precarious transition from the natural fact of the war of all against all to the Natural Law norm of the civil state. He himself held this transition to be causally necessary and thereby became entangled in the deep ambiguity of his concept of nature: he demanded of the causal order in the state of nature those norms he required for the foundation of his civil state. But the wholly mechanistic understanding of nature had actually inherited these norms from a prior transference of normative categories, which it had thereupon suppressed.

Hobbes calls *both* of these Natural Law: the *causal* connections of man's asocial instinctual nature *prior* to the contractual constitution of society and the state; and the *normative* regulation of their social cohabitation *after* this constitution. The difficulty here is evident: Hobbes has to derive from the causality of human instinctive nature the norms of an order whose function is precisely to compel the renunciation of primary satisfaction of these instincts.[46]

In an important passage Hobbes presents the distinction between the compulsion of natural desires and the commandments of natural reason:

> And I found the reason was, that from a community of goods there must needs arise contention, whose enjoyment should be greatest. And from that contention all kinds of calamities must unavoidably ensue, which by the instinct of nature every man is taught to shun. Having therefore thus arrived at two maxims of human nature: the one arising from the *concupiscible* part, which desires to appropriate to itself the use of those things in which all others have a joint interest; the other proceeding from the *rational,* which teaches every man to fly a contra-natural dissolution, as the greatest mischief which can arrive to nature: which principles being laid down, I seem from them to have demonstrated by a most evident connexion, in this little work of mine, the absolute necessity of leagues and contracts, and thence the rudiments necessity of leagues and contracts, and thence the rudiments both of moral and of civil prudence.[47]

The uninhibited satisfaction of natural needs brings with it the dangers of the conflict of all against all. When, however, the natural concern for self-preservation grows to the point where the fear of violent death is transformed into the fear of living continually in fear, then natural reason points the way to a satisfaction of needs, mediated by rules of social life, and to this extent inhibited, but therefore also freed from danger. If, as Hobbes assumes, the commandments of natural reason—thus understood as natural laws in the normative sense—necessarily grow out of a compulsion of natural desires—that is, natural laws in the causal-mechanical sense—then the problem lies precisely in interpreting this necessity itself causally—for actually, as will be seen, it can only be conceived as a "practical" necessity. Hobbes, under the mechanistic presuppositions fundamental to the theory of science of his time, had to reject as meaningless a "necessity" experientially derived from the conditions of praxis; and therefore he could only avoid the difficulty by means of an equivocation, that was almost methodical, in the use of the term "law of nature."

This problem complex, so laboriously suppressed in the transition from the state of nature to the social state, erupts again in the concept of an order of government designed according to the Natural Law. If it resulted initially from the derivation of the norms of natural reason from the mechanics of natural desires, it now returns again in the question: how can the commandments of Natural Law be made to prevail against the continually active compulsion of instinctive human nature?

The first antinomy: the sacrifice of the liberal content in favor of the absolute form of its sanction

The rationale for Hobbes's absolutist state, constructed according to Natural Law, is a liberal one. For the laws of natural reason developed under the title of freedom do not only obligate the conscience and goodwill of men inwardly; they also form the basis of the social and governmental contract of the citizens in such a manner—as is shown in the thirteenth chapter of *De Cive* —that those who hold political power are in principle obligated to a compliance with the liberal intention of Natural Law. In this respect Hobbes is the real founder of Liberalism. As evidence for this thesis we need merely point to these crucial principles:

(1) Government is instituted for the sake of peace, and peace pursued for the sake of the general welfare. This welfare does not merely consist in the preservation of life as such, but in the most pleasant life possible. But this is not the fruit of virtue, as is the "good life" of the classical tradition, but rather the fruit of the enjoyment of freely disposable property.[48]

(2) By his laws the sovereign cares for the welfare of the

citizens. These laws form the basis and regulate the order of property, so that "others may not hinder us from the free use and enjoyment of our own, and we may not interrupt others in their quiet possession of theirs." [49] Penal law sanctions this order, but is restricted, as is law in general, to a purely instrumental significance, rather than for the punishment of guilt, for protection, correction, and prevention. [50]

(3) The laws have the character of formal and general norms. The formality of the law ensures the citizens freedom in the sense of liberality. [51] In contrast to Natural Law, which permeates the whole of life, formal law separates the legal order from the order of life and creates areas of free scope which are legally neutral and not in their content subject to norms for the legitimate pursuit of private interests. [52]

Furthermore, the generality of the laws guarantees a formal equality of rights and duties, [53] above all an equal distribution of the tax burdens. [54] And aside from this, it ensures the predictability of the actions of others, thus an expectancy of behavior conforming to universal rules—and it is only this which makes civil intercourse possible.

(4) The sovereign must see to it that he enables as many citizens as possible to live as comfortably as human nature permits, by means of the fewest possible laws. [55] He maintains peace internally and defends the peace against external enemies, so that every citizen can be "enriched" and "enjoy a harmless liberty." [56]

Hobbes constructs sovereignty in accordance with Natural Law, because the legitimating reason of the state is to make possible a liberal society. But that is only one side of the matter. [57] For in order to bring about such a society he must construct sovereignty in the form of *absolute power;* this is explained by his Machiavellian presuppositions: a state of nature which is completely political, in which everyone fears death and therefore seeks to assert himself by all possible means in a life-and-death struggle. This condition can only be terminated by a state of peace, when the fear of all men, that they must continually live in fear, induces them to invest a single authority with a monopoly of physical force, so that it can compel all to keep the peace. To be sure, they pay this price in the expectation that the absolute power will be exercised in the service of a liberal society. The authority of the state must be absolute, absolved even from this latter expectation, if the natural force of the political is to be tamed at all—an argument which even Kant found unanswerable, to the extent that he disavowed any right of resistance to the power of the state. However, Hobbes carries this argument still further. The dialectical way in which political natural force is tamed by means of a second nature, embodied in sovereignty founded in contract, requires, of course, that the laws of civil intercourse are to be provided, as it were, wholesale by the general clause of the social contract, and that these laws can only be given in the exclusive form of sovereign commands (*auctoritas non veritas facit legem*). But the dialectic is only fulfilled through the stipulation that the judgment itself, of whether these commands correspond to the expectations of the social contract, must be reserved exclusively for the sovereign. For without this proviso his sovereignty would not be absolute, and that, of course, was the initial presupposition.[58] The sovereign not only legislates all laws, but it is also he alone who determines whether they correspond with the Natural Law of the social contract. Not only can he never do an injustice, but he cannot even act in a *recognizably* immoral manner.[59] As a consequence, the distinction between monarchy and tyranny, between legitimate and despotic rule, is inadmissible in practice. ". . . He is said to be a king who governs well, and he a tyrant that doth otherwise. The case therefore is brought to this pass, that a king legitimately constituted in his government, if he seem to his subjects to rule well and to their liking, they afford him the appellation of a king, and if not, count him a tyrant." [60] In Hobbes too, Machiavelli in the end carries the day over More. In the end he cannot rid himself of the spirit he has conjured up at the beginning of his system. The liberal justification of the state is devoured by the state's absolutism,[61] and *in this* it is indeed a Leviathan.

This dialectic, in which the liberal contents of Natural Law are sacrificed to the absolutist form of its sanctions, can be related to the methodological difficulties that formed our point of departure. The norms of Natural Reason ultimately fall prey to the mechanics of natural desires from which they were initially derived. For obedience to these norms must be secured by means of sanctions which are calculated in terms of the physics of human nature: thus laws become commands in the sense of a psychologically calculated compulsive motivation. In the end the sanctioning force, compelling by natural laws in the causal sense, gains control over the natural laws in the normative sense, even if it does so in their name. In the preface to *De Cive* Hobbes warns his readers to respect this relationship in their practical conduct too.

> I persuaded myself . . . that you will esteem it better to enjoy yourselves in the present state, though perhaps not the best, than by waging war endeavor to procure a reformation for other men in another age, yourselves in the meanwhile either killed or consumed with age.[62]

The second antinomy: the practical impotence of the science of power as social technique

Only at this point, where Hobbes reflects on the relationship of his theory to the political praxis of his fellow citizens, is the truly problematic character revealed of that derivation of normative laws from causal ones, the founding of relationships of justice on the inviolable laws of nature, to which the attempt to found social philosophy as a science has led. Hobbes, too, pursues this science with the approach of a technician: he appropriates Bacon's maxim that science only serves power; theory only serves construction; and in the end all knowledge only is directed toward an action or an achievement.[63] Hobbes investigates the mechanics of social relations in the same way as Galileo investigates that of motion in nature:[64]

> For as in a watch, or some such small machine [an analogy by which nature as a whole was interpreted at that time— J.H.], the matter, figure, and motion of the wheels cannot well be known, except it be taken insunder and viewed in parts; so to make a more curious search into the rights of states and duties of subjects, it is necessary, I say, not to take

them insunder, but yet that they be considered as if they were dissolved; that is, that we rightly understand what the quality of human nature is, in what matters it is, in what not, fit to make up civil government, and how men must be agreed among themselves that intend to grow up into a well-grounded state.[65]

The relationship of theory and praxis is defined in accordance with the model of classical mechanics. The scientific analysis of the relationships of life, objectified as an object of nature, informs us about the causal lawfulness according to which existing states reproduce themselves; it is less interested in the factual history of the origins of specific institutions than in the general conditions for the functioning of human social life. The construction of Natural Law can be understood as a general physics of sociation. With its knowledge concerning the basic character and constitution of human nature, it specifies those institutional arrangements, the physically effective compulsive force of which can be expected to produce the natural modes of reaction that will lead to an orderly cohabitation of human beings. This is the mechanics of the societal state, while the state of nature is the epitome of all those disturbances which can be predicted with certainty when the institutions are ineffectual or totally lacking. As science also proceeds by means of causal analysis in the domain of social philosophy, the construction of Natural Law serves to explain the functioning of state apparatuses. This knowledge can be applied prognostically and can serve to reorganize a governmental order that is threatened.

Hobbes leaves no doubt about the technological self-understanding of a social philosophy established as a science: "Now the greatest commodities of mankind are the arts; namely, of measuring matter and motion; of moving ponderous bodies; of architecture; of navigation; of making instruments for all uses; of calculating the celestial motions, the aspects of the stars, and the parts of time. . . . Philosophy, therefore, is the cause of all these benefits." [66] And in the same way, a scientific social philosophy can be of use, to an even greater degree than the philosophy of nature:

But the utility of moral and civil philosophy is to be esti-
mated, not so much by the commodities we have by knowing
these sciences, as by the calamities we receive from not knowing them. Now, all such calamities as may be avoided by
human industry, arise from war, but chiefly from civil war;
for from this proceed slaughter, solitude, and the want of all
things. But the cause of war is not that men are willing to
have it; for the will has nothing for object but good, at least
that which seemeth good. Nor is it from this, that men know
not that the effects of war are evil; for who is there that
thinks not poverty and loss of life to be great evils? The
cause, therefore, of civil war is, that men know not the
causes neither of war nor of peace. . . . But why have they
not learned them, unless for this reason, that none hitherto
have taught them in a clear and exact method? [67]

Thus because, before Hobbes, the Cartesian demand for a method
had not been put forth regarding the foundations of social philosophy, the classical doctrine of politics could never attain real
knowledge. In possession of the new method, Hobbes for the first
time develops a physics of sociation. As soon as insight into the
mechanics of the societal state has been gained, the technically
required arrangements can be fashioned to produce the correct
social and political order.

To be sure, from this the difficulty arises that the technicians
who install the "correct" order must be drawn from the circle of
citizens who, at the same time, as members of an existing "faulty"
order, also constitute the objects of this scientific knowledge. The
same human beings whose behavior was initially conceived as an
object of nature, in the necessary causal interconnections of institutional compulsions and modes of reaction given with human
nature, must at the same time assume the role of subjects who,
with the knowledge of these interrelationships, are to fashion the
better arrangements. They are just as much objects of the conditions to be investigated, as subjects of the conditions to be
changed.

Thus the same difficulty which arose in the genetic approach
to considering the social contract, where the normative constraint

was to arise out of natural causality, is now repeated in the technological interpretation of the relation of theory to praxis. In the
first case, Hobbes can point to the heuristic character of the
artificially constructed state with the argument that all states
which in fact arose by virtue of despotic force can still be conceived *as though* the power of their sovereigns arose from a reciprocal contractual obligation. However, in the actual application
of his social philosophy Hobbes must again have recourse to the
fictional role of a constitutive assembly of citizens. For if his own
doctrine is to have any practical consequences, it must be generally published and accepted by the mass of the citizens. The
citizens must come to understand through public argumentation
and to recognize that under the name of "natural laws" his doctrine enunciates objective needs and recommends what is practically necessary in the general interest:

> But now on the contrary, that neither the sword nor
> the pen should be allowed any cessation; that the knowledge
> of the law of nature should lose its growth, not advancing
> a whit beyond its ancient stature; that there should still be
> such a siding with the several factions of philosophers, that
> the very same action should be decried by some, and as
> much elevated by others; . . . these, I say, are so many signs,
> so many manifest arguments, that what hath hitherto been
> written by moral philosophers, hath not made any progress
> in the knowledge of the truth; but yet hath took with the
> world, not so much by giving any light to the understanding
> as entertainment to the affections, whilst by the successful
> rhetorications of their speech they have confirmed them in
> their rashly conceived opinions.[68]

In this passage Hobbes polemicizes against the topical treatment of the subject matter in the old politics and against the
humanistic rhetoric of his contemporaries in whom the classical
tradition still lived on. Half a century later he was answered by
Vico's metacritique of the attempt to replace practical prudence
by a methodologically rigorous science of social philosophy, "as
they [the representatives of the new method] have not developed

the general sense and have never sought to establish the probabil-
ities, being quite content with the truth alone, so they do not consider what *men as a whole* think of these things and whether they
also have the impression of truth. . . . The ancient Roman therefore rightly asked what the case 'appears' to be and judges and
senators formulated their opinions so as to include the words 'it
seems.' " [69] Vico hits on the difficulty with which Hobbes has wres-
tled in vain. The scientifically established theory of social action
fails to include the dimension of praxis to which the classical doctrine offered direct access. Social philosophy constructed after the
model of modern physics, namely, with the attitude of the technician, can only reflect the practical consequences of its own
teachings within the limits of technological self-evidence. Hobbes
can only repeat in a stereotype manner:

> For were the nature of human actions as distinctly
> known as the nature of *quantity* in geometrical figures [that
> is, not only in geometry but also in the philosophy of nature
> rendered a science by the geometrical method—J. H.], the
> strength of *avarice* and ambition, *which is sustained by the
> erroneous opinions of the vulgar touching the nature of
> RIGHT and WRONG*, would presently faint and languish; and
> mankind would enjoy such an immortal peace, that . . .
> there would hardly be left any pretence for war.[70]

But both the mechanistic presuppositions of his method as well
as the absolutist consequences of his doctrine exclude the possibility that, out of their insight alone, men will be ready to submit to
the authority of the state. Hobbes presumes that the knowledge
provided by social philosophy, whose certainty obviates public
discussion, has practical results. But the possibility of these results
cannot be accounted for within the framework of his social philosophy itself—the relationship of theory to praxis can no longer
be explained theoretically.

From the perspective of this dilemma, Hobbes would have
to subject his doctrine to a revision, together with its claim to
complete certainty in questions of social action. For unlike the
mere technical application of scientific results, the translation of

theory into praxis is faced with the task of entering into the consciousness and the convictions of citizens prepared to act: theoretical solutions must be interpreted in concrete situations as the practically necessary solutions for the satisfaction of objective needs—indeed, they must be conceived from the very outset within this perspective of acting human beings. It is in this sense that Vico recommends the art of rhetoric, which "throughout deals with the audience to which it is addressed." This art knows that truths which are to have consequences require a consensus prudently attained: this is the "semblance" of truth in the *sensus communis* of citizens participating in public discussion. A theory which is explicitly designed, with the approach of the technician, to secure control over processes of nature will encounter a specific barrier when it is transferred to the domain of a pedagogically attuned moral philosophy. Control over the processes of nature is essentially different from control over social processes: even if in the end the latter were to be *carried out* in the same manner as the former (which is what social technical planning within advanced industrial society requires today) a prior mediation through the consciousness of the citizens who discuss and act [*verhandeln und handeln*] still is needed.[71] The act of the technical domination of nature is in principle a solitary and silent act —free from any negotiated agreement among active subjects who wish to control their social relations practically. Nevertheless, even in this respect scientific social philosophy, in its structure, remains designed for a technical application of its results. To be sure, in Hobbes the uncontrolled element in the communication between citizens discussing and acting together—by which the control over society is dialectically disrupted (except in the case of complete manipulation)—is preserved in the moment of concluding the contract, but this is retracted again immediately by mechanistically reducing the normative compulsion generated by the contract to the causal compulsion of instinctual human nature. This undigested element, which Hobbes was able to suppress within his theory, will not, however, be laid to rest; its resistance reappears anew in the attempt to interpret theory itself technologically as praxis. Hobbes's assurance that social philosophical insights only require methodological certainty in order to become, without any detours, the practical certainty of citizens endowed with political insight, only reveals the impotence of any thinking which abstracts away the distinction between controlling and acting.

The relation between theory and praxis in the social philosophy of the eighteenth century. The problem of a dialectical reversion of social theory to the experiential horizon of practical consciousness.

The further development of social philosophy during the eighteenth century can be comprehended as a reply to the questionable aspects, indicated here, of this first attempt to make classical politics into a science. For this continuation of the development, two trends are characteristic. The first is the attempt to ground the natural laws of the social condition directly in the laws of nature, in such a way that the precarious transition from the fact of nature, represented by a war of all against all, to the Natural Law norms of the civil state can be avoided, and in the same way, the antinomies which are linked to this transition. As is well known, Locke made the order of property of bourgeois society as such the natural basis of state power founded on contract; but he formulated the laws of bourgeois society and its state in terms of Natural Law. From there it was but a step to the conceptions of Political Economy, in the second half of the eighteenth century, which declared these laws to be the natural laws of society itself. When, finally, Kant again took up the problem of the origins as posed by modern social philosophy, which Hobbes had developed—in Kant's view, the problem is

. . . to organize a group of rational beings who together require universal laws for their survival, but of whom each separate individual is secretly inclined to exempt himself from them, the constitution must be so designed that, although the citizens are opposed to one another in their private attitudes, these opposing views may inhibit one another in such a way that the public conduct of the citizens will be the same as if they did not have such evil attitudes.[72]

—when Kant returned to this problem, he was already familiar with the economic answer to his question, which for rhetorical purposes he had once more formulated in terms of Natural Law. In the advanced Western countries the sphere of trade in commodities and of social labor had meanwhile become separated from the regulation by the supreme state authority, so that the "natural order" could now be understood in terms of the categories of the laws of motion governing this "civil society," the *société civile* itself.[73]

But still more significant for our problem is the *other* tendency, which, still only adumbrated in Locke, becomes prominent in the various economic schools of the eighteenth century: the theory of civil society is complemented by a doctrine of a public sphere of politics. Theory, which in its scientific structure is designed for technical application, fails to relate properly, as we have seen, to the praxis of citizens who deliberate and act: it therefore requires correction by a body of doctrine, appended in a peculiar manner; this appendage is, to be sure, not considered part of the theory itself, but merely as its practical complement. The Physiocrats' wish to install the monarch as in praxis the guardian of the "Natural Order" of society which they have analyzed theoretically; the monarch, however, does not gain insight into the laws of the *ordre naturel* directly—he must allow this insight to be mediated for him by the *public éclairé*. Hobbes papered over the dimension of the transfer of theory into praxis. Now it is opened up again under the title of "public opinion," the concept of which was precisely defined for the first time within the circle of the Physiocrats. *L'opinion publique* is the enlightened result of the common and public reflection, guided by the philosophers as the representatives of modern science—a reflection on the fundamental bases of the social order; it comprehends the natural laws of this order in the form of the practical certainty of active citizens; it does not rule, but the enlightened ruler will have to comply with its insight.

A liberalized version of this doctrine of the public sphere of politics can be found at the same time in the economists and sociologists who belong to the tradition of Scottish moral philosophy.[74] They go further than the Physiocrats and make the mediat-

ing function of public opinion a constitutive part of the theory of
civil society itself, which they extend in the direction of philosophy of history. The "natural history of civil society" is conceived
as the law-governed progress of mankind's civilization—"from
rudeness to civilized manners": it embraces the development toward a liberal society in the economic *and* in the political sense.[75]
In accordance with this a political public sphere unfolds to the
same degree as the natural laws of the market assert themselves,
with the ascendancy of the private, autonomous exchange of commodities; this will lead to the equalization of social rank and to
the extension of civil rights of equality. The evolutionary concept
of society thus assures the theory of a prior and unconstrained
correspondence with public opinion. Because the physics of sociation, in this version extended into the philosophy of history, also
conceives the progress of practical consciousness to be a necessary
one, it does not need to interpret its relation to praxis technologically. The sociology of the Scottish thinkers could confine itself
to an interplay with a political public sphere that was ready to
"meet it halfway" in order to give individual action an orientation, in furthering practically—in the narrow sense—the historical process. As the theory knew that it was in harmony with the
historical process, it did not have to instruct the citizens on how
they could organize social progress.

If we can attain the philosophical certainty concerning the
course of history as a whole to the same degree that physics can
for the course of nature, then the problem of the relation between
theory and praxis is not insoluble. In principle, the philosophy
of history can then extend its predictions to the consequences of
transferring its own teachings into the praxis of acting citizens.
On the other hand, it is easy to see that precisely this extravagant
height of knowledge is not to be attained by following the principles of rigorous science. The doctrine of the political public
sphere could not be integrated into the theory of civil society—
the relationship of which theory to praxis it was to clarify—without changing the structure of this theory itself. In their rather
facile evolutionism, the Scots were aware of this just as little as
were their French contemporaries in their linear philosophies of
history.[76]

The problem was now posed thus: if, in addition, Social Philosophy wishes to clarify its own relationship to praxis theoretically, and if this aim leads it into the dimension of anticipating, in the manner of a philosophy of history, the practical consciousness of politically active citizens—then obviously the methodological ignorance of the difference between control and action, on which the technically oriented science is based, cannot be allowed to continue. Instead, a scientifically founded social philosophy which reflects on itself in the manner of philosophy of history must be concerned with a methodological approach which, on the one hand, will correspond to a clarification of practical consciousness, but on the other, will not relinquish that methodical rigor which is the irreversible achievement of modern science. The problem which arose with Hobbes, which the Physiocrats sought to take into account and the Scots sought to solve; the problem which goes back ultimately to the deficiency of the modern method of investigation compared to that of the Ancients —as noted by Vico—is that the moderns achieved the rigor of their theory at the cost of access to praxis. This problem of a theoretically satisfactory mediation between theory and praxis obviously required a revision of scientific social philosophy from the specific viewpoint of the classical doctrine of politics, insofar as it was able to see itself as the prudent guide to praxis. And from the viewpoint of modern science, to be sure, methodological rigor in pursuit of this perspective is not to be sacrificed.

Vico still assigned to the old politics the topical procedure of rhetoric; this procedure never claimed to represent a scientific method. The only method that, at least as far as the name was concerned, was practiced both in theoretical as well as in practical philosophy, was the art of disputation—dialectics.[77] To be sure, according to the studies of Kapp[78] there can hardly be any doubt that for Aristotle science does not in principle, or for systematic reasons, depend on the employment of dialectics, but uses it only for pedagogic purposes: it serves to introduce the student to knowledge, and of course the scientist, too, insofar as he still remains a student. Seen from this point of view, dialectics is the discourse of instruction and merely a prolegomenon to rigorous analysis. But in the context of practical philosophy, dialectics did not seem to exhaust its function within such propaedeutics. Thus, rhetoric indeed served the end of effective recommendation and warning; it aimed at decision, at the action of the citizens. In those cases, however, where rhetoric was involved with the actual matter under discussion, the orator was engaged in the philosophical transaction of practical prudence within the specific sphere of Politics. For this Aristotle recommends the topical procedure as a dialectical one; taking as its point of departure something familiar to us, such as traditionally or authoritatively legitimized and accepted points of view, commonplaces, and rules, it leads dialectically to their confirmation in the practical tasks of a given situation. The logical force of such *topoi* is validated in the subordination of particular cases under rules, rules which in turn can only be explained in terms of their schematic application to concrete particulars. In so doing, dialectics does not aim at establishing premises, as do the propaedeutic preparations to an apodictic science. As exercise of reflective judgment in which both parties mutually instruct each other, it instead accomplishes the subsumption of specific cases under schemata gained by prior understanding, and is more suitable to the hermeneutics of situations experienced in life and for the purposes of attaining a consensus among politically active citizens.

Obviously this is the form of the dialectic from which Hegel departs.[79] But Hegel stands abreast of modern science. He invokes dialectics for the methodically certain reflection of science on itself; the primacy of topics over analytics, which the rhetorician Vico only asserted pedagogically against the theoreticians of his time (for the sequential order of their studies), Hegel, much more boldly, turns into the methodological primacy of the dialectical procedure over the analytic in the investigation of the things themselves. In this way he can also attack, in a wholly novel manner, that difficulty which prevented social philosophy from carrying out successfully its scientific approach. For as we saw, social philosophy was deprived ultimately of its really meaningful achievement, the certainty of universally valid statements, even by its own criteria, because it was only able to make reassuring claims about the practical consequences of its own teachings, without being able to attain theoretical certainty in the most important point: how "the furthering of human life" could actually be brought about by putting theory into praxis. By comprehending history dialectically—and with that we are saying, within the experiential horizon of practical consciousness—Hegel is able to resolve [sublate] scientifically based social philosophy into a dialectical theory of society, and thereby select and develop the categories in such a way that this theory at every step is guided and permeated by the self-consciousness of its own relationship to praxis.

2

Natural Law and Revolution

"We should not therefore contradict the assertion that the Revolution received its first impulse from Philosophy." [1] This cautious observation by the older Hegel lends force to the French Revolution's understanding of itself: among the men of that time it had become a commonplace that the Revolution had transferred philosophy from books into reality. Philosophy here meant the principles of rational Natural Law and these were the principles of the new constitutions. A generation later the astonishment of philosophy itself still rings in the words of Hegel as he looks back at the unheard-of occurrence: that human beings had made philosophical thought their basis and had constructed political reality according to it. [2]

The bourgeois revolution's philosophical understanding of itself: the positivization of Natural Law[3] as the realization of philosophy

From the very beginning an intimate relationship existed between philosophy and the bourgeois revolution, no matter how much philosophers since then may have entertained suspicions as to the illegitimate nature of this relationship. The "evolution of Natural Law" was a philosophical concept which revolutionary theorists had formed about the revolution, as soon as, in the separation of the North American colonies from the mother country and the fall of the *ancien régime*, it was conceived of at all *as* a revolution. There are historical and sociological reasons for applying the concept of the bourgeois revolution objectively to much earlier events; thus, for example, those which led to the secession of the Netherlands from the Spanish Crown. But subjectively the appeal at that time was to the preservation of the privileges of the estates (for example, the declaration of independence of July 26, 1581); for on the basis of classical Natural Law, violent resistance against the established government could only be legitimized in terms of the continuity of an ancient and at the same time eternal law, for example, the restoration, regeneration, or reformation of a tradition of law which had been interrupted. A century later it was still the landing of William of Orange and not the declaration of Parliament on the succession to the English throne which had given the Glorious Revolution its name. The Declaration of Rights itself was considered to be an affirmation of ancient rights and freedoms. The appearance of William and the flight of James may have seemed to contemporaries events of the magnitude and the inevitability of destiny astronomically controlled, so that just for this reason it was compared to the revolutions of the stars. It was thus not credited to an actual political act of those engaged in the events; the objectively oriented concept of revolution did not recognize any revolutionaries. In Edmund Burke's memorable polemics against the French Revolution,[4] the distinction, which was self-evident in 1689, still finds its echo: the Glorious Revolution gains its significance as a sort of natural upheaval without the intervention of human arbitrariness and violence, in definitive contrast with the Great Rebellion, with its regicide and civil war, in the preceding decades.[5]

The appeal to classical Natural Law was not revolutionary, as the appeal to modern Natural Law has come to be. Indeed, it is not merely a concept of revolution which brings the revolution of the stars down to earth and which thus merely employs it as an image for the upheaval of the state, likening it to any other event in nature, but rather a concept of revolution which enters *as such* into the consciousness of active revolutionaries and which can be carried to its conclusion by these revolutionaries alone. Such a concept could only be ignited by rational Natural Law, could develop only in the act of translating this into positive constitutional law. What is it in this positivization that endows it with its violent character? In the first place, certainly, it is violent political force, without which the existing authority cannot be overthrown and a change in the basis for legitimation of any future authority cannot be brought about. But we shall leave aside the sociological concept of revolution. Rather we shall seek the immanent connection between modern Natural Law and the bourgeois revolution.

While in classical Natural Law the norms of moral and just action are equally oriented in their content toward the good—and that means the virtuous—life of the citizens, the formal law of the modern age is divested of the catalogues of duties in the material order of life, whether of a city or of a social class. Instead, it allows a neutral sphere of personal choice, in which every citizen, as a private person can egoistically follow goals of maximizing his own needs. Formal rights are in principle rights of freedom, because they must set free all acts which are not explicitly prohibited according to externally specified criteria. Hobbes had already enunciated clearly that under formal laws freedom consists in this indirect exemption.[6] And as is well known, Locke defines the purpose of such laws to be the right to dispose of private property, in which life and the freedom of one's person are included. Nor do the maxims of the Physiocrats,[7] which inspired all the later attempts to supplement the French declaration of the *rights* of men and citizens by a declaration of the corresponding *duties,* return to the commandments of virtue presented by classical Natural Law. For the supreme duty from which all rights derive, interpreted concretely in economic terms, is seen, in a most naturalistic manner, to be the obligation to self-preservation; its meaning is again the right to private autonomy. This Physiocrat doctrine of duties, especially, shows that formal law, once accepted, excludes any reference back to material morality. Legal duties are instead to be derived, for their part, only from the primary sense of being endowed with rights. If formal law accords spheres of activity to each individual choice, then the choice of each must be limited for the sake of all if these spheres are to be reconciled. But formal law frees the conduct of citizens within a morally neutral domain, releasing them from the motivations of internalized duties and liberating them to look after their own interests; therefore the limitations which result from this formal law can now only be imposed externally. Because it is in principle a law of freedom, formal law divorced from the informal order of life is *also* a law of coercion. The inverse of private autonomy, to which this law secures the right, is the psychological motivation of coercion, of obedience. When actually in force, formal law is sanctioned solely by physically effective force, and legality is fundamentally divorced from morality.

From this situation the act of the positivization of Natural Law as such incurs its peculiar difficulty as well as harshness. On the one hand, the positive assertion of compulsory law demands a sanctioning power which guarantees compliance. On the other hand, the positivization of Natural Law cannot be legitimately preceded by anything but the autonomy of isolated and equal individuals and their insight into the rational interdependence of Natural Law norms. In the doctrinal texts of Natural Law the original constitution of law has therefore always been conceived as though the power which guarantees the rights were produced by the will of all free individuals guided by a common and rational insight. The codifications of private law of the prerevolutionary eighteenth century presented no problem: here an established state power assumed the task of simultaneously establishing and asserting a system of formal laws, which, to be sure, was only a partial one. If now, however, the state power itself was to be reorganized from its very foundations in accordance with new principles, then that fictitious idea of a prior contract, which had been projected back to the threshold of the social state, had to serve as the interpretive scheme for revolutionary action. Because the goal was to create a system of compelling justifications, the sanctioning compulsion had to be conceived as originating in private autonomous insight and agreement.

The act by which the positivization of Natural Rights was initiated, in America as well as in France, was a declaration of fundamental rights. As a consequence of the revolutionary self-understanding, this declaration had to give evidence of both insight and will: the insight into the rational coherence of the fundamental norm; and the will to establish the authority of a sanctioning power that was itself bound by these norms. This act of declaration had to make the claim that it was generating po-

litical power solely from philosophical insight. The idea of the
political realization of philosophy—namely, the autonomous creation, by contract, of legal compulsion springing solely from the
compulsion of philosophical reason—is the concept of revolution
which followed immanently from the principles of modern Natural Law; under its other name of the social contract this concept
had been derived long before the bourgeois revolution, grown
conscious of itself, understood itself in terms of the positivization
of natural rights, and then linked this concept with its own name.
In this sense the slogan of the realization of philosophy had been
anticipated at the time of the Revolution, before its formulation
by the Young Hegelians.

Of course, in its precise sense this holds only for Paris and
not for Philadelphia. The appeal to philosophy in France corresponds to the appeal to common sense in America. In general,
the colonists did not carry out their emancipation from the
mother country with the strict awareness of making a revolution.
The talk of an American *Revolution* only became current *post
festum;* but by the outbreak of the French Revolution it had
already entered into common usage.[8] While Thomas Paine emphasized that which the two events, the American Revolution *and*
the French Revolution, had specifically in common, by pointing to
the universal foundation of the state in Natural Law, Robespierre
always reserved this fundamental claim of the bourgeois revolution for the French Revolution alone.[9] The Anglo-Saxon tradition of Natural Law, derived from Locke, on which the fathers of
the American Constitution based themselves, and to which
Thomas Paine then appealed explicitly to justify a revolution,
was never taken seriously as an essentially revolutionary doctrine
—not only by a French competitor like Robespierre, but also by
neither Burke nor Hegel. Hegel is so far from accepting the concept of an American Revolution that he can state, pointing to the
safety valve of internal colonization: "Had the forests of ancient
Germany still existed, then of course the French Revolution
would never have come to pass." [10] While the French Revolution
becomes the very key to the philosophic concept of World History
for him, Hegel would like to exclude North America entirely from
philosophical consideration, as a mere land of the future.

The meaning of "declaration" in the American and in the French Declarations of the Rights of Man

There are, in fact, unmistakable differences, even though the Americans, just like the French, appeal to the principles of modern Natural Law; and the common features, which the basis of legitimation displays, extend to a correspondence in wording, especially in the two declarations of fundamental rights.[11] But these two declarations have a different specific meaning, in spite of their substantive correspondence. With their recourse to the Rights of Man, the American colonists want to legitimize their independence from the British Empire; the French to legitimize the overthrow of the *ancien régime*. Certainly, in both cases a constitution is set up which remains within the framework of the declared fundamental rights. But already the value assigned externally by the position in the two documents of this declaration is not accidental: preceding the French Constitution as a preamble, merely attached to the American Constitution as amendments. The American Bill of Rights makes an inventory, in essence, of the existing rights possessed by British citizens. The form of its justification in terms of universal Natural Law only became necessary with respect to emancipation from the mother country. The Bill of Rights, which in substance is anticipated in the opening sentences of the Declaration of Independence, has as such the sense primarily of providing another basis of legitimation for the traditional substance of rights; the French declaration, in contrast, is intended to assert positively for the first time a fundamentally new system of rights. In France the revolutionary meaning of the declaration is to lay the foundation for a new constitution. In America, however, it is to justify independence, as a consequence of which, to be sure, a new constitution becomes necessary.[12]

When in 1822 John Adams raised against Thomas Jefferson, to whom, as the author of the Declaration of Independence, full honors of a *spiritus rector* were accorded, the objection that this declaration did not contain a single new idea, he received the characteristic reply from the object of his attack: yes, it may very well represent a compilation of commonplaces. And three years later Jefferson wrote to Richard H. Lee, who had called this declaration simply a plagiarism of Locke, that it had not been his task at that time to find new principles and arguments, "but to place before mankind the common sense of the subject." [13] A pamphlet by Thomas Paine which appeared at the beginning of 1776, and which invoked the tradition inspired by Locke for the current question of the impending emancipation and thus is said to have influenced Jefferson, bore the pithy title "Common Sense." For the American colonists Locke's conclusions had become commonplaces; in the place of learned arguments, their own experiences of government were sufficiently convincing; a government which remained perceptibly dependent on the parliamentary absolutism of a distant mother country solely with respect to trade policies. Under these circumstances a declaration could only have the significance of reasserting what was in any case a living common conviction: "It was intended to be an expression of the American mind. . . . All its authority rests then on the harmonizing sentiments of the day. . . ." [14]

When, on the other hand, the Abbé Sièyes composed his pamphlet on the Third Estate as the representatives of the nation during the Convention of Notables of 1788, he had to take his point of departure from an entirely different situation: "One cannot judge its demands according to the isolated remarks of a few authors, who to a lesser or greater degree have informed themselves about the rights of man. The Third Estate is still far behind in this respect, I say, not only behind the insight of those who have studied the social order, but also behind the mass of common ideas which form public opinion." [15]

In the presence of this gap between individual insight and majority opinion, the practical task falls to the *philosophe* to secure political recognition for reason itself by means of his influence on the power of public opinion. The philosophers must propagate the truth, must disseminate their unabridged insights publicly, for only when reason "hits the mark everywhere, does it hit it properly, for only then will it form that power of public opinion, to which one can perhaps ascribe most of those changes which are truly advantageous for the peoples." [16] In this one must

first attend to the division of labor between the philosopher and
the politician, which Sièyes points to in the motto of his polemic.
The philosopher must not let himself be inhibited by the prudent
conduct of the statesman, who must gauge his steps by the most
immediate difficulties, if his work is to clear a path for the statesman toward the goal. It is not the philosopher's task to put the
truth into effect, but only to present it, to explain it—*la déclarer*.
This is the path by which theory becomes a practical force:

> If all men thought the truth, then the greatest changes
> would present no difficulties, as soon as they represented an
> object of the public interest. What better can I do than to
> contribute with all my powers to the dissemination of the
> truth, which clears the paths? In the beginning they meet
> with a hostile reception, but gradually . . . they form public
> opinion, and finally in the execution of the principles one
> becomes aware of what at first were treated as insane
> fantasies.[17]

This duty to declare the truth is incumbent on the philosopher all the more when "public opinion finally even dictates the
laws for the lawgivers." [18] Sièyes borrows this formula directly
from the Physiocrats; according to their doctrine, the monarch
must allow himself to be instructed about the laws of nature by a
philosophically and economically enlightened public, and the
legislation must then take its direction from these laws. The
evidence of the natural order which attains power by publicity
is the sole basis on which a correct constitution can be founded.
Public opinion enlightened to the point of evidence, together
with a despotically asserted absolute rule of the laws of nature,
will guarantee the rightfulness of social conditions.[19] The public
instruction of the nation [*Volk*] was the core of Physiocratic
theory. Le Mercier, Mirabeau, and Dupont each drew up a plan
for the organization of popular education.[20]

The Physiocrats had done their preparatory work well:
there does not seem to be any doubt about the significance of
publicizing a Declaration of Human Rights, when it had finally

come to the point where public opinion could dictate laws to the legislators. The philosophers themselves had become legislators. It was already said of the first report of the committee constituted to prepare the Declaration of Rights (presented by Mounier) that the report was more appropriate for a philosophical society than for a National Assembly. And, according to contemporary reports, this assembly was transformed "en école de Sorbonne" during the discussion of the Rights of Man.[21] But once the philosophic insight was attained, this truth required propagation.[22] The Physiocrats had prepared the philosophic self-understanding of such a declaration in a still broader sense: to a legislator inspired by public opinion the Natural Laws must be so evident that the act of rendering them positive need only consist in declaring them. To the Physiocrat school *déclarer* had the technical sense of translating the *ordre naturel* into the *ordre positif* in such a manner that Natural Law would merely be implemented and applied in the laws derived from it.

Between July 9 and August 4, 1789, the subject of discussion in the National Assembly was whether and in what form a declaration of fundamental rights would be necessary. In these sessions the French sense of "declaration" as distinct from the American "declarations" which had preceded it was notably clarified. At first Lafayette had interpreted the function of such a declaration wholly in the sense of Jefferson, with whom he was in contact in Paris at that time. But the Anglophile faction of the Assembly immediately objected: "I beg you to consider, what an immense difference there is between a colonial people which breaks the bonds of a distant government, and one of the oldest nations on earth which for 1400 years has given itself its own form of government."[23] Later Champoin de Cicé, the Archbishop of Bordeaux, explicated this difference: the example of North America was not compelling, because there were only proprietors and equal citizens over there.[24] And finally, the delegate Malouet declared: the Americans had been able to declare their Natural Rights without any hesitation, because their society consisted in a majority of proprietors who were already accustomed to equality and who hardly knew the yoke of taxes and prejudice. Such people were without question ready for freedom, unlike the people in France at that time.[25] With that, Lafayette's interpretation was refuted, but his critics were not able to prevail with their warnings against any kind of declaration; they were only able to show what meaning such a declaration could *not* have in France.[26] The majority of the Assembly considered a declaration to be necessary, because the public required effectively publicized enlightenment. This meaning is unmistakably set forth in the preamble: a declaration is desired, because "the ignorance, forgetting and neglect of the rights of man are the universal causes of public misfortune and the corruption of the regime." In America the Declaration was itself the expression of "common sense"; in France it had first to form the *opinion publique*.

In America the positivization of Natural Law did not demand a revolutionary role of philosophy. A tension between theory and praxis, between Natural Law principles and their technical realization, considerations how philosophical insight could attain political power by way of public opinion—all this did not exist there. Indeed, the colonists who desired their independence and founded their own state behaved with respect to the Lockean tradition just as those who act politically have always behaved when they take their orientation from classical Natural Law: they were concerned with the prudent application of already given norms to a concrete situation. The philosophical minds of the National Assembly, on the other hand, had realized the break of modern Natural Law with the classical in a more rigorous fashion: at least as far as the decisive majority was concerned, their attitude toward the norms, no matter how they might be legitimized by nature, was no longer practical, but technical; they discussed the organizational means for the construction of a total order of society. Only thus did the positivization of Natural Law become a revolutionary task: philosophy was no longer to supply the orientation for politically prudent action under laws, but was to install a technically correct system of institutions with the aid of laws. Of course, not only is the meaning of the Declarations of Human Rights of the two countries different, but it can be shown that altogether, even where the wording corresponds, two different constructions of the Natural Law of bourgeois society are implied.

*The liberal construction of the Natural Law of bourgeois
society: John Locke and Thomas Paine*

Till that momentous controversy with the English Parliament in 1764, Americans had always been proud of being subjects
of the British Empire.[27] And even during the next decade, the
quarrel over the legislative competence of the English Parliament
had as premise the question: what rights do we Americans have as
British subjects? It was not till 1774 that a pamphlet appeared in
which James Wilson attempted to subordinate the English liberties of Common Law and the rights assured to the individual
colonies in their charters to a higher viewpoint of Natural Law:
the happiness of the society is the first law of every government.[28]
The Declaration of the First Continental Congress which assembled in the same year begins in a similar sense with the assertion that on the basis of the unchanging laws of nature, of the
fundamental principles of the English Constitution and various
contracts (charters and compacts), a series of rights are due to the
inhabitants of the English colonies in North America; to be sure,
this is followed immediately by Locke's formulation of the right
to life, liberty, and property. Sherman's famous statement, "The
Colonies adopt the common law, not as the common law, but as
the highest reason," still is wholly within the classical tradition.
This tradition had been preserved in America to a greater extent,
because the absence of an absolutist practice in government had
not made there the radical reinterpretation of Stoic-Christian
Natural Law as necessary, that had been carried through in the
mother country since Hobbes.[29] Thus Locke was still understood
within the continuity of classical Natural Law, even after emancipation had become unavoidable and nothing but modern Natural Law had remained as a basis for its justification; the
Christian presuppositions of his doctrine may have abetted this.[30]
The posture with which Locke was invoked remained the same
as that which Americans had assumed up to that time in appealing to their vested freedoms, and with which Englishmen themselves had appealed to their ancient rights since the time of the
Magna Carta. Like practical philosophy before him, Locke too

appeared to present the laws of the good life and prudent action and not the rules according to which the correct social order was now to be installed according to plan.[31]

This essentially unrevolutionary view was supported from the other side by precisely those elements of the Lockean doctrine that are simply irreconcilable with classical Natural Law. Because, in contrast to Hobbes, Locke proceeds from the premise that men preserve their life primarily by labor rather than by aggression and defense, he interprets the fundamental right of self-preservation as the right of property.[32] Locke's derivation of human rights is simple. In the state of nature personal labor for individual use alone provides the rightful title to private property. This natural right, which together with property also secures life and freedom, each man can exercise directly and maintain against all others, for in any case it is measured by his physical powers and skills. Insecurity and therewith the need for state authority, thus the motive for sociation, only arise with a mode of production determined by the market; for this requires the security of private property beyond those goods produced personally and for one's own consumption—the state of nature becomes untenable. Men associate under a government which is capable of protecting private property to an extent beyond the immediate physical powers and dispositions of the individual. This government must guarantee a legal order, which in its substance had always been based on private property, even prior to the state, but which now, in view of the increasing collisions arising from property expanded to the possession of capital, has to be explicitly sanctioned. Thus every possible government is "entrusted with the condition and for this end, that men might have and secure their properties." [33]

The natural rights to freedom, life, and property are not suspended in the social state; they are only, as it were, exchanged for state-sanctioned civil rights, as the powers of the individual no longer suffice for their assertion.[34] The government may have the power to regulate the commerce between the owners of private property, but never so much power that it can intervene against the property rights of even a single person without his agreement, "for this would be no property at all." [35]

When the American colonists invoked the authority of this doctrine against the encroachments of the English Parliament, they were brought to a revolutionary self-understanding neither by the modern justifications of their demands flowing from natural rights nor by the transposition of Locke back into classical Natural Law. For the liberal construction of Natural Law, that of bourgeois society, which was implicit in the rights received from Locke and declared against England, had merely the restrictive meaning of protecting the private autonomous sphere of social intercourse against state intervention. How little *this* tradition of Natural Law compels philosophic insight to prepare for revolutionary action has been shown, though against his will, by the very author who untiringly sought to place the American and French Revolutions on the same level—Thomas Paine.

In the second part of his book on the rights of man, published in 1792, Paine repeats the thesis that the emancipation of America would have had little significance had it not been accompanied by a revolution in the principles and practice of government.[36] However, he maintains that this revolution has nothing to do with the political act of realizing Natural Law, in the sense of constructing a constitution which organizes the total society; on the contrary, its sole aim is to limit political power to a minimum. Natural Law is not rendered positive by means of a revolution; it does not gain its validation subjectively through the consciousness of politically active citizens, but objectively through the effect of the uninhibited workings of society's immanent natural laws. For Paine identifies the natural rights of man with the natural laws of commodity exchange and social labor. He explicitly states the specific interconnection between Locke and Adam Smith; he sees that the classical economics of the eighteenth century project into the natural basis of society the same natural laws which in the seventeenth century were still conceived as the norms of formal law: "By the simple operation of constructing Government on the principles of Society *and* the rights of man, every difficulty retires." [37]

The distinction between the state of nature and the state of society has been replaced by that between society and the state. The limits on the powers of all government imposed by Natural

Law, which, according to Locke, were carried over from the state of nature into the social state, have become the laws of a natural society, one which is no longer based upon a contract. The government constituted according to nature, and above all, limited, now comes "out of society," just as previously it came "out of the social compact"; Paine uses both expressions as synonyms. With classical economists, such as Adam Smith, he shares the conviction, that as a system of needs based on the division of labor, society will naturally follow a harmonious development as long as it can be protected against the despotic intervention of government. The confrontation of the spontaneous forces of societal cohesion and self-regulation with the formal means of coercion of a repressive state power anticipates a conception of society as a living totality, which only accords validity to the state as one element split off from the whole, a particularity that has made itself independent. His polemical pamphlet of 1776 begins with an emphatic indication of the heterogeneous origins of society and government;[38] society is brought forth by our needs, the government by our weaknesses. Every social state is full of blessings, but even under its best constitution government remains a necessary evil; for the evil of oppression is the consequence of the political inequality of masters and servants, and not the social differences between rich and poor. Indeed, Paine's liberalism does not shy away from anarchistic consequences: society, he says in one place, begins to act spontaneously at that moment when the formal power of government is abolished—then a universal association arises, and the common interest creates universal security.[39]

The positivization of Natural Law is not a matter of revolutions, as soon as the rights of man coincide with the principles of society under the common name of Laws of Nature. Natural rights will find their reliable counterpart in the laws of trade and commerce; but these laws are obeyed by private persons because this is immediately in their interest and not because the state imposes formal laws under the threat of punishment. The practice of a universal free trade will therefore give stronger guarantees to the rights of man than any theory which has attained political power by virtue of public opinion, which dictates laws and thus positivizes Natural Law. Philosophy does not have to make any effort for the realization of this Natural Law.

The French, however, had a political economy of their own, in terms of which they could interpret the Natural Law doctrine of their own Locke, even if in the National Assembly this could not be formed into the unbroken coherence which the Anglo-Saxon tradition attained in the hands of a Thomas Paine. There is no doubt that both in form and content the American declarations were the model for the *Déclaration des droits de l'homme et du citoyen;* and certainly Lafayette, who was the first to hand in a draft, was not the only deputy influenced by the Americans. However, this influence was not so strong that the American spirit could have gained acceptance in the French formulation, but it served as a catalyst which made possible the peculiar combination of the doctrines of Rousseau and the Physiocrats, initially so contradictory. From this arose a different Natural-Law construction of bourgeois society; and this construction did indeed inspire a revolutionary self-understanding in the politically active citizens.

The dissemination of competing Natural-Law constructions of bourgeois society: Rousseau and the Physiocrats

After Mirabeau had presented a report before the Plenum of the National Assembly on August 17, reporting for the Committee of Five, which had been assigned the examination of the project submitted to it, for a declaration of the rights of man, the discussion was opened by the delegate Crenier, one of the most articulate adherents of Rousseau, as were Biauzat and the Count Antraigues.[40] He expressed the opinion, with reference to the American model, that this declaration could not have the form of a deduction from principles, for a right was the result of a contract and not a principle from which true statements could be deduced. In earlier sessions Crenier had already wished to identify the declaration of human rights with the act of concluding a social contract. In the state of nature man is neither master nor slave, he has neither rights nor duties; the natural independence and self-preservation of each could only be elevated to the natural right to freedom and equality by a social contract. The declaration of the rights of man is therefore equivalent to the constitution of the general will, to the formation of which all contribute and before the laws of which all are equal. During the further course of the debate Démeunier opposed this conception with an argument which deserves attention: "That is the system of Hobbes, which has been rejected by all of Europe." [41]

Indeed, Rousseau was in agreement with Hobbes in believing that the compulsion for sociation had to be derived from a state of universal mistrust and from the precarious insecurity of a universal and violent competitive struggle. This characterization, put forward in a number of passages, does not only, to be sure, fit that state of nature which immediately precedes the social state, but also—in principle—the civilized society of contemporary France, and this is by no means accidental. For *against* Hobbes Rousseau insists that the state dominated by natural political evils which make sociation necessary is not by any means abolished in a social state which is the result of despotic compulsion, but these evils live on in the competition of private interests within a restless and strife-torn system based on the division of labor and expanded needs. In Rousseau the social contract is to perform the same task as in Hobbes: the natural political evil of a universal self-assertion of all against all is so substantial that the positive validity of general norms can only be enforced by an absolute power. But the total cession of proprietary rights [*Übereignung*] and submission is the same only in its form. The alienation of self [*Selbstentäusserung*] in Hobbes means submission to a compulsion which, though set up by men themselves, still remains an irrevocably *external* compulsion, but in Rousseau it means the transformation of corrupted human nature into the moral person of the citizen. For thus sovereign power itself can become *internalized,* be brought back from the externally compulsive sovereignty of the prince to an internally present sovereignty of the people. In the face of the presupposition they held in common, it was consistent that these two solutions appeared to Rousseau as completely alternative. In his famous letter of July 26, 1767, to Mirabeau, the Physiocrat, he therefore confesses: I can see no viable middle path between the rawest democracy and the most complete Hobbesian system.

It was to this that the delegate Démeunier was obviously al-
luding, in order to remind his audience that human rights could
not be based on Hobbes at all. But it is not only in the determination of the fundamental natural evil that Hobbes is distinguished from Locke; as the one considers weapons to be the
primary means of self-preservation, while the other sees these in
food, clothing, and shelter, so for Hobbes socially organized self-
preservation requires an order of coercion against internal and
external enemies, whereas for Locke it requires an order of property which protects against hunger and want. And the Natural-
Law basis of state power is different too; because, according to
Locke, men overcome the economic natural evil in the same
manner, in principle, *before* their sociation as after—by individual labor—and therefore property rights in their substance
are prior to the state. The government is only to remove certain
risks, so that the natural form of self-preservation can be better
maintained. Hobbes, however, requires a sovereign power for the
complete liquidation of the state of nature. For obedience, the
fear which liberates from fear, is a product of sociation, and does
not have its origin in nature, as does labor, the pain which removes pain.[42] Thus legal limits against the will of the Hobbesian
sovereign cannot be set by a nature *against* which he is constituted, no more than they can against the democratically inverted
and morally internalized sovereignty of the general will in Rousseau—unless, of course, the natural rights follow from the nature
of this will itself. This indeed is what the delegate Crenier wanted
to assert. Freedom and equality, and in consequence also life,
security, and happiness, these the citizens do not owe to the automatism, secured by private law, of either natural rights or social
intercourse based in nature. Rather, that these principles of freedom and equality cannot be violated is based solely on the structure of the *volonté générale,* although this will as the *pouvoir
souverain* is free to enact whatever laws it likes—as long as they
are *laws.*

As acts of the general will, these legal conventions must have
the character of universal laws; there can be no law concerning a
singular case. At the same time, the subjects, who participate in

the formation of the general will, only obey themselves and each other mutually:

> From this one sees that the sovereign power—as absolute, as sacred, as inviolate as it is—does not transgress the limits of universally obligatory conventions, nor can it do so; furthermore that each man can have complete disposition over that of his property and his freedom which is left to him by these conventions. In this way the sovereign never has the right to impose more burdens on one subject than on another, for then the matter becomes a particular one and therefore his power is no longer competent.[43]

Compared to the liberal construction of human rights, the material automatism of a Natural Law fulfilled by the natural laws of society is replaced by the formal automatic operation of the general will, which, because of its own nature, can violate the interests of society just as little as the freedom of even one individual. In itself the sole author of a total constitution organizing the state and society, it is in the general will that the Natural Law is founded, and not in the functioning, according to its own lawfulness, of an order that is prior to the state, whether this be the state of nature or a society that has its origin in nature. These are the consequences drawn by Crenier. His proposal for a declaration of the rights of man only contains nine propositions. To the question of what are these natural rights, whose promulgation alone can form the act of constitution of a nation, he replies: the exclusive subjection to general laws and the collaboration in the general will from which these laws proceed exclusively. Against this, Mirabeau defended the specifically enumerated rights of man drawn up by the Committee of Five with a reference to the Natural-Law principles of his father. The natural order of the Physiocrats appeared to give a more solid foundation to the declaration than the general will of Rousseau. The proposal of Rousseau's partisans, in any case only a handful of the delegates, was a hopelessly weaker position; above all, the form of the declaration was not influenced by them. But in substance their arguments were salvaged precisely by their opponents, inspired by the Physiocrat conception of Natural Law.

The Physiocrats did not know, any more than the English economists who were their contemporaries, of a rigorous distinction between the state of nature and the state of society; society itself is a piece of nature and by no means arose out of a contract. Le Mercier speaks of a *société naturelle, universelle et tacite,* in which certain rights and duties are tacitly in force. To be sure, it then is differentiated into various *sociétés particulières et conventionnelles* as soon as landed property becomes the basis of social reproduction. From then on, internal order and external security must be secured by the power of the state. In order that the economic circulation of a society based on agrarian production can take place in a natural way, the protection of landed property, as well as the free exercise of the rights of property in general, must be organized and thus the transition of society to a "political society" must be carried out. The material interrelationships of life are subject to the laws of physical nature and on the whole obey an *ordre naturel.* In contrast to the liberal conception of a natural harmony, however, the Physiocrats are convinced that at the stage of development at which agriculture and political organization have become necessary for the reproduction of a more extensive and richer life, the natural laws of society no longer assert themselves with the necessity of an *ordre physique.* Rather, in the *ordre positif* the *ordre naturel* must be made to dominate *on the basis* of philosophical insight and *by means of* political power and its assertion, which must then be maintained despotically. The political society is a creation of the state, dictated by insight into the natural laws of motion of material life.

Just like Locke, Quesnay recognizes the right of property as the core of Natural Law; and as is well known, he anticipated Adam Smith's insight of "laissez-faire," which Le Mercier celebrated as the "glory of our century." In the free competition between the individual interests of private proprietors, the total interest of society was to find its satisfaction. But here, as also in general, the Physiocrats are to be distinguished from the liberals in a decisive point: the desired harmony would not result *naturally* from the egoistic interplay of *immediate* interests, but only from the *enlightened* self-interest within the framework of a natural order *organized by the state.* As long as the citizens remain captive to controversial opinions and have not advanced to recognizing the evidence of the natural order, they cannot emerge from the depraved state of society. Only by an enlightened despot, who in accordance with natural maxims asserts his sovereign power to render positive the order of Natural Law, can the natural order of society be created and stabilized. The Physiocrats are in agreement with Rousseau that human rights can exist only *as* citizens' rights, freedom only *within* a political state. The natural order of society is actualized solely by means of political power, but, of course, in distinction to Rousseau, this power proceeds on the basis of laws which have been established from philosophical insight into the nature of the things themselves.

Meanwhile, now that a declaration of the rights of man had to be derived from the undisputed basis of political freedom and equality, a peculiar combination of the two theories suggested itself. I do not maintain that in the intellectual antechambers of the National Assembly such a relationship was explicitly established. Still, not only are the basic traits of these two theories to be recognized in specific statements of the declaration in its final form, but the concept of a positivization of these basic rights was articulated in terms of a tacit interplay of the two traditions.

The relationship of state and society in the two constructions of Natural Law

In order to bring about and secure the natural order of society politically, the sovereign who was instructed by a Physiocratically enlightened public, and thus by public opinion, had to positivize the natural rights of man—this was the substance of legal despotism, so quickly discredited. In 1789, however, it was desired to put into effect democratically what had previously been attempted despotically. The inverted despotism of the general will could bridge the gap which discredited the system all the more readily, the more the ultimately economic justification of Physiocrat Natural Law had paled. For what remained of it in the philosophic consciousness of the time was merely the idea of a natural order which could attain existence solely within the framework of a political society—and which now was to be realized from below, by revolution, instead of from above, despotically. The Abbé Sièyes had already transformed the public opinion which enlightens the sovereign about natural laws into an authority which was to dictate laws to the legislator of the day; during the course of the Revolution, public opinion became the sovereign itself. With respect to what is to be understood by a democratic sovereign, the *Contrat Social* at that time enjoyed canonical authority. The draft of the declaration prepared by the Committee of Five, which Démeunier defended against Crenier, and which Mirabeau also supported, contained in the second article the contract of submission almost in Rousseau's own words: "Every individual in common places his person and his capabilities under the supreme direction of the general will, and at the same time the society incorporates him as a part." [44] And Article 6 of the ratified version lays the basis for this formula with the sentence: "The law is the expression of the general will." On the other hand, the National Assembly did not wish to base the natural rights as such on the nature of the general will. However, if the rights of man are a prior given in any manner, and yet are to be compatible with the sovereignty of the general will, then their natural foundation can only lie in the society itself. Wherever these correspond, even literally, with the prepolitical and purely negative rights of the American declaration, with its liberal basis, they still are only considered as fundamentally political rights. That is in fact the way Natural Law was conceived of by the Physiocrats, and that is the way it was understood by the great majority of the National Assembly.

In this way the often noted "intermixture" in the French declaration of the rights of man, the rights of citizens and the principles of constitutional law offers no real difficulty—from the outset Natural Law is conceived as the law of society. In Article 2 the state can be defined as the institution ensuring *all* the rights of man, because these are tacitly regarded as the rights of a politically constituted society. In any case, the three fundamental rights mentioned by name are but a repetition of a formula,

which had the validity of a political sacrament for the Physiocrat school: *la liberté, la propriéte, la sûreté.*

Later, in the Declaration of Rights of June 24, 1793, the
right of security is explicated in a manner which clarifies the implicit meaning of the underlying Natural Law construction of
bourgeois society. Security, it says in Article 8, consists of the
protection accorded *by the society* to every one of its members
for the preservation of his person, his rights, and his property.
"Society" is thus named as the subject which organizes the interrelationships of human life as a whole. It can neither be understood as a government which sanctions a legal order with the
mandate and the limited authority of the united individuals, nor
as that union of individuals themselves, which confronts the government as a contracting party. Otherwise the converse of the
principle in Article 34 would have no meaning: that the oppression of any single individual destroys the legal order as a whole;
for in that article it says: the oppression of each individual takes
place when the body of society is oppressed. *Corps social,* Rousseau's concept, signifies, just like the *société politique* of the Physiocrats, a total constitution organized by the institutionalization of
natural rights, which embraces the state and society politically. No
state of nature is found in this constitution—as it is in Locke's
conception; this constitution is not based on interrelationships
of social intercourse originating in nature, such as would have
corresponded to the conceptions of Adam Smith or Thomas
Paine. No substantial basis prior to this constitution exists for it,
for this order which the National Assembly itself now wishes to
produce politically for the first time—though to be sure, according to the principles of nature—did not exist in the state of nature, prior to all politics.

Therefore it was no contradiction when the catalogue of
the rights of liberty of 1793, which laid the foundation for a society with a liberal structure, incorporated the rights of social
participation.[45] For this construction places the total social interrelationships of life under the control of a political will—to be
sure, one enlightened in terms of Natural Law. If the right to
security once again imposes upon the total subject of the society

the obligation to guarantee the fundamental rights, then (as Article 28 reciprocally complements Article 8) the society for its part can only be guaranteed by the active "collaboration of all, in order to assure to each the enjoyment and preservation of his rights; this guarantee is based on the sovereignty of the people."

In the liberal construction of Natural Law the fundamental rights correspond to the laws of intercourse developed prior to the state; the substance of this intercourse originates in a state of nature or in a society rooted in nature and is preserved intact within the framework of the political order. Indeed, the political order has the exclusive purpose of preserving these laws. Under these circumstances it is sufficient to charge the government, in a manner that can be revoked, with the commission of sanctioning the natural rights. The members of the society reserve the right of instituting the government and of supervising whether it is working in a trustworthy manner. This is the sole act of political decision-making, which the American Declaration of Independence defines in the form of the "consent of the governed." Uninterrupted recourse to the continual implementation of the political decision-making is not needed. This "active collaboration of all" (*l'action de tous*), based by Rousseau in the sovereignty of the people, is only required when the institutionalization of fundamental rights does not merely preserve a substance prior to the state, but must first create, assert, and maintain an organized total constitution, however it may accord with the principles of nature, against a depraved social intercourse. For this, omnipotent political power is required and therefore also the democratic integration of this power in an ever present political will.

It is not as though one conception recognized the democratic principle and the other denied it. The two are not distinguishable primarily with respect to the organization of state power, but by their interpretation of the relationship between the state and society. Jefferson can only conceive of a radicalization of democracy in such a way that the domination of public opinion (Locke's Law of Opinion) makes a government based on formal laws entirely superfluous: "public opinion is in the place of laws and restrains morals as powerfully as laws ever did anywhere." [46] Jefferson not only prefers a condition where there are newspapers but no government to a government without newspapers; he is even convinced that it is such a condition which will first fully realize democracy. The repressive power of the state as such may die away, together with formal laws, as soon as society organizes itself. In contrast to this, Sièyes cannot conceive of a democratically enthroned public opinion in any other way than as the sovereign of a legislative machine; and the Jacobins, too, as apt disciples of Rousseau, conceive of democracy, even in its radical form, in such a way that the general will exercises its sovereignty by means of formal and general laws. For the French do not take a natural basis of society, distinct from the state, into their calculations; the liberation of a sphere of commodity exchange and social labor from state intervention must itself be realized and asserted, they believe, within the framework of a total constitution which always embraces society itself.

From this specific distinction between the Natural-Law construction of bourgeois society which was dominant in America, and that dominant in France, the different interpretations of the revolutionary task necessarily follow: how to positivize Natural Law and actualize democracy. The revolutionary act itself cannot have the same significance, when in the one place it is a matter of setting free the spontaneous forces of self-regulation in harmony with Natural Law, while in the other, it seeks to assert for the first time a total constitution in accordance with Natural Law against a depraved society and a human nature which has been corrupted. In the one place, revolutionary force is mobilized for the restriction of despotically unrestrained power; in the other, for the construction of a natural order which cannot count on a natural basis which will meet it halfway. In the one place, the Revolution can let the uncurbed egoism of natural interests work for it; in the other, it has to mobilize moral incentives.

Revolutionary self-awareness in Jacobin France and in Jefferson's America: Robespierre and Paine

Here is how Rousseau saw the issue: the transformation of natural man suited to an isolated and autarchic life into a citizen capable of peaceful cooperation was conceivable only as a conversion. Therefore the social contract requires denaturing an original natural existence to make it into a moral one; the contract is a moral act as such. Because of that, Rousseau considers a constitution in accord with the principles of the social contract to be possible for small nations at a primitive stage of development—for example, Corsica, where trade and industry had hardly evolved yet, where property was broadly and equitably distributed, and where pure and simple mores prevailed.[47] For the great states in an advanced stage of civilization he did not consider a republican transformation applicable. His doctrine was not revolutionary; it had yet to be interpreted in a revolutionary manner. The pupils did not respect the limits of this model's application, which the teacher himself had drawn; they wanted to bring about a republican constitution also in advanced society within a large state, by revolution; or more precisely, to carry the revolution which had already broken out toward its goal in accordance with this plan.

No one was more aware of the immanent difficulty which this entailed in theory than Robespierre. He held fast to the principle that the establishment of Natural Law by means of the power of an internally coercive sovereign guaranteeing freedom and equality, was possible, only on the basis of virtue and not on that of interest. Consequently, the problem of a successful completion of the Revolution was posed for him in the following form: how can the sentiments of virtue be generated among the mass of the population? "The society would bring forth its crowning work if with respect to moral concerns it created a vivid instinct in men, which would induce them to do good and avoid evil without the additional aid of thought." [48] At the end of the century whose intellectual energies had been devoted to the unmasking of priestly deception more than to any other matter, Robespierre sees himself driven to the questionable restoration of a rational belief in God, for the sake of a virtue which no longer would sprout forth of itself from the soil of an uncorrupted people. For reasons of state he wants to decree a quasi-clerical cult of the "Supreme Being"; in so doing, Robespierre is not in doubt as to what is involved in attempting to reproduce something that is supposed to be aboriginal: "The idea of the Supreme Being and the immortality of the soul is a constant appeal to justice; thus it is social and republican." [49] Sorel's political myth is already anticipated by this new cult and its national festivals—they present the staged dramatization of brotherhood and produce revolutionary moral sentiments, soon within the very shadow of the guillotine.[50] Thomas Paine, on the other hand, to whom but a few years before French patriots had given the key to the Bastille so that he might present it to George Washington, did not have to import virtue into his revolutionary calculus— particularly not virtue coerced by manipulation and ultimately terror. Every effective improvement in the conditions of life, he emphasized, must be mediated by the personal interests of all individuals.[51]

This statement is contained in the *Rights of Man,* which meanwhile, as we learn from the letters of Jefferson to Paine, had become the textbook of the Republicans, while the Federalists held to Burke's writings. In the United States the scene had changed. There too men's views were divided by the French Revolution. Only now did the ideology of civil war and its social conflicts begin to be imported from Europe—to such a small extent had the American emancipation known the divisiveness and confrontation of civil war in the strict sense. Jefferson, who had returned from France at the high point of the Revolution, now interpreted the events of 1776 in terms of the articulated categories of 1789 and formed the Republican organization against the government. The latter included the great representatives of American independence, whose ambivalent attitude toward the French Revolution betrayed only too clearly how little they themselves had formerly understood their appeal to Natural Law, the universal founding of the constitutional state as a revolutionary break with classical Natural Law and the historical rights of the English tradition.[52]

On the other hand, the revolutionary interpretation of their opponents was by no means *solely* a projection backward. In the same manner as the American model had been a catalyst for French self-understanding, so now the Americans could discern the revolutionary aspect of the foundation of their own government more clearly in the mirror of the French Revolution. Actually the consciousness of an American Revolution, the traditional image that has come to prevail today, was formed only with the election of Jefferson as President (which was therefore called the "Revolution of 1800"). In this image are preserved the traits of a revolution which had its genuine descent from the Anglo-Saxon tradition of Natural Law and could not be confused with the revolutionary self-understanding of the European continent. In 1794, Robespierre proclaimed before the National Convention that one half of the revolution was already realized, while the other still had to be carried out. This revolution, whose completion he conceived as the realization of philosophy,[53] is not the same as the revolution whose concept Thomas Paine interpreted so effectively for republican America.

To the traditional states Paine opposes the new systems of rule based on Natural Law; while the former arose by pure force, normally by conquest, the latter are based on the laws of a society separate from the state and at the same time on the rights of men, who, as members of a society in which they share in common, commission the government with the care of their common affairs, but are not themselves incorporated into the state. A revolution in the strict sense thus has the task of overthrowing those "governments out of power" and in their place setting up "governments out of society"—or more precisely, of letting such governments come to be established. For it is sufficient to remove repressive force in order for the principles of society to enter into effect and produce a government which serves the spontaneous development of "society, civilization, and commerce." Through the interests of liberated private persons these principles will assert themselves with the same natural force as the laws of nature and the instincts of animals. One consideration which Paine brings to bear proves that he does not expect the positivization of Natural Law, insofar as it is to realize the abstractly formulated construction of the Natural Law of bourgeois society, to arise from revolutionary action as such:

It is possible that an individual can work out a system of principles according to which a state can be erected on any possible territory. That is no more than an operation of the mind . . . acting on the basis of such principles and their application to the numerous and varied circumstances of a nation, to agriculture and manufacture; commerce and trade require a different sort of knowledge. This can only arise from the various parts of society itself; it is an ensemble of practical experiences which no individual person has at his disposal.[54]

At best the revolution can remove obstacles; its appeal to natural rights is legitimized solely by the expectation that the natural laws of society will correspond to these. Indeed, Paine even arrives at the conclusion that inversely, the state will not be able to resist being revolutionized according to the principles of Natural Law as soon as the sphere of commodity exchange and labor achieves autonomy. An emancipation of society can precede the revolution of the state just as well as it can be set in motion by revolution: "If commerce were permitted to act to the universal extent it is capable then it would . . . produce a revolution in the uncivilized state of governments." [55] Just as the revolutionary abolition of political force was the precondition in France for turning the market society over to the immanent laws of commercial exchange, according to liberal principles, so a liberal economic structure can induce societal processes which will bring about a political revolution in their wake.[56]

The Marxist critique of liberal Natural Law and a dialectical concept of the bourgeois revolution

From this ultimate point which the liberal self-understanding of the bourgeois revolution attains in Thomas Paine the Marxist interpretation could take its direct point of departure two generations later. For initially Marx conceives the bourgeois constitutional state in no other way than it has understood itself in the liberal tradition: "Due to the emancipation of private property from the commonwealth the state gained a separate existence beside and external to bourgeois society; it is nothing else

than the form of organization which the bourgeois necessarily
accord themselves, externally as well as internally, for the mutual
guarantee of their property and their interest. . . . The most
perfect example of a modern state is North America." [57] Therefore the state can be conceived as the guarantor of a contract by
all the members of a society concerning those conditions "within
which individuals had the enjoyment of chance. This right to
enjoy chance undisturbed within certain conditions has up till
now been called personal freedom." [58] Now this liberal construction of Natural Law itself had considered political economy to be
the crucial test of its truth: the natural laws of society were to
fulfill the promise of the natural rights of man. If Marx could
therefore prove for political economy that the free commerce of
private proprietors among each other necessarily excluded the
enjoyment of equal opportunity for personal autonomy on the
part of all individuals, then he had at the same time furnished
the proof that the formal and general laws of the bourgeois private legal order must be economically deprived of their professed
justice. The interests of the bourgeois [*Bürgerlichen*] can no
longer be identified with that of all citizens [*Bürger*]; precisely
those general laws in which the formal rights are expressed serve
only to assert the particular interest of one class:

> The individuals who rule under these conditions . . . must
> give a general expression to their will, determined by these
> specific conditions, as the will of the state, as the law. . . .
> Their personal rule must at the same time constitute itself
> as a common rule. Their personal power is based on condi-
> tions which develop as conditions common to many, the
> maintenance of which they have asserted as rulers against
> others and at the same time as valid for all. The expression of
> this will determined by their common interests is the law.
> Precisely the assertion of individuals independent of each
> other, the assertion of their own wills, which on this basis
> are their behavior towards each other, renders self-denial
> necessary in laws and rights. Self-denial in the exceptional
> case, self-assertion of their interest in the average case. [59]

Because in serving the interests of the private proprietors the state does not serve the interests of society as a whole, it remains an instrument of domination; the repressive power cannot wither away, cannot return to a society which regulates itself spontaneously. Marx only has to confront the expectations of the liberal, Natural-Law construction of bourgeois society with the developmental tendencies of this society itself in order to confront the bourgeois revolution polemically with its own concept. Because this revolution had philosophically formed a concept of itself, it could be taken at its word by its critics. The astonishing combination of philosophy and economics is not the peculiar distinctiveness of the *Paris Manuscripts*—it was already anticipated in the philosophic self-understanding of the bourgeois revolution.

In consonance with the linguistic usage of the Hegelian philosophy of right, Marx comprehends the bourgeois revolution as the emancipation of citizens [burgher] but not of human beings: recognized before the law as free and equal legal persons, still at the same time the citizens are at the mercy of the natural conditions of a society of exchange, which has been set free.

> Man, such as he is as a member of bourgeois society, the nonpolitical man, appears necessarily however as the natural man. The *droits de l'homme* appear as *droits naturels,* for self-conscious activity is concentrated on the political act. The egoistic man is the passive result of a dissolved society in which he is merely presented as a given phenomenon. . . .
>
> The political revolution dissolves bourgeois life into its component parts, without revolutionizing these parts themselves and subjecting them to a critique. It is related to bourgeois society, to the world of needs, of labor, of private interests and private law, as to the basis of its existence, as to a precondition which requires no further justification—therefore as to its natural basis.[60]

The polemical concept of a merely political emancipation, which at the same time is recognized "as a great step forward," [61] thus turns critically against the central presupposition underlying the

Anglo-Saxon tradition of Natural Law. To be sure, Marx never made an explicit distinction between the liberal construction and the competing one going back to Rousseau and the Physiocrats, which recognized no separation in principle of human rights from citizens' rights, of fundamental rights prior to the state from those conferred by the state. Therefore it had to remain inexplicable to him

> that a nation which has just begun to liberate itself . . . solemnly proclaims the justification of egoistic man, separate from his fellowmen and the community (in the *Déclaration de 1791*), and even repeats this proclamation at the very moment . . . when the sacrifice of all interests of bourgeois society have been made the order of the day and egoism must be punished as a crime (*Déclaration de 1793*).[62]

As has been shown, the liberal doctrine of Natural Law could not, indeed, have served as the basis for the self-understanding of the French Revolution. For the latter had as it basis the idea of a political society, an organization embracing both state and society. Without knowing it, Marx himself stands within this tradition, and takes his departure from its concept of revolution, though, to be sure, giving this concept a new content. While the political revolution had emancipated the citizen legally, the future proletarian revolution was to emancipate man socially. As is well known, Marx constructed an interpretation of the Paris revolt of June 25, 1848, as the indication of such a proletarian revolution; he compared it with the outbreak of the February Revolution of that same year in terms of the formula: "After June revolution means: the overthrow of bourgeois society, while prior to February it had meant: the overthrow of the political form of the state." [63] The proletariat should use the political power it had gained in order to organize a revolution from above ("by means of despotic intervention in the bourgeois relations of production") and should thus now organize also the socially derived natural basis of the state which the bourgeoisie had revolutionized politically. In this, of course, it was no longer a question of positivizing Natural Law; instead, the revolution relies on carrying out a justice extracted dialectically from natural history. In the framework of a world history deciphered as a structure of guilt, Hegel had sacrificed abstract Natural Law to what seemed to him a more living judgment of destiny. Therefore to the statement, adopted approvingly, that the revolution had received its first stimulus from philosophy, he had at the same time added the limitation: "But this philosophy is only abstract thought, and not the concrete comprehension of absolute truth, which constitutes an immeasurable difference." Marx, with his critique of ideology applied to the bourgeois constitutional state and with his sociological resolution on the basis of natural rights, went beyond Hegel to discredit so enduringly for Marxism both the idea of legality itself and the intention of Natural Law as such that ever since the link between Natural Law and revolution has been dissolved. The parties of the internationalized civil war have divided this heritage between themselves with fateful unambiguity: the one side has taken up the heritage of revolution, the other the ideology of Natural Law.

Fundamental rights as principles for a total constitutional order in the welfare state

In the welfare states of the mass democracies of a highly industrialized and bureaucratically highly organized society, the recognized human and citizens' rights occupy a peculiarly ambivalent position. Three aspects are characteristic of this:

(1) On the one side, the guarantee of fundamental rights is the recognized foundation of constitutionality, of an order in terms of which the exercise of authority, the use of force, and the distribution of power must legitimize themselves. On the other side, Natural Law itself is devoid of any and every convincing philosophcial justification. To be sure, the teachers and practitioners of law actually do have recourse to the tradition of Natural Law, whether of the Christian or the rationalistic persuasion; not only are the systems to which they appeal controversial, but they have lost their credibility in the pluralism of the attempts to justify them, and in general they have remained far below the level of contemporary philosophy. Thus Scheler's and Hartmann's

material ethics of value [*Wertethik*], for example, by no means belong to the current "store of philosophic knowledge"—if one can speak of anything like that at all.

(2) Furthermore, to a great extent the social basis on which the still prevailing liberal interpretation of the catalogue of fundamental rights would rest has been withdrawn. As consequence of the tendencies toward the interdependence of state and society, which have been predominant since the last quarter of the nineteenth century, the sphere of commodity exchange and social labor has been removed from the autonomous control of private individuals to the same degree to which the state has taken over interventionist tasks. The property order and the business cycle are no longer merely given as the natural basis of the welfare state. The economic preconditions of a depoliticized society have disappeared. The classical separation of human rights and citizens' rights, the sharp distinction between private and public rights thus have lost the foundations from which they were once derived in the liberal tradition.[64]

(3) Finally, the accretion of functions of the welfare or social state has led, on the part of legislators, governments, and administrations, as well as those parties and organizations which participate informally in influencing and exercising political power, to the preparation of their decisions by means of the scientific analysis of factual social conditions. As long as the activity of the liberal state was essentially limited internally to the maintenance and development of a private legal order, in principle determined in terms of fundamental rights, political action remained "practical": at most, one needed only the recourse to juridical expertise. Today, on the other hand, instruction derived from social-technical expertise has become indispensable. The consequence of this has been a scientification of government praxis: the social sciences which now are consulted for this no longer proceed hermeneutically, but rather analytically. They can furnish technical recommendations for effective instrumentalities, but can no longer normatively give any orientation with respect to the goals themselves; they abstain rigorously from any cogent enlightenment about practical necessities in given situations, about the selection of aims, the priority of goals, the application of norms.

Both of these aspects—fundamental norms of political action for which a scientific legitimation can no longer be found, and scientifically rationalized methods of purely technical control over social processes, which methods, as such, are devoid of practical orientation—have become separated in an abstract manner. The theoretical interconnection between the two aspects, which had always remained preserved in the doctrines of Natural Law and the natural society, from Hobbes and Locke down to Marx, is now broken; the positivistic adaptation to a basic philosophy of *"dirigisme"*—of pure control and manipulation—cannot take the place of these.[65]

When these points have been sufficiently taken into consideration, the historical comparison of the two competing Natural-Law constructions offer several conclusions which are applicable also to a systematic analysis of fundamental rights under present-day conditions. For what at the end of the eighteenth century was a difference in interpretation becomes later, under changed social conditions, a distinction in the life-process of the political constitution itself. If one considers the fundamental rights during the liberal phase solely with a view to their sociological function, then fundamentally the same picture emerges for Europe as for America. These rights guarantee society as the sphere of private autonomy; confronting it, a public power limited to a few central tasks; and, as it were, between the two the domain of private persons gathered together to form the public who as citizens mediate between the state and the needs of bourgeois society.[66] As a consequence the human rights could be interpreted in a liberal manner: they protect against interventions and usurpations by the state in the domain reserved in principle for private persons bound by the general rules of legal intercourse. But the fundamental rights could be *interpreted just as well* as the principles of a constitution organizing society and the state. They by no means had only a *limiting* effect. For, given the social basis for which the liberal constitutions were conceived, the fundamental rights had to become effective for offering as positive guarantees for participation with equal opportunity in the process of the production of social wealth, as well as that of the formation of public opinion. In the interplay of a commercial society, which was presupposed by the National Assembly, just as it was by the Physiocrats, the granting of equal opportunity in participating in social rewards (by way of the market) and in participating in the political institutions (as part of the general public) was to be attained only indirectly by means of guaranteeing freedom and security vis-à-vis the power concentrated in the state; thus the positive impact of the fundamental rights was to be attained only by way of their negative effect.

The objective functions of positivized Natural Law at that time were neutral with respect to the two dominant interpretations. However, through a change in function, they have meanwhile, on a different social basis, lost this neutrality. In industrial society constituted as a welfare state, the fiction of the prepolitical character of the subjective rights of freedom is no longer tenable, nor is the fundamental distinction between human rights and citizens' rights, which was already lacking in the French declarations. No one can any longer expect that the positive fulfillment of fundamental rights which have negative effect will "automatically" take place. The natural laws immanent in society did not oblige individuals by compensating for spheres free from state intervention with even approximately equal chances to participate in social rewards as well as in political institutions. Therefore, not only have fundamental social rights and provisions been added as supplement, but indeed the human rights themselves can no longer be interpreted in any other way than as political rights. As Ernst Rudolf Huber had already shown for the Weimar constitution, the fundamental rights were once, in the liberal manner, understood as the recognition and not as the conferring of natural freedom belonging to an autonomous private domain, external to the state, but now they can derive their specific meaning only from the context of objective principles constituting a total legal order which encompasses both state and society.[67]

What can no longer be guaranteed indirectly by a delimitation, must now be granted positively: participation in social achievements and in political public life.[68] The group of fundamental rights, which, with the institutional guarantee of property as their core, confirmed the basic freedoms of private law and thus also the free choice of profession, of employment, and of education, now assume in part the character of rights of participation, and in part they are limited by other guarantees of the welfare state. The other group of fundamental rights, which assure a politically functioning public life, are transformed in their function into positive guarantees of participation and supplemented by legal principles of rights covering the organization of the mass media, political parties, and public associations. Even the fundamental rights which guarantee the integrity of the most intimate sphere, of the immediate family and the personal status of freedom, once they are related to a materially interpreted right of the free development of the personality, lose the purely negative character of which they provided the prototype during the transition from the older feudal rights of the "estates" to the bourgeois rights of freedom.[69]

Finally, a triple function of the fundamental rights is also legitimized by the fact that in an industrially advanced society private autonomy can be maintained and assured only as the derivative of a total political organization. The rights to freedom, property, and security, when they have been transformed in function socially or in the context of the welfare state, are no longer based on legal relations naturally stabilized by the interests of free commodity exchange; instead, they are based on an integration of the interests, of all the organizations acting in relation to the state, and in turn controlled by an internal as well as external public sphere. This integration has to be continually reconstituted in a democratic manner.

The norms of fundamental rights, to which the praxis of the welfare state is also obligated, are related dialectically to the constructions of Natural Law by which they were once legitimized. These norms are adhered to unwaveringly as far as their original intention is concerned, but at the same time their function must be transformed with a view to the social conditions under which they have to be actualized today. Just that linking by the liberals of the construction of Natural Law to the political economy of bourgeois society has provoked a sociological critique, which teaches that we cannot isolate formal right from the concrete context of social interests and historical ideas, and, as it were, ground it independently—whether ontologically, transcendentally-philosophically, or anthropologically—in nature (the nature of the world, of consciousness, or of man)—an insight by which Hegel, in the Jena *Philosophie des Geistes,* had already anticipated what Marx stated in the *Deutsch-Französische Jahrbücher.* To be sure, we do not conceive the fundamental rights historically, in terms of the organization of social life, merely in order to devalue them as pure ideology, we do so precisely to keep the ideas from losing their meaning, once their basis in life has been removed, and thus coming to justify precisely that from which they were once to liberate mankind: the unattenuated substantial force of political domination and social power, which is neither willing nor able to be legitimized in terms of publicly discussed and rationally justified purposes. Thus conversely, the same dialectical relationship presents itself as follows: on the one hand, the revolutionary significance of modern Natural Law cannot simply be reduced to the social interrelationship of interests, and, on the other hand, the idea of Natural Law which points beyond the bourgeois ideology, though it cannot be salvaged by these means, can only be realized seriously by an interpretation in terms of the concrete social relations. The natural, unreflected structures of these relations can be eliminated—within the norms of the total constitution of a political society, founded firmly in fundamental rights—only to the degree to which they also are operative within that society.[70]

We can go back to the construction of Natural Law of the French National Assembly, inspired equally by Rousseau and the Physiocrats, insofar as there the fundamental rights were conceived as the principles of a political constitution which, together with the state, also encompassed society. But only because it was believed that the naturalness of such a total order of rights and of its principles could be vindicated, was it to be carried out for all times by a revolutionary act against a depraved society. This revolutionary self-understanding was facilitated by the fundamental ambiguity of the Physiocrats' concept of nature. For it was the immanent laws of a bourgeois society emancipated from the state which were called natural; at the same time, however, they required legal regulation and despotic revolutionary enforcement, because the natural laws of society do not operate with the absolute inviolability of the laws of physics, but rather are laws which must be made to rule by political means in the face of the corruption of human nature. In contrast to this, the liberal interpretation had seen through the illusory naturalness of an emancipated market society. As the natural basis of a liberal state, market society could be set free by political power, but it would enter into a total political constitution only if private persons, as citizens, were to influence the condition of the social reproduction of their life politically, throughout ever more extensive spheres, and in principle bring these under their control. To be sure, this idea was only realized in the transformation of the liberal constitutional state into the welfare state: the revolutionary element contained in the positivization of Natural Law has been resolved into a long-range process of democratically integrating the fundamental rights.[71]

In the meantime these rights have been divested of the abstractness of natural rights, because we know that they can do justice to their intention only within the material formations of social conditions. And with that their character also changes. The French Declaration had contained the tacit premise that a compulsory order of formal and general norms would be translated directly into organizing the conditions of social life; it shared this legal prejudice with the whole of the tradition that derives from Hobbes. However, as soon as the expectations invested in bourgeois formal right were no longer fulfilled by the immanent laws governing the autonomous private sphere of commodity exchange and social labor with sufficient credibility, a divergence arose between the immediate normative effect of the fundamental rights for the legal persons subsumed under them and the positive directions given by these principles for a total constitutional order, in which an assimilated society first must be divested of its character of having a basis in nature.

In the welfare state, political praxis is constrained to proceed according to the criteria presented by the fundamental rights. It is not only bound to them as legal norms but at the same time depends on guiding the process of transformation *by means of* these rights acting as maxims for the formative process. Thus praxis will take its orientation from the norms of fundamental rights precisely to the degree to which it allows itself to be informed at the same time by social science concerning the actual conditions under which the possibilities for their functioning must take place. But this form of commitment also reacts back on the social sciences themselves. In *this* form a scientification of politics, which has become unavoidable, would also require reflection on the part of the sciences on their own political consequences—a reflection which until now has been anxiously avoided. A positivistically limited social science cannot allow itself to go beyond the level of dissolving the empty formulas of Natural Law by means of the critique of ideology.[72] On the level of self-reflection about its commitments to a political praxis operating under the obligation of fundamental rights, however, it will not be able to remain content with the postulates of ethical nihilism or abstinence. Instead, it will then have to understand itself as a component of the practical interrelationships of life—as an agent within them.

3

Hegel's Critique of the French Revolution

"There is no other philosophy which is so much and so deeply in its innermost impulses the philosophy of revolution as that of Hegel." This thesis, which has been defended emphatically by Joachim Ritter,[1] I would like to amplify with a second thesis: in order not to sacrifice philosophy to the challenge posed by the revolution, Hegel elevated revolution to the primary principle of his philosophy. Only after he had fastened the revolution firmly to the beating heart of the world spirit did he feel secure from it. Hegel did not curse the French Revolution and its children into oblivion; he celebrated them into oblivion. During all the years of his life, according to one tradition, he honored the Revolution with a toast on the anniversary of the fall of the Bastille. If this ritual did indeed take place, then its magical character would be quite undeniable: the celebration would have been an exorcism. For did not Hegel, by then almost resigned, confess at the end of the *Philosophy of History* that the unrest set in motion by the Revolution, and subsequently arising continually anew, was a knot which history would have to unravel in the future—and only then? [2] Hegel celebrates the revolution because he fears it; Hegel elevates the revolution to the primary principle of philosophy for the sake of a philosophy which is to overcome the revolution. Hegel's philosophy of revolution is his philosophy *as* the critique of revolution.

In 1817 in the *Heidelberger Jahrbücher* a polemic appeared

against the assembly of the Württemberg estates [*Landstände*] which, after long discussions, had rejected a constitution offered by the king.[3] The pamphlet was understood by contemporaries to represent a reactionary support for the monarch. The latter, however, proved to have a sharper vision of the confused political polarities of the day, for he mistrusted his uninvited supporter—in any case, he did *not* offer the author the post in the state service for which he had hoped. The author was Hegel. The thrust of his critique could offer as little comfort to the king as to the assembled estates; for it took just that direction which the Revolution itself had taken a quarter century before.

Hegel did not criticize the demand of the estates that they receive more extensive rights than those which the new constitution accorded them; instead, he condemned as their most fundamental error the justification they presented for this demand. For the Assembly had appealed to the privileges contained in the ancient constitution of Württemberg, and had demanded the restoration of the old freedoms held by the estates. With that they had returned to the tradition of the classical Natural Law, and had thus regressed behind the level attained by revolutionary Natural Law. For the latter refuses to recognize in the positive mass of privileges which have become historical an order proclaimed for all eternity. The reason of rational Natural Law has stripped away the traditional continuity of those prevailing customs among the burghers and the functioning institutions of communal life; before this reason it is solely the abstract freedom of the legal person in the equality of all men under formal and general laws which has validity. From such a viewpoint, the practical reason of the old "Politics," which discerned what was natural *in terms of* traditions, had to be reduced to mere traditionalism: "Whether what is called ancient right and constitution is actually right or not cannot depend on its antiquity. For the abolition of human sacrifice, of slavery, of feudal despotism and innumerable other infamies was also the abolition of what had been an ancient right." [4] Hegel conceives the French Revolution as the world-historical event that for the first time had conferred real existence and validity on abstract right. Looking back on the decades which had passed since that event, as a partisan of the revolutionary order he expresses his contemptuous judgment of the Revolution's opponents: "There can hardly be a more terrifying mortar to crush the false concepts of right and false prejudices about constitutions, than the tribunal (*Gericht*) of these last twenty-five years, but this assembly of estates seems to have emerged from it quite undisturbed." This recognition, to be sure, betrays, in this very statement, the duality of the basis on which it rests: for the validity of the abstract Right that Hegel asserts so rigorously against the positive mass of what has merely come to be in history is subjected to the course of world history as the supreme court of judgment ("the tribunal of these last twenty-five years").

Hegel legitimizes the objective reality of abstract right in terms of world-history. Thereby he undermines the basis of justification claimed by Natural Law itself; he separates the validity of abstract Right from its actual realization; the order produced by the Revolution from the Revolution itself; he separates the abstract freedom which has gained positive assertion in the sphere of bourgeois society (Code Napoléon) from that abstract freedom which wishes to actualize itself (Robespierre). For the latter is ensnared in the contradiction of the absolute freedom entertained by a consciousness which remains merely subjective: in the fullest development of its power it necessarily experiences its own frailty. As such a negation of abstract freedom exaggerated to the point of absolute freedom Hegel understands the Jacobin Terror. It is toward this that the critique of the French Revolution is directed. Thus Hegel welcomes in Napoleon both the conqueror of the French Revolution and the protector of the revolutionary order, the general who is actually victorious over Robespierre and the patron of the new bourgeois code of law. One brief instant sufficed to acclaim this figure of the world spirit on horseback; but a whole life hardly sufficed to think out this affectively induced acclamation, namely: to conceptually legitimize the revolutionizing of reality without Revolution itself.

I

Let us first recognize in terms of the historical situation the specific significance which the French Revolution had to attain in the self-understanding of modern Natural Law.[5] The Revolution appears to resolve in fact difficulty which had always adhered to the doctrine of Natural Law theoretically as an unresolved residue. Virtually overnight an unforeseen upheaval accomplishes that peculiar translation of theory into praxis which could not have been thought out within the framework of this theory itself. For along the road to scientific rigor the modern doctrine had lost that capacity which the old politics had once possessed as prudence, namely: practical orientation with respect to what is to be done, correctly and justly, in a given situation.[6]

The social philosophy which Hobbes had founded in the spirit of Galileo desires to specify once and for all the conditions for the correct order of state and society. Therefore what is required in the knowledge of these general conditions is not the practically prudent action of men toward each other, but the correctly calculated generation of rules, relationships, and institutions. The engineers of the correct order can disregard the categories of moral relations and can confine themselves to the conditions which will compel men to conform to a specific behavior. But the same men who are to be the material of this order are, as its technicians, to process this material. This defines the difficulty: how is this theory to become practical?

Hobbes's assurance, untiringly reiterated, that social philosophical insight merely requires methodological certainty, in order to become immediately the practical certainty of citizens possessed of political insight—this itself betrays the impotence of thought which abstracts from the difference between control and action. Differing in this respect from the merely technical application of scientific results, the translation of theory into praxis confronts the task of becoming incorporated in the consciousness and the moral attitudes of citizens prepared to act. Theoretical solutions must be proven as practically necessary solutions for the satisfaction of objective needs under concrete conditions, if they have not already, from the outset, been conceived within this perspective by those who are involved in action.[7] It is precisely *this* difficulty which the Revolution now seems to remove for theory. The actualization of abstract right has been carried out by history itself, so to speak, behind the back of theory. In the comprehension of contemporaries, therefore, the Revolution appears as, in the words of Kant, the evolution of Natural Law.

To be sure, this division of labor between theory and history did not actually present a solution. For what could no longer be appropriately reflected in the theory, the actualization of abstract Right, by no means asserted itself in the Revolution unreflectingly as simply an objective event. The French Revolution was the first revolution, which, although it erupted initially like a natural catastrophe, was soon incorporated into the will and the consciousness both of its partisans and its opponents. Since 1789 there have been revolutions which have been defended as such, driven forward, directed, and completed by their revolutionary-minded advocates. But with these advocates, ideologues, and "men of principles" [*Prinzipienmänner*], as Hegel calls them contemptuously, that precarious becoming-practical of the theory in turn enters into the political planning of the acting individuals; for these again are engineers, acting within the mode of actual producing, who desire to confer immediate reality to the general norms. This is comprehended by the *Phenomenology of Mind* as the "terror of absolute freedom." The direct actualization of the abstract Right that had been outlined in theory, presents the problem of mediating a simple, unbending, cold generality with the absolute brittleness and obstinate punctiliousness of self-consciousness as it exists in reality. But as both of these extremes have been extracted from the continuity of the practical interrelationships of life and thus are absolute, for themselves, relationship between them can "send out no part towards the middle by which they could link up." The revolutionary activity authorized by subjective consciousness is therefore the negation of the individual in the general. Its sole work is death and indeed "the coldest, most insipid death, with no more significance than chopping through a head of cabbage or gulping down water." [8]

Hegel acclaims the Revolution, insofar as it helps what Kant conceived as the condition of Right to achieve external existence. However, at the same time he criticizes the revolutionaries who incorporate the condition of Right into their action as the immediate goal. [9]

Hegel cannot retreat from this aim itself; therefore he is dis-

tinguished in principle from the first critic of the French Revolution, Edmund Burke. He can no longer refer the problem of
constitutional law back to the prudence of state, as Burke did, as
a "question of dispositions, and of probable consequences—wholly
out of the law." [10] Burke's "prudence," which derives from the
classical tradition of politics by way of Cicero's *prudentia* and
Aristotle's *phronesis,* this practical prudence, which is invoked
once more by Vico against the methodical rigor of modern science, can no longer suffice for Hegel. And indeed he only criticizes
the ambitious self-understanding of the Revolution: to seek to
realize reason itself by the power of a subjective consciousness
which is not capable of going beyond the abstractions of the understanding. The claim of the Revolution as such ". . . that
man's existence centers in his head, i.e. in thought, inspired by
which he builds up the world of reality." [11]—this claim Hegel
takes seriously. He has to legitimize the revolutionizing of reality
without legitimizing the revolutionaries themselves. That is why
he undertakes the magnificent attempt to understand the actualization of abstract Right as an objective process.

II

Abstract Right gains its logical force and its ontological
status from the fact that it abstracts away from all that has merely
come to be historically; but the philosophy which comprehends
it conceives it as a moment within the historical totality in order
to justify it precisely in its abstract character in terms of the concretely universal.

To be sure, the architecture of Hegel's Philosophy of Right
leads one to misconstrue his peculiarly historical concept of abstract Right. In the first part, which stands distinctly under the
title of Natural Law, the elements of abstract Right, possession,
property, and contract are introduced as principles independent
of history and devoid of presuppositions—this they claim to be
according to their modern self-understanding, and this they also
must be, in their character of critical criteria for the annihilation
of all right that has merely come to be historically. A certain difficulty results in the transition from the contract to injustice

[*Unrecht*] and punishment; for only a right which has the force of law can be violated. However, abstract Right, which Hegel first develops here as right in itself [*Recht an sich*], attains such validity in bourgeois society. In the third part of the Philosophy of Right *actualized* abstract Right therefore appears under the unpretentious title of jurisprudence [*Rechtspflege*]. It has only come into existence here as positively asserted private Right; only here is it manifested as *the* form in which the private sphere of social labor, thus modern society, becomes secure in its own power. But the concept of abstract Right and that of the system of human needs are independent of each other and each has been developed on its own [*für sich*]; this creates the appearance that the completed social content enters into a ready-made legal form.[12] The Philosophy of Right, elaborated in the shadow of the Logic, withholds information concerning the actual process by which abstract Right originated out of the historical interrelationships of social labor, and concerning its actualization in industrial society. The younger Hegel had furnished this information in detail: the *System of Morality* and the two versions of the Jena *Realphilosophie* preserve the traces of the course which Hegel's labors took in bringing the abstractions of Natural Law back down to the ground of historical experience, the ground which political economy had prepared.[13] He had reconstructed Locke in terms of Adam Smith and had shown how possession is initially appropriated in the work performed upon an object, how surplus possessions are then exchanged in trade, and how in this exchange it is then recognized mutually as property; how then finally the generalization of the relationship of exchange, and therefore of contract, produces a legal state, in which the will of each individual is constituted with private autonomy in the will of all individuals.

Hegel sees through the historical and at the same time systematic interconnection between specific processes of social labor and the free exchange by the producers, on the one hand, and, on the other, those formal rules of transactions in private law, the principles of which have been elaborated in rational Natural Law, codified in the civil law books since the eighteenth century[14] and formulated by Hegel in terms of the concept of abstract right. By comparing the Natural-Law doctrines of modern social philosophy with the contemporary doctrines of natural society developed by political economy, he discovers as their essential interconnection that the freedom of legal persons and their equality under general laws literally have been won by labor [*erarbeitet*]. Abstract Right documents a concrete liberation: for social labor is that process in which consciousness makes itself into a thing, in order thereby to form itself into its own proper form [*sich zu sich selbst bilden*], and finally, as the offspring of bourgeois society, to divest itself of its servile guise. In this process of socialization the abstract right of the modern state becomes actualized; the fiction of a social contract and contract of government by which all the individuals initially constitute the state abstracts from the historical process of a consciousness that must emancipate itself from compulsive force, of natural origin; this consciousness does so by way of the developed systems of needs and thus first develops itself to the point where it can attain the autonomy of a partner in the contract.[15]

Thus the French Revolution could bring about the positive assertion of abstract right, almost overnight, only because the individuals had during the preceding centuries advanced themselves by their labor to become the true children of a bourgeois society in the modern sense and thus had matured to the formal freedom of legal persons. With this concept of abstract right reinserted into the historical context, Hegel was able to legitimize the revolutionary order and still at the same time to criticize revolutionary consciousness. The problem would have been solved and Napoleon properly understood if this solution itself had not suggested certain consequences of the relation of theory and praxis.

We have seen that the revolutionary consciousness that appeals to the principles of rational Natural Law remains abstract with respect to the existing conditions which it wishes to overthrow; either it remains caught, impotent, in the contradiction between what it reasonably demands and that which resists this demand—or it deploys its unlimited power in the destruction of reality and together with it destroys its hopes. Now instead of this, the historical concept of abstract right makes possible a dialectical relation between theory and praxis; this Hegel develops in the draft of the introduction to his pamphlet against the constitution of the Holy Roman Empire, written just shortly before Napoleon actually did destroy it.[16] The transformation which to begin with is experienced as practically necessary must be understood in its historical necessity: "The feeling of the contradiction between nature and the existing state of life is the need that this contradiction be removed [*gehoben*]; [but] this will [only] happen when the existing life has lost all its power and worth, when it has become something purely negative." As soon as theory can prove such a negative character to hold true for the world which is maintaining itself, then the theory itself gains practical force. For then the idea is joined and supported by interest. In the mass of the people "the contradiction between the unknown which human beings unconsciously seek and the life which is offered and permitted them" grows. At the same time, this practical striving draws closer to critical theory, which is the longing for life of those who have worked to elevate nature to an idea within them: "The needs of the ones to attain a consciousness concerning that which holds them captive and the unknown which they demand, corresponds with the need of the others to make the transition from their idea to life." This is one of the central passages for which Karl Löwith's observation, of which he has given systematic proof, is appropriate: that the positions of the Young Hegelians were anticipated by the young Hegel himself.[17] Thus Marx raises as criticism of Hegel's Philosophy of Right what Hegel himself had formulated long before in his text on the German constitution: "Will theoretical needs be directly practical needs? It is not enough that thought strive to actualize itself; actuality must itself strive towards thought." [18] To be sure, Hegel warns of the application of revolutionary force; only reform with insight can remove completely with honor and peace that which is tottering. When only force is employed against the force of a petrified life then this act must remain imprisoned in a historical process which precisely in its necessity is not a reflective one: for "external force is the particular against the particular." Theory can only become a practical force behind the back of this life, by depriving that which exists of the status of the universal, namely, of that recognizable right which it still claims for itself: "The limited [*Beschränkte*] can be attacked in terms of its own truth . . . and brought into contradiction with this truth; it does not base its rule on the force employed by particular men against particular men, but on universality; this truth, the right by which it seeks to vindicate itself, must be taken from it and conferred on that part of life which is being demanded."

As early as 1798, in a critique of the deficiencies of the Württemberg Municipal Constitution [*Magistratsverfassung*], Hegel had unmistakably assigned this practical task to theory. Change, conceived in its historical necessity and legitimized as objective justice, must assume the guise of a conscious reform. To be sure, if this necessity is one that is merely felt, while men timidly strive to retain what they possess, then change will grow to outstrip them and become revolutionary in spite of them: "After having attained the cool conviction that a change is necessary, they must not fear to go into specifics in their investigation, and the abolition of what they find to be unjust must be demanded by those who suffer the injustice, and those who are in possession unjustly must voluntarily sacrifice what they have." [19] Precisely that penetrating theory, which criticizes what exists by showing that the pretended universality of its own concept is untenable, forces the sacrifice from the particular interests. Philosophy cannot compel by external force, but it can attack what is limited with the latter's own truth. By reflection of the contradiction in which this limited existence stands to its own truth philosophy can make it surrender itself [*Selbstaufgabe*].

Insofar as in so doing philosophy criticizes the moral world as fragmented in itself, it thus asserts the "atheism" of this world. But how can the high-handed judgment which Hegel pronounces in the preface to his *Philosophy of Right* on just this atheism of the moral world be reconciled with this? Obviously he has revised the position he had espoused in the earlier political writings. Philosophy, in any case, always arrives too late to instruct, because it comprehends its time in thought only after reality has completed itself—a theory such as that is exempted entirely from praxis by the old Hegel.[20] He had relinquished the dialectical relation between the two because of the intimation that this becoming-practical of theory, once liberated from the abstractions of the understanding, even if cautiously limited to reform, will still bear the stigma of revolution within its heart. Still, in any case, theory was to prove the corruption of the existing world by confronting it with its own concept, was to weigh the scales critically in favor of a future life over that life which is dying off, and thus could very well have developed its political force indirectly.

Hegel had traced back the subjective revolutionary actualization of abstract right to the objective revolutionary process, the social emancipation of laboring individuals, in order to legitimize the revolutionizing of reality, while discounting the revolution itself. But now he traded off for this the dangerous potential of a theory which still understood its own critical relationship to praxis. Hegel wished to defuse this potential. And he could do so by recalling that other meaning which he *also* had always attributed to the actualization of abstract right. While Hegel now conceived the abstractions of the new private right as the seal set on the self-liberation of the individual by means of social labor, formerly he had attacked the abstractions of Roman Law as the signs marking the progress of a tragedy in the moral realm. Abstract right appears not only as the form in which modern society emancipates itself, but also as that form in which the substantial world of the Greek *polis* had disintegrated. From these competing connotations, as a form in which social labor emancipates itself, on the one hand, and as the product of a dissolved morality in decay on the other, abstract right receives its deep ambiguity, which echoes Hegel's ambivalence with respect to the French Revolution.

III

Hegel, taking his orientation from Gibbon's depiction, untiringly reiterates the decay of the absolute morality of the Greek *polis* into the formal legal relations of the Roman universal monarchy. Together with political freedom, interest in the state is extinguished, the citizens are confined to their private existence, at the same time made rigidly into individuals and posited as absolute. As person, the individual has departed from individuality's immediate living unity with substance. The spirit of substantial universality, which has died and split up into the atoms of many absolute isolated individuals, has decayed to become the formalism of law. Hence a distorted image of emancipatory freedom under general and formal laws arises. As the product of the decay of morality, abstract right displays those characteristics of crisis, the model of which the youthful Hegel worked out in his theological confrontation with the Mosaic religion of law.

The universality of norms confronts living subjectivity as the rigid, impersonal, and indestructible positive. By conferring upon certain duties the character of universal commandments, the law abstracts from the specificity of the individual and the concreteness of his situation; the domination of law suppresses life. As long as laws are the supreme authority [*das Höchste*], that which is individual cannot find itself within the universal to which it is being sacrificed. The punishment of violated law remains an external compulsion; even when it has been paid, the penalty cannot reconcile the criminal with the law. On the other hand—and this was a consideration rich in consequences—when instead of the abstract law, concrete life itself appears as the punishing reality, then the punishment is experienced as destiny, as itself something individual, which the subjectivity that suffers it can confront as a hostile power, as it would an enemy. Because in this enemy the violated and alienated life is at the same time experienced as a *life,* even if as a separated one, the criminal can also reconcile himself with the power which he has armed against himself.

From this confrontation of punishment as compulsion and punishment as destiny, Hegel gains the concept that is decisive for the mediation between abstract right and substantial morality. In the completed tragedy of the moral, the universality of law, petrified into positivity, can only be surmounted if it is dethroned, as the highest authority, that is, if it falls back into the arena of historical life as a specific right in competition with another right and thus becomes involved in a *struggle for right;* and so war is the highest sign of the downfall of abstract right brought on by the self-assertion of a concrete state:

. . . in the combat over rights there lies a contradiction; . . . in the same way, the combatants are opposed to each other as real, living beings of two different sorts, life in the struggle with life. By the self-defense of the injured party the attacker is equally attacked and thus placed in the right of self-defense, so that both are right, both find themselves in the state of war which gives them both the right to defend themselves." While under the peaceful rule of law, right and reality are not properly mediated, and those engaged in war let force and strength decide their right; thus "the two (right and reality) are intermixed and make the former dependent on the latter." [21]

By war and by individuals' sacrifice for what is morally universal, which Hegel includes in his concept of war, right is again rooted in the soil of reality; as a living entity struggling with a living entity, it is itself awakened to life.

In comparison to abstract right, the assertion and validation of which cannot be free of injustice in the face of the unmediated particular which is subsumed under it, concrete right appears to be actualized only historically in the struggle between powers, above all in war between states. As a universal which is mediated into the particular, without violating its particularity, the concrete right comes into being behind the backs of living individuals, as a result of the struggle of interests between powers whose uppermost principle is the unwritten law of concrete self-assertion.

With this conception, the claim by revolutionary consciousness of directly realizing the universalities, reasonably formulated in the Natural-Law theories, is rejected conclusively. On the other hand, the possibility that theory may become dialectically practical, which Hegel once had considered, is also rejected. With the dictum that concrete justice can only generate itself by the partisan struggle of life with life, every critique which seeks to rise above this divisiveness of the specific is also condemned, when it seeks to unmask its mere pretension to universality in an interest petrified into particularity, in order then to decipher in it the physiognomy of a true interest, that is as yet merely being demanded. Hegel thus condemns every critique that seeks to steal from the dead the power they unjustly retain, in order to confer it upon a future life as its right.

Instead, in world history, one right shapes itself in terms of the other and ultimately loses its abstract character only in the existentialism of the national spirits [*Volksgeister*]. By conceiving abstract right as the product of a dissolved morality's decay, instead of as the form of emancipation of social labor, Hegel had tacitly changed his approach to the problem. Not the actualization, but the reconciliation of abstract right has now become the subject of discussion—and with it the revocation of that sphere, which was to confer positive validation on private right, the revocation of bourgeois society, of which it had already been said in the Jena *Realphilosophie*:

> Needs and labor raised to this level of generality form, in themselves, an immense system of communality and mutual dependency within a great nation, a life of the dead that bears its own motion within itself, that oscillates in this motion blindly and in an elemental manner, and which, like a wild animal, requires constant taming and strict domination.[22]

IV

Has Hegel thereby joined the counterrevolution? Has he in the end rejected, together with the revolution itself, also the order of abstract right and bourgeois society, as the sphere of private right? Has the concept of a morality of the state, restored through the revolution, in which Hegel so distinctively combined the classical concept of the political with the modern one, namely the Aristotelian doctrine of virtue with the rules of self-assertion by force, developed from Machiavelli down to Hobbes, has this concrete justice absorbed the abstract one—has the revolution lost its rights to the idea of morality?

That is indeed how the conservative interpreters present Hegel. For evidence of this tradition, the glorious academic predominance of which still casts its shadow today, I cite only one statement of Karl Larenz: "The relation of right to the community means . . . that the content of a specific positive right must correspond to the national spirit [*Volksgeist*] involved, its moral consciousness, the morals of that folk." [23] And even if with that the door has not been opened to "the idea of the folk community as the guiding principle of right," [24] then still, right in its abstract character has been cast out altogether, along with the atheism of morality.

Against this, the liberal interpreters can show how Hegel always maintained that every present and future constitution must respect the revolution's universal principle of freedom, namely, abstract freedom by means of equality under formal and general laws. But the point of this interpretation has been revealed by Joachim Ritter. The legally abstract form of social intercourse by private proprietors amongst each other emancipated men indirectly; for legal persons, limited in the preservation of their external life to their natural will, are set free by this sort of reduction precisely for the encroaching interrelationships of life:

> As objective world of labor, modern society (ordered by private law) not only frees men from the power of nature, but together with the objectification . . . of the relations of labor it raises . . . freedom to a general principle; it sets free for the person in itself, as personality, its self-existence [*Selbstsein*] and the actualization of this.[25]

Against such a conception the Left Hegelians, in turn, have been able to raise objections; for they point—and here I only mention Herbert Marcuse[26]—to the fact that, after all, Hegel's critique of abstract right, when measured against substantial morality, must be taken more seriously than the fiction of a private autonomy, protected as inalienable precisely by a law which is external and compulsive, would wish to recognize. The power of reified society is so penetrating that its divisiveness leaves no zone of inviolability which can be formally safeguarded for subjectivity. On the other hand, as the conservative interpretation shows, the substantive morality of a sphere of private right and of abstract society, absorbed [*aufgehoben*] into the state, threatens to disavow the revolution's universal principle of freedom, to which the liberal interpretation rightly adheres; therefore these Left Hegelian interpreters become critics of Hegel. As is known, they maintain that the social emancipation which was confirmed in the order of private right created by the revolution must be pushed further, into the sphere of social labor itself, to the point where abstract right is transformed into concrete right. New, as against Hegel, is the demand to conceive the morality of concrete right (now, to be sure, cut loose from its substantial ground) exclusively as the form of emancipation of social labor. But with that the dialectical relation between theory and praxis is re-established, from whose revolutionary potential Hegel himself drew back in fear.

We only wish to recall briefly these three interpretations of the sublation of right and society into morality, because in these competing arguments the tensions of Hegel's own deeply ambivalent relationship to the French Revolution are developed more fully; therefore these interpretations also form themselves in accordance with the political fronts of the European civil war which has raged in Europe during our century and which still determine our relationship to the Revolution down to the present day. Finally, I would still like to risk asking how these interpretations relate to Hegel himself. For only in posing the question thus will the thesis be demonstrated that Hegel elevates the revolution to the main principle of his philosophy for the sake of a philosophy which overcomes the revolution as such. The assertion that Hegel can justify all three interpretations as elements within his own representation is more than a literary extravagance of the neo-Hegelians. The fantastic effort—fantastic in the literal sense—required to force all three elements into dialectic unity, however, only betrays too clearly that Hegel did not achieve mastery over the complex of his critique of the French Revolution without leaving some scars.

Concrete right cannot be anticipated abstractly in the subjective consciousness, and then be asserted in a revolutionary manner; for Hegel has seen that a formal and general law must suppress individuality and disrupt the interrelationships of life to precisely the degree to which it abstracts from the richness of life, as soon as this abstraction attains positive force. A justice which is yet free from this immanent injustice of abstract right, can only be actualized by destiny; it must arise out of the polemic of the competing national spirits. Whereupon, however, the question is posed: if not revolutionary consciousness, then what or who will guarantee the revolutionary direction which world-history takes in the struggle of life with life, in order to actualize reason, in order to establish concrete right? The concept of life is historically too ill defined; it must unfold logically into the life of the concept.[27] From this complex of interrelations, therefore, one would have to derive why Hegel reintroduces on the level of objective spirit what he rejects on the level of subjective spirit: for, after all, he designates Robespierre, whom he has rejected, as world spirit. This world spirit, as is known, is permitted to use history as a blood altar on which the happiness of nations, the wisdom of states, and the virtue of individuals are offered up as sacrifice. Here the guillotine is rehabilitated, as an instrument which decapitates the figures of the *objective* spirit. The world spirit, which is at the same time that place where the Logic exposes its mythical core, is marked by a contradiction which is not sublated and not justified.

For Hegel defines the spirit, which he recognizes again in history as the spirit of the world, in the following manner:

> The first remark we have to make . . . is that what we call principle, aim, destiny or the nature and idea of Spirit, is something merely general and abstract. Principle—plan of existence—Law—is a hidden, undeveloped essence, which as such—however true in itself—is not completely real. Aims, principles, etc., have a place in our thoughts, in our subjective design only; but not yet in the sphere of reality. That which exists for itself only, is a possibility, a potentiality; but has not yet emerged into existence. A second element must be introduced in order to produce actuality—viz. actuation, realization; and whose motive power is the Will—the activity of man in the widest sense.[28]

Thus Hegel vindicates for the world spirit precisely that structure of consciousness which he criticized so devastatingly in the French Revolution. The ground thereby is pulled away from under the subjectively oriented concept of revolution, in that, by the interpolation of a world spirit, an objectively revolutionary event is comprehended in categories that are borrowed from subjective revolutionary consciousness, but are now only to be valid for the subject of history as a whole. Only in this way can history be comprehended as a step-by-step realization of the demands raised by the revolution for the actualization of right, without at the same time having to legitimize the revolutionary activity of subjective consciousness.

On the other hand, having gained the benefit of this conception, Hegel cannot, without stumbling into the dialectic of revolutionary consciousness, accept its consequence: that the world spirit can first know in advance as an abstract universal and subsequently actualize the principle of history with which it informs the world in a revolutionary manner. Therefore, Hegel subsequently reduces the inwardly known principle to a self-subsistent being of natural origin: "World-history begins with its general aim, that the concept of Spirit be satisfied, only in itself, *that means, as nature;* this aim is its inner—its innermost—unconscious instinct, and the entire business of world-history is . . . the labor of bringing this to consciousness." The world spirit is allowed to know the goal of history beforehand as the abstract universal just as little as the revolutionary of 1789 was allowed to have his abstract Right in his head, if he wanted to keep it on his shoulders.

The contradiction contained in the construction of the world spirit, which is by no means a dialectical one, thus consists in the following: on the one hand, in order to guarantee the realization of the revolutionary demand in history, a subject must be substituted for this history, which invents the ultimate aim of history as an abstract universal, in order then to actualize it. On the other hand, this universal must not have the character of a theoretically predesigned plan; it is therefore degraded to a self-subsistent being of natural origin, which only "comes to itself"—is realized—after it has objectified itself in the course of history.

The world spirit must not be recognizable as revolutionary consciousness. The world spirit is a fiction invented in order to give the cunning of reason a name; but only after this cunning has been carried out can there be a world spirit which could have such cunning thoughts. In the world spirit as the revolutionary who is not yet allowed to be a revolutionary, Hegel's ambivalent relation to the French Revolution is once again brought into focus: Hegel desires the revolutionizing of reality, without any revolutionaries. The world spirit has accomplished the revolution, reason has already become practical, before the absolute spirit—above all, philosophy—recognizes the reality of its reasonableness. The hypothesis of the world spirit underlies the paradoxical character of an objective spirit which nevertheless has borrowed its knowledge from the Absolute.[29] Onto it alone is projected what the old Hegel strictly prohibited for politicians as well as for philosophers: at the same time to act *and* to know. Only after the spirit has revolutionized reality practically and has made reason actual, can philosophy attain consciousness of the revolutionized world, the world become reasonable. A communication between philosophers, who have insight into reason in history and the level of actualization it has attained, on the one hand, and politically active subjects on the other, simply cannot exist. Hegel makes revolution the heart of his philosophy in order to preserve philosophy from becoming the procurer of revolution. With that he has once more salvaged the dialectic as ontology, has preserved its origin in theory for philosophy, and has withdrawn theory from mediation by historical consciousness and social praxis. He has done this although, and indeed because, he was the first philosopher to lead philosophy into this dimension, and that much more deeply than historicism and pragmatism—the professional destroyers of metaphysics who came after him—were capable of doing. In spite of this, philosophy today appears to have penetrated so deeply into this dimension, and will have to penetrate still so much more deeply, that not even such an already half-forced return of philosophy to *theoria,* in the lofty Greek sense, as Hegel attempted, can be foreseen.[30]

Together with the positivity of Christian religion, the young

Hegel had criticized its eschatology, as a compensation for the impotence of a dissociated morality. In its time, in Hellenism, the realization of the moral idea could only be a wish, but no longer something actually willed: "For such a revolution, to be accomplished by a divine being and in which human beings conduct themselves wholly passively, the first disseminators of Christian religion hoped; and when this hope finally disappeared, men contented themselves with expecting this revolution of the whole at the end of the world." [31] The old Hegel opposed to this expectation of a deferred revolution the memory of one actually carried out. But by his own criteria, does the one not remain as abstract as the other? The bad Utopia of a deliverance from all evil to take place objectively in the future, just as much as the compulsory identification of a present that is merely subjectively unsatisfied with a reality that is viewed rationally and recognized in its rationality—both have in common that "the realization of an idea is set outside the bounds of *human* power." [32] No matter whether the as-yet-to-be-expected realization of the moral idea becomes something that can only be desired, or whether the already accomplished realization need only be recognized, it is all the same: a revolutionizing of reality can "no longer be actually willed."

To be sure, the old just as much as the young Hegel criticizes the powerlessness of subjective belief. But while Hegel criticizes the moment of belief in the eschatological expectation, because it grants dispensation from one's own participation in action, from accomplishing it oneself, he criticizes the moment of belief on the level of absolute spirit, because it once more presumes to active participation and to the accomplishing of the realized good:

> This repetition of the presupposition of the unrealized end after the actual realization of the end consequently also determines itself in the following manner: the subjective attitude of the objective Notion is reproduced and perpetuated. . . . The objective Notion is still limited to its own view of itself, which vanishes by its reflection upon what its actualization is *in itself*. By this view it stands only in its own way, and in this matter must turn, not against any other actuality, but against itself. [33]

Once the young Hegel—in a quite Young Hegelian fashion—would have accused this reconstitution of theory of the same resignation (in the fundamental *post hoc* character of absolute knowledge) of which he had accused the Christian expectation of salvation, internalized back into contemplation and turned over to an external transcendent authority. To theory as concept, as to eschatology, he would have counterposed a concept of theory which would not have to leave praxis "behind," either because of the superior power of theory or its impotence. For then he was still at one with Feuerbach and Marx in the conviction that "it has been reserved for our times above all to vindicate, at least in theory, those treasures which were formerly wasted by relegating them to the heavens; but which age will have the strength to enforce this right, and to take possession of it?" [34]

4

Labor and Interaction: Remarks on Hegel's Jena *Philosophy of Mind*

During 1803–1804 and 1805–1806, Hegel held lectures on the Philosophy of Nature and of Mind at Jena. The *Philosophy of Mind* is linked to the *System of Morality,* which was only worked out in a fragmentary manner. These works of Hegel [1] still are under the influence of the study of political economy which Hegel was pursuing at the time. Marxist studies of Hegel always have pointed to this fact.[2] In spite of this, the distinctive position of the Jena *Philosophy of Mind* within the Hegelian system has not till now received adequate consideration. The conception which Lasson set forth in the preface to his edition of the Jena lectures continues to predominate: these works are regarded as a preparatory stage for the *Phenomenology* and the parallels to the later system are emphasized. In contrast to this, I would like to present the thesis that in the two Jena lecture courses, Hegel offered a distinctive, systematic basis for the formative process of the spirit, which he later abandoned.

The categories language, tools, and family designated three equally significant patterns of dialectical relation: symbolic representation, the labor process, and interaction on the basis of reciprocity; each mediates subject and object in its own way. The dialectics of language, of labor, and of moral relations are each developed as a specific configuration of mediation; what is involved are not stages constructed according to the same logical form, but diverse forms of construction itself. A radicalization of

my thesis would read: it is not the spirit in the absolute movement of reflecting on itself which manifests itself in, among other
things, language, labor, and moral relationships, but rather, it is
the dialectical interconnections between linguistic symbolization,
labor, and interaction which determine the concept of spirit. The
locus within the Hegelian system of the categories named would
speak against this; they do not appear in the logic but in the
Realphilosophie. On the other hand, at that time, the dialectical
relations still adhere so sensuously [*anschaulich*] to the basic
patterns of heterogeneous experience, that the logical forms diverge according to the material context from which they are
drawn: externalization [*Entäusserung*] and alienation [*Entfrem-
dung*], appropriation and reconciliation are not yet integrated.
In any case, the tendency of the Jena lectures is that only the
aggregate of the three dialectical patterns of existing consciousness can render spirit transparent in its structure.[3]

I

In the introduction to the *Subjective Logic,* Hegel recalls to
mind that concept of the "I" in which his fundamental experience of the dialectic is contained:

> "I" . . . is that initially pure unity relating to itself, and
> this it is not immediately, but in that it abstracts from all
> determinateness and content and, in the freedom of un-
> limited self-equality, passes back into itself. Thus it is uni-
> versality; unity which is unity with itself only due to that
> negative comportment, which appears as abstraction, and
> which therefore contains all the determinateness, dissolved
> within itself. Secondly, "I" is singularity just as immediately
> as it is the negativity which relates to itself; it is absolute
> being-determinate which confronts the other and excludes
> it; individual personality. The nature of both the "I" and
> the concept consists both of this absolute universality, which
> is just as immediately absolute singular individuation
> [*Vereinzelung*], as well as a being-in-and-for-itself, which
> is simply being-posited, and which is this being-in-and-for-

itself only through its unity with being-posited. Neither the "I" nor the concept can be comprehended if the two above-mentioned moments are not conceived simultaneously in their abstraction and in their perfect unity.[4]

Hegel takes as his point of departure that concept of the "I" which Kant had developed under the title of the original synthetic unity of apperception. There the "I" is represented as the "pure unity relating to itself," as the "I think," which must be capable of accompanying all of my inner representations. This concept articulates the fundamental experience of the philosophy of reflection: namely, the experience of ego-identity in self-reflection, thus the experience of self of the knowing subject, which abstracts from all possible objects in the world, and refers back to itself as the sole object. The subjectivity of the "I" is determined as reflection—it is the relation of the knowing subject to itself. In it the unity of the subject as self-consciousness constitutes itself. At the same time, Kant interprets this experience of self-reflection in terms of the presuppositions of his theory of knowledge: he purifies the original apperception, which is to guarantee the unity of transcendental consciousness, of all empirical contents.

Fichte furthers the reflection of self-reflection, *prior* to its distribution among the spheres, as the foundation of which it is, after all, to serve, father, and encounters the problem of the foundation [*Begründung*]—indeed of the ultimate foundation—of the "I." In this he pursues the dialectic of the relation between the "I" and the "other" within the subjectivity of self-knowing.[5] Hegel, on the other hand, confines himself to the dialectic of the "I" and the "other" within the framework of the intersubjectivity of spirit, in which the "I" communicates not with itself as its "other," but instead with another "I" as its "other."

The dialectic of Fichte's *Wissenschaftslehre* of 1794, which is expressed in that the "I" simply posits itself, remains confined within the condition of solitary reflection. As a *theory of self-consciousness,* it resolves the aporias of that relation in which the "I" constitutes itself by knowing itself in terms of *(bei)* an "other" identified as itself. Hegel's dialectic of self-consciousness passes over the relation of solitary reflection in favor of the complementary relationship between individuals who know each other. The experience of self-consciousness is no longer considered the original one. Rather, for Hegel it results from the experience of interaction, in which I learn to see myself through the eyes of other subjects. The consciousness of myself is the derivation of the intersection [*Verschränkung*] of perspectives. Self-consciousness is formed only on the basis of mutual recognition; it must be tied to my being mirrored in the consciousness of another subject. That is why Hegel cannot answer the question of the origin of the identity of the "I" as Fichte does, with a foundation of self-consciousness returning into itself, but solely with a *theory of spirit*. Then spirit is not the fundament underlying the subjectivity of the self in self-consciousness, but rather the medium *within* which one "I" communicates with another "I," and *from* which, as an absolute mediation, the two mutually form each other into subjects. Consciousness exists as the middle ground on which the subjects encounter each other, so that without encountering each other they cannot exist as subjects.

Fichte only deepens Kant's transcendental unity of self-consciousness; the abstract unity of synthesis is resolved into the original action which produces the unity of the opposition of the "I" and the "other," by which the "I" knows itself. Hegel, on the other hand, retains Kant's empty identity of the "I"; but he reduces this "I" to a moment, by comprehending it under the category of the universal. "I" as self-consciousness is universal, because it is an abstract "I," that is, it has arisen from the abstraction of all contents given to a subject that knows or has mental representations.[6] In the same way as it abstracts from the manifold of external objects, an "I" which retains itself as identical must abstract from the succession of inner states and experiences. The universality of the abstract "I" is displayed in that, by means of this category, *all possible* subjects, thus *everyone* who says "I" to himself, are determined as individuals. But on the other hand, the same category "I" is also an instruction in each case to think a specific subject, which, as it says "I" to itself, asserts itself as an inalienably individual and singular subject. Thus the identity of the "I" does not mean only that abstract universality of self-consciousness as such, but at the same time the category of singularity. "I" is individuality not only in the sense of a repeatable identification of a "this-there" [*Diesda*] within specifiable coordinates, but in the sense of a proper name, which signifies that which is simply individuated. "I" as category of singularity excludes the reduction to a finite number of elements, for example, to the currently known number of elementary components constituting the genetic substance.

While Fichte comprehends the concept of "I" as the identity of "I" and "not-I," Hegel from the outset comprehends it as the identity of the universal and the singular. "I" is the universal and the singular in one. Spirit is the dialectical unfolding of this unity, namely, moral totality. Hegel does not select this term arbitrarily, for "Spirit," with which we are familiar in ordinary language as in the spirit of a nation, of an epoch, or team spirit, always extends beyond the solitary self-consciousness. The "I" as the identity of the universal and the singular can only be comprehended in terms of the unity of a spirit which embraces the identity of an "I" with an other not identical with it. Spirit is the communication of individuals [*Einzelner*] in the medium of the universal, which is related to the speaking individuals as the grammar of a language is, and to the acting individuals as is a system of recognized norms. It does not place the moment of universality before that of singularity, but instead permits the distinctive links between these singularities. Within the medium of this universal—which Hegel therefore called a concrete universal— the single beings can identify with each other and still at the same time maintain themselves as nonidentical. The original insight of Hegel consists in that the "I" as self-consciousness can only be conceived if it is spirit, that means, if it goes over from subjectivity to the objectivity of a universal in which the subjects who know themselves as nonidentical are united on the basis of reciprocity. Because "I" in this precisely explicated sense is the identity of the universal and the singular, the individuation of a neonate, which within the womb of the mother has been an exemplar of the species as a prelinguistic living being, and thus could be explained biologically in terms of a combination of a finite number of elements quite adequately, once born can only be conceived as a process of socialization. To be sure, here socialization cannot be conceived as the adaptation to society of an already given individuality, but as that which itself produces an individuated being.[7]

II

The *moral relationship* was clarified by the young Hegel in terms of the relationship between lovers: "In love the separated entities [*das Getrennte*] still exist, but no longer as separated—as united [*Einiges*] and the living feels the living." [8] In the second Jena lectures Hegel explains love as the knowing [*Erkennen*] which recognizes itself in the other. From the union of distinct entities [*Unterschiedener*] results a knowledge which is characterized by "double meaning":

> Each is like the other in that wherein it has opposed itself to the other. By distinguishing itself from the other it thereby becomes identical [*Gleichsetzen*] with it; this is a cognitive process precisely in that . . . for the being itself the opposition is transformed into sameness, or that the one, as it looks at itself in the other, knows itself.[9]

To be sure, Hegel does not explicate the relation of recognizing oneself in the other, on which in turn the concept of the "I" as an identity of the universal and the singular depends, directly from the relations of intersubjectivity, through which the complementary agreement of subjects confronting each other is secured. Rather, he presents love as the result of a movement, love as the reconciliation of a preceding conflict. The distinctive sense of an ego-identity based on reciprocal recognition can be understood only if it is seen that the dialogic relation of the complementary unification of opposing subjects signifies at the same time a relation of logic *and* of the praxis of life. That is shown in the dialectic of the moral relationship, which Hegel develops under the title of the *struggle for recognition*. It reconstructs the suppression and reconstitution of the dialogue situation as the moral relationship. In this movement, which alone may be called dialectical, the logical relation of a communication distorted by force itself

exercises practical force. Only the result of this movement eradi-
cates the force and establishes the noncompulsory character of the
dialogic recognition of oneself in the other: love as reconciliation.
What is dialectical is not unconstrained intersubjectivity itself,
but the history of its suppression and reconstitution. The distor-
tion of the dialogic relationship is subject to the causality of split-
off symbols and reified logical relations—that is, relations that
have been taken out of the context of communication and thus
are valid and operative only behind the backs of the subjects. The
young Hegel speaks of a causality of destiny.

In the fragment on the *Spirit of Christianity* he demonstrates
this causality by the example of the punishment which strikes the
one who destroys a moral totality. The "criminal" who revokes
[*aufhebt*] the moral basis, namely the complementary interchange
of noncompulsory communication and the mutual satisfaction of
interests, by putting himself as individual in the place of the
totality, sets in motion the process of a destiny which strikes back
at him. The struggle which is ignited between the contending
parties and the hostility toward the injured and oppressed other
makes the lost complementary interchange and the bygone friendliness palpable. The criminal is confronted by the power of defi-
cient life. Thus he experiences his guilt. The guilty one must
suffer under the power of the repressed and departed life, which
he himself has provoked, until he has experienced the deficiency
of his own life in the repression of others' lives, and, in his turning away from the lives of others, his own alienation from himself.
In the causality of destiny the power of suppressed life is at work,
which can only be reconciled, when, out of the experience of the
negativity of a sundered life, the longing for that which has been
lost arises and necessitates identifying one's own denied identity
in the alien existence one fights against. Then both parties recognize the hardened positions taken against each other to be the
result of the separation, the abstraction from the common interconnection of their lives—and within this, in the dialogic relationship of recognizing oneself in the other, they experience the
common basis of their existence.

In the Jena lectures the dialectics of the struggle for recognition is removed from the context of "crime"; here the point of

departure is the sensitive relationship between subjects who attach their whole being to each detail of a possession they have labored to gain. The struggle for recognition they conduct as a life-and-death struggle. The abstract self-assertion of parties contemptuous of each other is resolved by the combatants risking their lives and thus overcoming resolving and revoking (sublating) the singularity they have inflated into a totality: "Our knowledge that the acknowledged total consciousness only exists by sublating itself, now is known by this consciousness itself; it itself performs this reflection of itself within itself, that the single totality, in which it [the reflection] wants to preserve itself as such, absolutely sacrifices itself, sublates itself, and thereby does the opposite of what it sets out to do. The totality itself can only exist as a sublated one; it cannot preserve itself as an existing one, but only as one that is posited as sublated." [10] Destiny avenges itself on the combatants, not, to be sure, as destiny did in the case of the criminal, as punishment, but still in the same manner, as destruction of the self-assertion which severs itself from the moral totality. The result is not the immediate recognition of oneself in the other, thus not reconciliation, but a position of the subjects with respect to each other on the basis of mutual recognition—namely, on the basis of the knowledge that the identity of the "I" is possible solely by means of the identity of the other, who in turn depends on my recognition, and who recognizes me.[11] This Hegel calls the absolute salvation of singularity, namely, its existence as "I" in the identity of universality and singularity:

> This being of consciousness, that exists as single totality, as one which has renounced itself, perceives itself [*schaut sich an*] precisely on that account in another consciousness. . . . In every other consciousness it is what it is immediately for itself, by being in another—a sublated totality; by this singularity has been saved absolutely.[12]

Hegel's concept of the "I" as the identity of the universal and the singular is directed against that abstract unity of pure consciousness relating solely to itself, the abstract consciousness of original apperception, to which Kant had attached the identity of consciousness as such. The fundamental experience of the dialectic, however, which Hegel develops in the concept of the "I," derives, as we have seen, not from the experiential domain of theoretical consciousness, but from that of the practical. The consequences of the new departure for the critique of Kant were therefore first drawn by the young Hegel in a critique of moral doctrine.

Because Hegel conceives self-consciousness in terms of the interactional structure of complementary action, namely, as the result of a struggle for recognition, he sees through the concept of autonomous will that appears to constitute the essential value of Kant's moral philosophy. He realizes that this concept is a peculiar abstraction from the moral relationships of communicating individuals. By *presupposing* autonomy—and that means the will's property of being a law unto itself—in practical philosophy in the same way as he does the unassailable and simple identity of self-consciousness in theoretical philosophy, Kant expels moral action from the very domain of morality itself. Kant assumes the limiting case of a pre-established coordination of the acting subjects. The prior synchronization of those engaged in action within the framework of unbroken intersubjectivity banishes the problem of morality from the domain of moral doctrine —namely, the interplay of an intersubjectivity which has been mediated by overidentification and loss of communication.[13] Kant defines moral action according to the principle, "to act according to no other maxims than that which can have itself as universal law as its object." [14] Universality of moral law here not only means intersubjective obligation as such, but *the* abstract form of universal validity which is bound *a priori* to general agreement. Every single subject must *attribute* its maxims for action to every other subject as equally obligating maxims of action, doing so as it examines their suitability as principles of a universal legislation: "It is not enough that . . . we attribute freedom to our will when we have not sufficient reason to attribute just this same freedom to all rational beings. Morality can only serve as a law for us as rational beings, and thus it must be valid for all rational beings." [15] The moral laws are abstractly universal in the sense that, as they are valid as universal for me, *eo ipso* they must also be considered as valid for all rational beings. Therefore, under such laws interaction is dissolved into the actions of solitary and self-sufficient subjects, each of which must act as though it were the sole existing consciousness; at the same time, each subject can still have the certainty that all its actions under moral laws will necessarily and from the outset be in harmony with the moral actions of all possible other subjects.

The intersubjectivity of the recognition of moral laws accounted for *a priori* by practical reason permits the reduction of moral action to the monologic domain. The positive relation of the will to the will of others is withdrawn from possible communication, and a transcendentally necessary correspondence of isolated goal-directed activities under abstract universal laws is substituted. To this extent moral action in Kant's sense is presented, *mutatis mutandis,* as a special case of what we today call strategic action.

Strategic action is distinguished from *communicative actions* under common traditions by the characteristic that deciding between possible alternative choices can in principle be made monologically—that means, *ad hoc* without reaching agreement, and indeed must be made so, because the rules of preference and the maxims binding on each individual partner have been brought into prior harmony. The completely intersubjective validity of the rules of the game is part of the definition of the situation within which the game is played, in the same way as the *a priori* validity of the moral law is guaranteed by practical reason on the transcendental level in Kant's moral doctrine. Both cases eliminate problems of morality, which arise solely in the context of an intervening communication and the intersubjectivity that emerges among actors on the always precarious basis of mutual recognition. From the moral viewpoint we must disregard the moral relationship in Hegel's sense, and not take into consideration that the subjects are involved in a complex of interactions as their *formative process.* We must disregard what enters into the dialectical course of violent communication and what results from it; thus we must first abstract from the concrete consequences and ramifications of action guided by moral intentions; furthermore we must abstract from the specific inclinations and interests, from the "welfare" [*Wohl*] by which the moral action is motivated and which it can serve objectively; and finally, we must abstract from the content [*Materie*] of duty, which is only determined within a specific situation.[16] This threefold abstraction had been criticized by the young Hegel in the statement: "As long as laws are the highest [instance] . . . the individual must be sacrificed to the universal, i.e., it must be killed." [17]

III

Because Hegel does not link the constitution of the "I" to the reflection of the solitary "I" on itself, but instead understands it in terms of formative processes, namely the communicative agreement [*Einigung*] of opposing subjects, it is not reflection as such which is decisive, but rather the medium in which the identity of the universal and the individual is formed. And Hegel speaks of the "middle," or medium, by passing through which consciousness attains existence. After our considerations up to this point, we can expect that Hegel will introduce communicative action as the medium for the formative process of the self-conscious spirit. And in fact in his Jena lectures he uses the example of the shared existence of a primary group, namely family interaction, to construct the "family possession" [or welfare—*Familiengut*] as the existing middle of reciprocal modes of contact. However, besides the "family" two further categories are to be found, which Hegel develops in the same manner as media of the self-formative process: language and labor. Spirit is an organization of equally original media: "That first dependent existence—consciousness as middle—is the spirit's existence as language, as tool and as the (family) possession, or as the simple unity [*Einssein*]: memory, labor, and family." [18] These three fundamental dialectical patterns are heterogeneous; as media of the spirit, language and labor cannot be traced back to the experiences of interaction and of mutual recognition.

Language does not already embrace the communication of subjects living together and acting; rather here it means only the employment of symbols by the solitary individual who confronts nature and gives names to things. In immediate perception

[*Anschauung*] the spirit is still animalistic. Hegel speaks of the nighttime production of the representational faculty of imagination, of the fluid and not yet organized realm of images. Only with the appearance of language, and within language, do consciousness and the being of nature begin to separate for consciousness. The dreaming spirit, as it were, awakens when the realm of images is translated into the realm of names. The awakened spirit has memory; it is capable of making distinctions and at the same time of recognizing that which it has distinguished. Following the conceptions of Herder's prize essay,[19] Hegel sees the essential achievement of the symbols to be representation: synthesis of the manifold is bound to the representational function of features that permit the identification of objects. Naming and memory are but two sides of the same thing: "The idea of this existence of consciousness is memory, and its existence itself, language." [20]

As the name of things, the symbol has a double function. On the one hand, the power of representation consists in making present something that is not immediately given through something else that is immediately given, but which stands for something other than itself. The representational symbol indicates an object or a state of affairs as something else [*ein Anderes*], and designates it in the meaning that it has for us. On the other hand, we ourselves have produced the symbols. By means of them speaking consciousness becomes objective for itself and in them experiences itself as a subject. This relation, too, of the reflexive perception of the subject in language had already been characterized by Herder. In order that nature can constitute itself into the world of an "I," language must thus achieve a twofold mediation: on the one hand, of resolving and preserving the perceived [*angeschaut*] thing in a symbol, which represents it, and on the other, a distancing of consciousness from its objects, in which the "I," by means of symbols it has produced itself, is simultaneously with the thing and with itself. Thus language is the first category in which spirit is not conceived as something internal, but as a medium which is neither internal nor external. In this, spirit is the *logos* of a world and not a solitary self-consciousness.

Labor Hegel calls that specific mode of satisfying drives which distinguishes existing spirit from nature. Just as language breaks the dictates of immediate perception and orders the chaos of the manifold impressions into identifiable things, so labor breaks the dictates of immediate desires and, as it were, arrests the process of drive satisfaction. Like symbols in language, here the instruments, in which the laborer's experience of his objects is deposited, form the existing middle. The name is that which has permanence [*das Bleibende*] as against the ephemeral moments of the perceptions; in the same way, the tool is that which is general as against the ephemeral moments of desire and enjoyment: "It is that wherein working has its permanence, that alone which remains of the laborer and the substances worked upon, and in which its contingency is eternalized; it is inherited in the traditions, while that which desires, as well as that which is desired, only subsist as individuals and as individuals pass away." [21] The symbols permit recognizing again the identical [*des Selben*], the instruments retain the rules according to which the domination of natural processes can be repeated at will: "In the tool the subjectivity of labor has been elevated to something universal; everyone can imitate it and work in precisely the same manner; thus it is the constant rule [*Regel*] of labor." [22]

Of course, the *dialectic of labor* does not mediate between subject and object in the same manner as the *dialectic of representation*. It begins not with the subjection of nature to self-generated symbols, but, on the contrary, with the subjection of the subject to the power of external nature. Labor demands the suspension of immediate drive satisfaction; it transmits the energies of human effort [*Leistungsenergien*] to the object worked on under the laws imposed by nature on the "I." In this twofold respect Hegel speaks of the subject making itself into a thing—reifying itself—in labor: "Labor is the this-wordly [*diesseitige*] making oneself into a thing. The splitting up of the "I" existing in its drives (namely into the reality-testing ego and into the repressed instinctual demands—J.H.) is precisely this making oneself into an object." [23] By way of my subjection to the causality of nature, the results of my experience come into being for me in the tools, by means of which I can in turn let nature work for me. As consciousness gains the unintended fruit of its labor through technical rules, it returns back to itself from its reification, and, indeed, it returns as the cunning [or artful] consciousness which, in its instrumental action, turns its experience of natural processes against these processes themselves: "Here the drive withdraws entirely from labor. It lets nature wear itself down, quietly watches it do so, and only with a slight effort controls the whole: cunning. The broad flank of brute force is attacked by the sharp point of cunning." [24]

Just like language, the tool is a category of the middle, by means of which spirit attains existence. But the two movements pursue opposing courses. The *name-giving consciousness* achieves a different position with respect to the objectivity of the spirit than does the *cunning consciousness* that arises from the process of labor. Only in the limiting case of conventionalization can the speaker have a similar relation to his symbols as the worker to his tools; the symbols of ordinary language penetrate and dominate the perceiving and thinking consciousness, while the artful consciousness controls the processes of nature by means of its tools. The objectivity of language retains power over the subjective spirit, while the cunning that outwits nature extends subjective freedom over the power of objective spirit—for in the end the labor process too terminates in mediated satisfaction, the satisfaction in the commodities produced for consumption, and in the retroactively changed interpretation of the needs themselves.[25]

Against Kant's abstract "I," the three patterns developed in the Jena lectures, of a dialectical relation between subject and object, bring out the self-formative processes of the developed identity of the naming, the cunning, and recognizing consciousness. Corresponding to the critique of morality, there is also a critique of culture. In the methodological doctrine of the teleological capacity of judgment,[26] Kant treats culture as the ultimate aim of nature, insofar as we can understand it as a teleological system. Culture, Kant calls the bringing forth of the fitness [*Tauglichkeit*] of a rational being for any purposes whatsoever. Subjectively, this means skill in the purposive-rational choice of suitable means; objectively, culture is the epitome of the technical control over nature. Just as morality is conceived as a purposive activity according to pure maxims, which disregards the embeddedness of the moral subjects in an emergent intersubjectivity, so Kant also conceives culture as a purposive activity according to technical rules (that is, conditional imperatives) which abstracts in the same manner from the subject's involvement in the labor process. The *cultivated "I"* to which Kant attributes the fitness for instrumental action is conceived by Hegel, in contrast, as a result of social labor, and in fact, as a result which changes world-historically. Thus in the Jena elaboration of the Philosophy of Spirit he never misses the opportunity to point to the development which cunning consciousness, arising from the employment of tools, undergoes, as soon as labor becomes mechanized.[27]

What is valid for the moral and the technical consciousness, is valid, by analogy, for theoretical consciousness. The dialectic of representation by means of linguistic symbols is directed against Kant's concept of the synthetic achievements of a transcendental consciousness, conceived apart from all formative processes. For the abstract critique of knowledge conceives the relation of the categories and the forms of intuition to the material of experience according to the model of the artisan's activity, already introduced by Aristotle in which the working subject forms material; the terms employed themselves show this. If, however, the synthesis is not achieved by means of the superimposition of the categorial forms, but is bound initially to the representational function of self-generated symbols, then the identity of the "I" can just as little be supposed to be prior to the process of knowledge as to the processes of labor and interaction, from which the cunning and the recognizing consciousness first arise. The identity of the knowing subject is one that has first to be formed, to the same degree as the objectivity of the recognized objects first arises with language, within which alone the synthesis of the divergent elements, of the "I" and of nature, is possible as a world of the "I."

IV

Kant proceeds from the identity of the "I" as an original unity of transcendental consciousness. In contrast to this, Hegel's fundamental experience of the "I" as an identity of the universal and the singular has led him to the insight that the identity of self-consciousness is not an original one, but can only be conceived as one that has developed [*geworden*]. In the Jena lectures, Hegel works out the threefold identity of the naming, the cunning, and the recognizing consciousness. These identities are formed in the dialectic of representation, of labor, and of the struggle for recognition, and thus contradict that abstract unity of the practical will, of the technical will, and of intelligence, with which both Kant's *Critique of Practical Reason* and of *Pure Reason* begin. From this viewpoint we can actually see the Jena *Philosophy of Spirit* as a preparatory study for the *Phenomenology*. For the radicalization of the critique of knowledge carried out as a science of appearing [*erscheinende* = phenomenal] consciousness consists precisely in relinquishing the viewpoint of a "ready-made" or "completed" subject of knowledge. Above all, the skepticism of critique, which is doubting that is not impervious to despair, and the skepticism of reflection, which is the penetration of illusion until consciousness itself is reversed, requires a radical beginning in a new sense. For we must drop even the fundamental distinction between theoretical and practical reason, between descriptively true statements and normatively correct decisions, and begin without any presupposition of standards at all—although just this beginning without theoretical presuppositions cannot be an absolute beginning, but must depart from natural consciousness. If we look back from this point to the Jena *Philosophy of Spirit*, then indeed the question of the *unity of the self-formative process* forces itself upon us, as this is initially determined by *three heterogeneous patterns of formation*. The question of the coherence of that organization of media is posed with special urgency once we recall the historical effects of Hegelian philosophy and call to mind the divergent interpretations that elevate each of the three fundamental dialectical patterns to the chief interpretative principle of the whole. *Ernst Cassirer* takes the dialectic of representation and makes it the guiding principle [*Leitfaden*] of a Hegelianized Kant interpretation, which at the same time is the foundation of a philosophy of symbolic forms. *Georg Lukács* interprets the movement of intellectual development from Kant to Hegel along the guideline presented by the dialectic of labor, which at the same time guarantees the materialistic unity of subject and object in the world-historical formative process of the human species; finally, the neo-Hegelianism of a thinker such as *Theodor Litt* leads to a conception of the stepwise self-development of spirit which follows the pattern of the struggle for recognition. The three positions have in common the method, employed by the Young Hegelians, of appropriating Hegel at the cost of surrendering the identity of spirit and nature claimed by absolute knowledge. However, for the rest, they have so little in common that they only give evidence of the divergence of the three approaches, and that means of the conception of the dialectic underlying them. How, therefore, is the unity of a formative process to be conceived, which, according to the Jena lectures, goes through the dialectic of language, of labor, and of interaction?

Under the title *language* Hegel rightly introduces the employment of representational symbols as the first determination of abstract spirit. For the two subsequent determinations necessarily presuppose this. In the dimension of actual spirit, language attains existence as the system of a specific cultural tradition:

> Language only exists as the language of a people [*Volkes*]. . . . It is something universal, something granted recognition in itself, something that resounds in the same manner in the consciousness of all; within it every speaking consciousness immediately becomes another consciousness. Language, in the same way, only becomes true language, as to its contents, in a people, it becomes the enunciation of that which everyone means.[28]

As cultural tradition, language enters into communicative action; for only the intersubjectively valid and constant meanings which are drawn from tradition permit the orientation toward reciprocity, that is, complementary expectations of behavior. Thus interaction is dependent on language communication which has established itself as part of life. However, instrumental action, as soon as it comes under the category of actual spirit, as social labor, is also embedded within a network of interactions, and therefore dependent on the communicative boundary conditions that underlie every possible cooperation. Even disregarding social labor,

the solitary act of using tools is also dependent on the employment of symbols, for the immediacy of animalistic drive satisfaction cannot be moderated without the creation of distance from
identifiable objects, provided by naming consciousness. Instrumental action, at least when solitary, is monologic action.

More interesting and by no means as obvious as the relation
of the employment of symbols to interaction and to labor, however, is the *interrelation of labor and interaction.* On the one
hand, the norms under which complementary action within the
framework of a cultural tradition is first institutionalized and
made to endure are independent of instrumental action. Technical rules, to be sure, are first elaborated under the conditions of
language communication, but they have nothing in common with
the communicative rules of interaction. Into the conditional imperatives which instrumental action follows, enters in solely the
causality of nature and not the causality of destiny. A reduction
of interaction to labor or derivation of labor from interaction is
not possible. On the other hand, Hegel does indeed establish an
interconnection between the *legal norms,* in which social intercourse based on mutual recognition is first formally stabilized and
processes of labor.

Under the category of actual spirit, interactions based on
reciprocity appear in the form of an intercourse, controlled by
legal norms, between persons whose status as legal persons is
defined precisely by the institutionalization of mutual recognition.
However, this recognition does not refer directly to the identity of
the other, but to the things which are subject to his powers of
disposition. The institutional reality of the ego identity consists
in the individuals' recognizing each other as proprietors in the
possessions produced by their labor or acquired by trade. "Not
only my possession [*Habe*] or my property is posited here, but my
person, because in my existence lies my all [*mein Ganzes*]: my
honor and my life." [29] Honor and life are recognized, however,
solely in the inviolability of property. Possession as the substrate
of legal recognition arises from the labor process. Thus instrumental action and interaction are linked in the recognized product of labor.

In the Jena lectures Hegel constructs this interconnection

quite simply. In the system of social labor, the division of the labor process and the exchange of the products of labor are posited. From this arises a generalization of labor as well as of needs. For with respect to its content, the labor of each is general labor for the needs of all. Abstract labor produces goods for abstract needs. Thereby the produced goods receive their abstract value as exchange value. Of the latter, money is the concept brought to existence. The exchange of equivalents is the model for reciprocal behavior. The institutional form of exchange is the contract; the contract therefore is the formal establishment of a prototypical action in reciprocity. The contract "is the same thing as an exchange, but an ideal exchange. It is an exchange of declarations, not of things, but it has the same validity as the thing. For both the will of the Other as such has validity." [30] The institutionalization of the reciprocity actualized in exchange is accomplished by virtue of the spoken word being accorded normative force; complementary action is mediated by symbols, which fix the expectations of obligatory behavior:

> My word must have validity, not for moral reasons—so that inwardly I can remain the same for myself and may not change my moral attitudes, convictions, and so forth—no, indeed I can change this; but my will only exists insofar as it is recognized. I contradict not only myself, but the fact that my will is recognized. . . . The person, the pure being-for-oneself, thus is not respected as single and solitary, as will separating itself from the common will, but only as the common will.[31]

Thus the relation of reciprocal recognition, on which interaction is based, is brought under norms by way of the institutionalization of the reciprocity established as such in the exchange of the products of labor.

The institutionalization of ego-identity, the legally sanctioned self-consciousness, is understood as a result of *both* processes: that of *labor* and that of the *struggle for recognition*. The labor process, by means of which we free ourselves from the immediate dictates of natural forces, thus enters into the struggle for recognition in such a manner that the result of this struggle, the legally recognized self-consciousness, retains the moment of liberation through labor. Hegel links together labor and interaction under the viewpoint of emancipation from the forces of external as well as internal nature. He does not reduce interaction to labor, nor does he elevate labor to resolve it in interaction; still, he keeps the interconnection of the two in view, insofar as the dialectics of love and conflict cannot be separated from the successes of instrumental action and from the constitution of a cunning consciousness. The result of emancipation by means of labor enters into the norms under which we act complementarily.

It is true that Hegel developed the dialectical interconnection between labor and interaction, taking his departure from a consideration presented in his *System of Morality*,[32] only one more time extensively, namely, in a chapter of the *Phenomenology of Mind*: the relationship of the one-sided recognition of the master by the servant [*Knecht*] is overturned by the servant's power of disposition over nature, just as one-sidedly acquired by labor. The independent self-consciousness, in which both parties recognize that they recognize each other, is constituted by way of a reaction, which the *technical* success of an emancipation by means of labor exerts on the relationship of *political* dependency between master and servant. To be sure, the relationship of dominance and servitude also gained admittance into the philosophy of subjective spirit after, and by way of, the *Phenomenology*. In the *Enzyklopädie*[33] it designates the transition to universal self-consciousness and thus the step from "consciousness" to "spirit." However, already in the *Phenomenology* the distinctive dialectic of labor and interaction has been deprived of the specific role which was still attributed to it within the system in the Jena lectures.

This can be explained by the fact that Hegel soon abandoned the systematics of these lectures and replaced it by the subdivisions of the *Enzyklopädie*, into subjective, objective, and absolute spirit. While in the Jena lectures, language, labor, and action in reciprocity were not only stages in the formative process of spirit, but also principles of its formation itself, in the *Enzyklopädie*, language and labor, once models of construction for dialectical movement, are now themselves constructed as subordinate real conditions [*Realverhältnisse*]. Language is mentioned in a lengthy passage (§459) in the philosophy of subjective spirit at the point of transition from the faculty of imagination to that of memory, while labor, as instrumental action as such, is deleted entirely and instead, as social labor, under the title of the system of needs, designates an important stage in the development of objective spirit (§§524ff.). However, the dialectic of moral relationships has retained its specific role for the construction of spirit as such in the *Enzyklopädie*, just as it did in the Jena lectures. Yet when we look at this more closely, we will recognize in it not the dialectic of love and conflict, but rather that dialectic which Hegel developed in his essay on *Natural Law* as the movement of absolute morality.

V

We have sought the unity of the formative process of spirit in an interconnection of the three fundamental dialectical patterns, thus in the relation between symbolic representation, labor, and interaction. This distinctive interconnection, which, limited to one stage, is taken up again in the relationship between domination and servitude, does not reappear later. It is tied to a systematics which Hegel appears to have tried out only in the Jena period. To be sure, the Jena lectures incorporate a tendency that makes understandable why the specific interconnection of labor with interaction loses its significance. For in the Jena lectures Hegel proceeded from that absolute identity of the spirit with nature, which prejudices the unity of the spirit's formative process in a particular manner. In these lectures Hegel constructs the transition from the philosophy of nature to the philosophy of spirit no differently than he does in the *Enzyklopädie*: in nature, spirit has its complete external objectivity, and it therefore finds its identity in the sublation of this externalization. Spirit thus is the absolute presupposition [*absolut Erste*] of nature:

> The *manifesting* [*Offenbaren*] which . . . is the *becoming* of nature, as the manifesting of spirit, which is free [in history], is the *positing* of nature as the *spirit's* [*seiner*] world; a positing which as reflection is at the same time *presupposing* [*Voraussetzen* = prepositing] of the world as independent nature.[34]

Under the presupposition of this thesis of identity Hegel has always interpreted the dialectics of representation and of labor idealistically: together with the name we enunciate the being of objects, and, in the same manner, that which nature is in truth is incorporated in the tool. The innermost part of nature [*das Innere*] is itself spirit, because nature only becomes comprehensible in its essence and "comes to itself" in man's confrontation with it: the interior of nature is expressed only in the realm of its names and in the rules for working upon it. If, however, hidden subjectivity can always be found in what has been objectivized, if behind the masks of objects, nature can always be revealed as the concealed partner [*Gegenspieler*], then the basic dialectical patterns of representation and of labor can also be reduced to *one* common denominator with the dialectics of moral action. For then the relationship of the name-giving and the working subject to nature can also be brought within the configuration of reciprocal recognition. The intersubjectivity in which an "I" can identify with another "I" without relinquishing the nonidentity between itself and the Other, is also established in language and in labor when the object confronting the speaking and the working subject is from the outset conceived idealistically as an opposite [*Gegenüber*] with which interaction in the mode of that between subjects is possible: when it is an *adversary* [*Gegenspieler*] and not an *object* [*Gegenstand*]. As long as we consider each of these determinations of abstract spirit by itself, a specific difference remains. The dialectic of representation and of labor develops as a relation between a knowing or an acting subject on the one hand, and an object as the epitome of what does not belong to the subject on the other. The mediation between the two, passing through the medium of symbols or of tools is conceived as a process of externalization of the subject—a process of external-

ization (objectification) and appropriation. In contrast to this, the
dialectic of love and conflict is a movement on the level of intersubjectivity. The place of the model of *externalization* is therefore
taken by that of *separation* [or division—*Entzweiung*] and alienation, and the result of the movement is not the *appropriation*
of what has been objectified, but instead the *reconciliation,* the
restoration of the friendliness which has been destroyed. The
idealistic sublation of the distinction between objects as objects
[*Gegenstände*] and as adversaries [*Gegenspieler*] makes possible
the assimilation of these heterogeneous models: if interaction is
possible with nature as a hidden subject in the role of the Other,
then the processes of externalization and appropriation formally
match those of alienation and reconciliation. The unity of the
self-formative process, that operates through the medium of language, the tool, and moral relations, then does not have to be
tied first to the interconnections of labor and interaction, still
central for the Jena *Philosophy of Spirit.* For the unity of this
process already subsists in the dialectic of recognizing oneself in
the Other, in which the dialectics of language and of labor can
now converge with that of morality: under the presuppositions
of the philosophy of identity they are only apparently heterogeneous.

To be sure, the dialectic of recognizing oneself in the Other
is bound to the relationship of interaction between antagonists
who are in principle equal. As soon as nature in its totality is
elevated to an antagonist of the united subjects, however, this
relation of parity no longer holds; there cannot be a dialogue
between spirit and nature, the suppression of the dialogic situation between the two, and a struggle for recognition which results in a constituted moral relationship—absolute spirit is solitary.
The unity of absolute spirit with itself and with a nature, from
which it differentiates itself as its Other, in the end cannot be
conceived in terms of the pattern of the intersubjectivity of acting
and of speaking subjects, by which Hegel initially attained the
concept of the "I" as the identity of the universal and the singular. The dialectical unity of spirit and nature, in which spirit does
not recognize itself in nature as an antagonist, but only finds itself
again as in a mirror image [*Gegenbild*], this unity can more

readily be constructed from the experience of the self-reflection of consciousness. Therefore Hegel conceives of the movement of absolute spirit in terms of the model of self-reflection, but in such a way that the dialectic of the moral relationship, from which the identity of the universal with the singular originates, enters into it: *absolute spirit is absolute morality.* The dialectic of the moral relationship which accomplishes itself on the criminal with the causality of destiny in the same way as on those who struggle for recognition, now proves to be the same movement as that in which the absolute spirit reflects itself.

The process of destiny, which in the theological works of Hegel's youth was conceived from the viewpoint of the members of a moral totality, as a reaction evoked by the subjects themselves through the suppression of the dialogic relationship, can subsequently be reinterpreted all the more readily within the framework of self-reflection as a self-movement of the totality, because Hegel can link it to the *dialectic of the sacrifice* [*Opfer*] which is already developed in the earliest fragments: "For the power of the sacrifice consists in the perceiving [*Anschauen*] and objectivating of the involvement with the inorganic; by which perception this involvement is dissolved, the inorganic is separated out and recognized as such, and thereby is itself incorporated into the indifferent [*Indifferenz*]: the living, however, by placing what it knows to be a part of itself within the same [the inorganic] and offering it up to death in sacrifice, at the same time has recognized the rights of the inorganic and separated itself from it." [35] The division of the moral totality now represents no more than the destiny of the Absolute, which sacrifices itself. According to this model of absolute morality, which Hegel first developed in the essay on *Natural Law* as the accomplishment of tragedy in the moral realm, spirit is conceived as identical with nature as its Other, and the dialectic of self-consciousness is united with the dialectic of moral relationships. The Logic merely presents the grammar of the language in which the tragedy is written, which the Absolute acts out with itself eternally:

> that it eternally gives birth to itself into objectivity, and in this its character of objectivity thereby surrenders itself to

suffering and death, and from its ashes ascends to glory. The divine in its shape [*Gestalt*] and objectivity has an immediately dual nature and its life is the absolutely united being of these two natures.[36]

But the essay on *Natural Law* and the *Logic* [*Grosse Logik*] are not linked by a continuous development. In the three parts of the Jena *Philosophy of Spirit* which we have discussed, Hegel's study of contemporary economics is reflected in such a manner that the movement of the actual spirit does not mirror the triumphal sacrificial march of the Absolute, but develops the structures of spirit anew, as interconnections of symbolically mediated labor and interaction. The dialectic of labor does not readily fit into the movement of such a spirit conceived as absolute morality, and therefore forces a reconstruction. This Hegel relinquished again after Jena, but not without it leaving its traces. The position which abstract Right occupies within the system does not flow directly from the conception of moral spirit. Rather, elements of the Jena *Philosophy of Spirit* are retained in it. Other elements of the concept developed in Jena are not, to be sure, incorporated in the later constructions of right.

Up to the essay on *Natural Law,* Hegel had conceived the domain of formal legal relations as the result of the decay of free morality, basing himself in this on Gibbon's depiction of the Roman Empire; this free morality the young Hegel had seen as realized in the idealized constitution of the Greek *polis*. In 1802 he still asserts that, historically, private law first evolved in the form of Roman Law, within a condition of the citizen's depoliticization, of "decadence and universal degradation": the intercourse of privatized individuals, subject to legal norms, compares unfavorably with the destroyed moral relation. In the movement of absolute morality, law belongs to that phase in which the moral becomes involved with the inorganic and sacrifices itself to the "subterranean powers."

In contrast to this, in the Jena *Philosophy of Spirit,* the state of legality [*Rechtszustand*], which now is also characterized in terms of modern bourgeois private law, no longer appears as a product of the decay of absolute morality, but, on the contrary, as the first configuration [*Gestalt*] of constituted moral relationships. Only the intercourse of individuals acting complementarily and subject to legal norms, makes an institution of ego-identity, namely the self-consciousness which recognizes itself in another self-consciousness. Action on the basis of mutual recognition is only guaranteed by the formal relationship between legal persons. Hegel can replace the negative definition of abstract Right by a positive one because meanwhile he has come to know the economic interrelation of private law with modern bourgeois society and has seen that these legal categories also incorporate the result of *liberation through social labor*. Abstract Right places its seal on a liberation which literally has been worked for.[37]

Finally, in the *Enzyklopädie* and the *Philosophy of Right*, abstract Right once again changes its role within the system. It retains its positive determinations, for only within the system of these universal norms can free will attain the objectivity of external existence. The self-conscious and free will—the subjective spirit on its highest level—as a legal person becomes subject to the more rigorous determinations of objective spirit. However, the interrelationship between labor and interaction to which abstract right owes its true dignity is dissolved; the Jena construction is given up, and abstract right is integrated into the self-reflection of spirit, conceived as absolute morality. Now bourgeois morality is considered to be the sphere of disintegrated morality. In the fragmented system of needs, the categories of social labor, the division of labor and of commerce based on exchange, which make possible abstract labor for abstract needs under the condition of an abstract intercourse of isolated individual competitors, all have their place. But although abstract right determines the form of social intercourse, it is introduced from the *outside* under the title of jurisprudence. It constitutes itself independently of the categories of social labor, and only *after the fact* enters into its relationship with the processes to which, in the Jena lectures, it still owed the moment of freedom, as a result of liberation through social labor. It is solely the dialectic of morality which guarantees the "transition" [*Übergehen*] of the as yet internal will to the objectivity of law. The dialectic of labor has been deprived of its central role within the system.

VI

Karl Löwith, to whom we owe the most penetrating analysis of the intellectual break between Hegel and the first generation of his pupils,[38] has also pointed to the subterranean affinity between the positions of the Young Hegelians and themes in the thought of the young Hegel. Thus without any knowledge of the Jena manuscripts, Marx had rediscovered that interconnection between labor and interaction in the dialectic of the forces of production and the relations of production, which for several years had claimed Hegel's philosophical interest, stimulated by his study of economics. In a critique of the last chapter of the *Phenomenology of Mind,* Marx maintained that Hegel had taken the viewpoint of modern political economy, for he had comprehended labor as the essence of man, in which man has confirmed himself. It is in this passage of the Paris Manuscripts that the famous dictum is to be found:

> What is great in Hegel's Phenomenology and its final results is that Hegel comprehends the self-generation of man as a process, the objectification as the process of confronting objects [*Entgegenständlichung*], as externalization and as sublation of this externalization, that he thus comprehends the essence of labor and conceives objective man, the true because the actual man, as the result of his own labor.

From this point of view Marx himself attempted to reconstruct the world-historical process by which the human species forms itself in terms of the laws of the reproduction of social life. The mechanism of change of the system of social labor he finds in the contradiction between the power over natural processes, accumulated by means of social labor, and the institutional framework of interactions, that are regulated in a "natural" [*naturwüchsig*], that is, primitive and pre-rational, way. However, a precise analysis of the first part of the *German Ideology* reveals that Marx does not actually explicate the interrelationship of interaction and labor, but instead, under the unspecific title of social praxis, reduces the one to the other, namely: communicative action to instrumental action. Just as in the Jena *Philosophy of Spirit* the use of tools mediates between the laboring subject and the natural objects, so for Marx instrumental action, the productive activity which regulates the material interchange of the human species with its natural environment, becomes the paradigm for the generation of all the categories; everything is resolved into the self-movement of production.[39] Because of this, Marx's brilliant insight into the dialectical relationship between the forces of production and the relations of production could very quickly be misinterpreted in a mechanistic manner.

Today, when the attempt is being undertaken to reorganize the communicative nexus of interactions, no matter how much they have hardened into quasi-natural forms, according to the model of technically progressive systems of rational goal-directed action, we have reason enough to keep these two dimensions more rigorously separated. A mass of wishful historical conceptions adheres to the idea of a progressive rationalization of labor. Although hunger still holds sway over two thirds of the earth's population, the abolition of hunger is not a Utopia in the negative sense. But to set free the technical forces of production, including the construction of cybernetic and learning machines which can simulate the complete sphere of the functions of rational goal-directed action far beyond the capacity of natural consciousness, and thus substitute for human effort, is not identical with the development of norms which could fulfill the dialectic of moral relationships in an interaction free of domination, on the basis of a reciprocity allowed to have its full and noncoercive scope. *Liberation from hunger and misery* does not necessarily converge with *liberation from servitude and degradation,* for there is no automatic developmental relation between labor and interaction. Still, there is a connection between the two dimensions. Neither the Jena *Realphilosophie* nor the *German Ideology* have clarified it adequately, but in any case they can persuade us of its relevance: the self-formative process of spirit as well as of our species essentially depends on that relation between labor and interaction.

5

On Hegel's Political Writings

Hegel, the author of the *Enzyklopädie,* has entered into the consciousness of the present epoch, which can no longer relate directly to the great tradition of philosophy, as the last creator of a system. But at the same time he was an involved and even a skillful political author and publicist. From the time when he served in Bern as a private tutor until he finally established himself as a university professor, the two roles are so closely linked, in spite of the different weight they assumed, that the impression has arisen among later biographers that Hegel aimed at a journalistic career side by side with a scholarly one. The connection between his philosophy and his journalistic writings, however, is not based on merely biographical considerations, such as Hegel's lifelong appreciation of the daily blessing of perusing the morning newspaper and his having been a newspaper editor.[1] This connection also is rooted in his thought. For as a whole Hegel's system can be comprehended as an elaborated proof which falsifies the fundamental ontological assumptions of Classical as well as modern philosophy, namely, the abstract opposition between essence and appearance, between eternal Being and Non-being, and between the permanent and the ephemeral. A philosophy which knows itself to be the result of the same formative process that it comprehends in terms of the interrelationship of nature and history cannot set itself outside the element of time. Spirit devours time, but time for its part can render judgment on an impotent spirit.

World-history is the medium of the experience in terms of which philosophy must test itself and on which it can also founder. According to Hegel's own criteria, expressed in the preface to the *Philosophy of Right,* a philosophy which shatters under the effort of comprehending its own time in thought is disgraced before the power of objective spirit which it has failed to subdue. If it turns out that it has not grasped its own epoch in its concept, then it is unmasked as a threadbare abstraction, which has intruded between reason as self-conscious spirit and reason as present reality. Certainly Hegel was not able to accept world-historical experience as an independent criterion of his theory's validity; that would have been irreconcilable with philosophy's autonomous foundation in itself [*Selbstbegründung*], with the preconception [*Vorbegriff*] which Hegel's logic has of itself.[2] But Hegel's system stands and falls with his philosophy of spirit, especially of objective spirit. It is a theory of society and a philosophy of history in one. And it has to prove itself by its claim as a theory of the contemporary age: its claim of comprehending the contemporary situation world-historically. Such a concept must be able to hold up under the world-historical changes of a progressing present.

Journalism defines the form of consciousness in which historical movements are initially reflected on the periphery of daily events. Hegel's political writing was the medium through which he appropriated the mass of experience provided by journalism.

The origins of the political writings

Hegel did not prove very lucky in his political writings.[3] In part they were not even published, in part they remained without any effect, and insofar as they did have political effects, these were hardly what the author desired.

(1) *The Confidential Letters Concerning the Former Constitutional Relationship of the Vaud to the City of Bern* was published in 1798 under the author's name, the Vaud lawyer Cart, who had emigrated to the United States by way of Paris, and who, incidentally, was still alive, despite the contrary assertion of

the subtitle of the German translation. Not till 1909 did Falkenheim identify the anonymous translator and editor as Hegel.[4] Cart's polemic is directed against the rule by the municipal aristocracy of Bern over this province, which had been independent since 1564. Cart does not argue on the basis of Natural Law; rather he criticizes the violation of historically established rights and liberties. The letters were published in the original after the suppression of the revolt of Vaud against the Bernese rulers. A few weeks before the appearance of the German edition in the spring of 1798 French troops marched into Switzerland—the government of Bern was overthrown and Vaud regained its political independence.[5]

During the period when he was a private tutor in Bern Hegel had become familiar with the rule of the families who had the right to sit on the council. As his knowledgeable comments on Cart's polemic show,[6] he had provided himself at this time with a precise empirical knowledge of the historical background and of administrative practice. Obviously the editor identified strongly with his author. The Bernese aristocracy seemed to Hegel to be the perfect model of an oligarchy which deserved the fate of a revolutionary overthrow. When the German translation appeared, it had in a way already been rendered obsolete by the invasion of the French troops. It had hardly any effect, and only a few copies are still preserved.

(2) The first of his own political writings Hegel did not publish. It was written in the first half of 1798 and only fragments of it are preserved: the introduction in manuscript, and several further statements as reported in the account by Haym,[7] who still had access to a copy of the original manuscript. The neutral title, "On the Most Recent Internal Conditions in Württemberg, Especially the Deficiencies of the Municipal Constitution [*Magistratsverfassung*]" is by the hand of another, replacing the original heading, which has been crossed out and which was formulated more programmatically: "That the magistrates must be elected by the people." Hegel had already softened this formulation himself, substituting "citizens" for "the people." The title pages bore the dedication: "To the people of Württemberg." The text itself does not appear to have contained a clear proposal of how

the elections to the state parliament [*Landtag*] were to be carried out. Still, the tendency of the pamphlet is clear: in the conflict between the duke and the estates it sides with the latter.

In the fall of 1796, when, before assuming his new post as private tutor in Frankfurt, Hegel spent several months in his native Württemberg, the Landtag had been convened—for the first time since 1770. Taxes had to be raised for the war indemnities to be paid to France. Furthermore, the Landtag could possibly break the power of the administrative bureaucracy of committees, who together with the privy council were endangering the pro-Austrian policy of the duke, then seeking the Electoral office. Under Duke Frederick, however, who assumed the throne at the end of 1797, the harmony between the duke and the estates did not last long. Calling the Assembly of the Estates had strengthened republican tendencies in the dukedom. Pro-French pamphleteers were already demanding that the estates be transformed into a parliament representative of the people. In the Assembly of the Estates itself, forces in favor of a Swabian republic were stirring; the example of Napoleonic Switzerland was having its effect. In this situation Hegel's criticism of the "presumption of higher officials" was in effect a demand to strengthen the position of the inadequately represented people against the government, in spite of his misgivings about democratic elections, and to broaden energetically the rights of the estates.

The inhibiting motives which restrained Hegel from publishing the pamphlet have not been plausibly explained to the present day. Haym tries to establish as the reason the insufficient political clarity and the weak argument of the work itself.[8] Rosenkranz tells of three friends of Hegel in Stuttgart, who advised him against publication.[9] E. Rosenzweig speculates that French diplomacy at the Rastatt Congress may have had a sobering and discouraging effect on the idealistic partisans of France, due to its naked politics of power.[10]

(3) During the Rastatt Congress Hegel was at work on the first draft of his *Constitution for the German Reich*. He actually wrote it at the beginning of the year 1799. Though the fragment of an introduction is of somewhat later origin, it still falls, with some certainty, into the Frankfurt period.[11] At Jena during the

winter of 1800–01 Hegel again took up the work on the constitu-
tion, which he had dropped. He revised the "original version"
[*Urschrift*] once more at the end of 1802. This "revised copy"
[*Reinschrift*] encompasses about one half of the whole treatise.
It breaks off at the point at which the difficult relationship be-
tween the state and the individual had to be clarified.

The war against the French Republic, the insufficient coordination between the German states, the unfortunate operations of the Reich and the Peace of Lunéville brought clearly to
awareness the state of affairs, which Hegel mercilessly calls by its
right name: Germany had ceased to exist as a state. Hegel saw the
military weaknesses as the symptoms of a deeper disorganization,
which was disrupting the Reich in its very substance. Yet Hegel
did not take into account the possibility, empirically so obvious
and then actually carried out by Napoleon, of a dissolution of
the Reich into sovereign territorial states. This essay has a programmatic aim, too: the root-and-branch reform of the Reich
under the leadership of Austria. Prussia was not even considered
as a candidate for this role: it had compromised itself too deeply
by its unilateral conclusion of the Peace of Basel. In addition, the
Prussian Assembly of Estates had become completely divested of
any political significance. Thus Hegel placed his hopes in the
representative bodies of Austria. In Hegel's conception the reform
of the Reich was to be accomplished by way of a reform of the
army and the methods for financing it. The core of his proposals
gives evidence, in spite of a great sharpness of vision in the analysis of details, of a wholly unrealistic evaluation of the actual
power relations. Though Hegel saw that against the resistance of
the territories a reform can only be compelled by the power of
a conqueror, it is still hardly fortuitous that the person of this
conqueror is designated by a mythical name, as a new Theseus—
Napoleon could hardly be envisioned in this fictitious role and
pragmatically there was certainly no other candidate for it. The
enactment of the delegates of the Empire (1803) soon made this
text, which Hegel had been at work revising, irrelevant; so this
work was also not published. In its entirety it was first published
by Mollat in 1893.

(4) Only once did Hegel as journalist attain any effect on

the political public, with his *Evaluation of the Proceedings, as Printed, of the Assembly of the Estates of the Kingdom of Württemberg in the years 1815 and 1816* [Beurteilung der im Druck erschienenen Verhandlungen in der Versammlung der Landstände des Königreichs Württemberg in den Jahren 1815 und 1816]. This pamphlet was written in the form of a review and appeared anonymously in the November/December number of the *Heidelberger Jahrbücher,* volume 10, at the end of 1817. The debate in the estates had been evoked by an edict of King Frederick, meanwhile deceased, who at the beginning of 1815 had promised his country a constitution solely "on his own initiative and without any external influences." It was in the interest of the king to forestall the decisions of the Congress of Vienna and to secure constitutionally his territorial domain, which had been considerably expanded under the French. Under Napoleon the king had ruled in the style of princely absolutism, which was reason enough for the estates to distrust the despot's conversion to constitutionalism. Thus it was politically understandable that the estates did not simply accept the proposal of a constitution but demanded democratic concessions and constitutional guarantees of their rights, although they appealed to the traditions of old Württemberg as the justification of these changes. According to this traditional right of the estates, the new constitution was not to enter into force as a decree of the king, but as a contract between the prince and the estates.

Hegel, concentrating essentially on this source of the conflict, and quite neglecting the negotiations which were taking place with Frederick's successor, who was more amenable to compromise, uses the opposition's appeal to tradition as the occasion to rebuke the estates in quite forceful formulations for their hesitancy. As in no other previous text, Hegel asserts the rational validity of abstract bourgeois law against the accidental historical character of the traditional rights of freedom of the estates. Thus philosophically he deploys the world-historical results of the French Revolution against those whose understanding of themselves lags patriarchally and uncomprehendingly behind the concept of the modern state. The ambivalence of his political position is revealed in that a theoretically superior and certainly progressive position was exploited in favor of the power of the king and his minister Wangenheim, who were playing a restorative role. The government saw to it that Hegel's pamphlet against the estates was disseminated in an inexpensive special printing. That Hegel was actually a collaborator on the *Württembergischen Volksfreund*, an opposition newspaper, I consider to be improbable.[12] The remark of his friend Niethammer, who viewed Hegel as brilliantly defending a bad cause, in any case aptly represents the reaction of the enlightened and liberally inclined public. The journalistic effect which Hegel attained on this occasion for the first and only time thus remains ambivalent when measured against his basic intentions.[13]

(5) Rosenzweig reports Hegel's reaction of anxiety at the news of the events in Paris in July 1830. For several days he was even troubled by the behavior of a student who had appeared wearing a red, white, and blue cockade; the young revolutionary, however, defused his demonstration in time, by pointing out that the red, white, and blue did not refer to the French tricolor but to the Brandenburg colors. In the following winter Hegel concluded his lectures on the Philosophy of History with a dubious look back at the renewed fall of the Bourbons. Although "after forty years of wars and immeasurable confusion" his old heart longs for a pacification of the revolutionary state of the world, Hegel can find no peace, foreseeing the continuing tumult of the conflict. This conflict appears above all to lie in the broadening of democratic principles:

> The will of the Many expels the Ministry from power, and those who had formed the opposition fill the vacant places; but the latter having now become the Government, meet with hostility from the Many and share the same fate. Thus agitation and unrest are perpetuated. This collision, this nodus, this problem is that with which history is now occupied, and whose solution it has to work out in the future.[14]

In England, too, the elections, under the impact of the July Revolution, had turned out in victory for the opposition. After the new cabinet had put forward the draft law for an election reform in March 1831, the philosopher, shortly before his death, for the last time took up the role of journalist and published a pamphlet against the English Reform Bill.

The first installment of the essay "On the English Reform Bill" appeared in the *Allgemeine Preussische Staatszeitung* on April 26, 1831. On the following days two further installments appeared; then the publication of the essay was discontinued. The last fourth of the essay could no longer be published. Shortly before, on April 22, the king of England used a right which had not been employed for many years, and, after an amendment to the government draft had unexpectedly met with success, dissolved Parliament. In this situation the Prussian king felt that foreign policy considerations had to prevail and ordered the article to be deleted. The pamphlet, which met with Frederick William's private approval, was circulated among friends and other interested parties in a specially printed edition. But it was not published in its entirety during Hegel's lifetime. Nor has it attracted great attention during subsequent years. As Rosenzweig remarks laconically, Hegel's greatest glorification of Prussia could find no place in the organ of the Prussian government.

The relation of theory and praxis

Within the dimension of their own contemporary history the political writings met with no real success. Hegel's journalistic enterprises must suffer the irony that they had less significance for their day, to which they addressed themselves, than they have now for his philosophical system. The mere fact that Hegel wrote political polemics throws a peculiar light on the relation of his theory to praxis. For how can the intention of changing reality—which is, after all, the reality of the moral idea—be reconciled with a theory which must reject as vain any such claim?

In the last section of the *Logic* the relation of subjective activity, directed toward a goal, to the idea of the good is defined unambiguously.[15] Where the idea of the good is conceived as a directive for such action, it is unavoidably admixed with subjectivity. For then theory as "a domain of transparent thought" abstractly confronts reality as an "undisclosed domain of dark-

ness." This viewpoint of subjective consciousness is abstract because it disregards the knowledge which always links us with
reality at this level of action. For praxis, which here means not
instrumental action and technical disposition over an objectified
nature, but instead morality in Hegel's sense, as political action
and interaction within a living context—this praxis always moves
within a reality which reason has imagined for itself. Theories
such as rational Natural Law, which first set up the goals subject
to which an existing reality is subsequently to be revolutionized,
fail to comply with the world of objective spirit. In this world,
in the life-interrelationships of the institutions, the good as such
[*an sich*] has already been realized:

> As the activity of the objective external reality [*Wirklich-
> keit*] is changed by the activity of the objective spirit, its
> merely phenomenal reality is taken from it . . . in this the
> presupposition is sublated altogether, namely, the determi-
> nation of the good as a merely subjective goal limited in its
> content, the necessity to as yet realize it by means of sub-
> jective activity, and this activity itself.[16]

If we still behave in the face of this reality as though, instructed
by better insight, we could change it willfully and consciously,
we fall prey to a fatal illusion [*Schein*]: for we repeat the presuppositions of the unactualized goal after the actual carrying out
of this goal. This Hegel calls the subjective attitude of the objective
concept:

> What still limits the objective concept is its own view of
> itself, which disappears through reflection on what its ac-
> tualization is in itself. With this view it stands only in its
> own way; thus it must direct itself not against an external
> reality, but only against itself.[17]

In the preface to the *Philosophy of Right* Hegel drew the
conclusions from these provisions of the *Logic*. Philosophy cannot instruct the world about what it ought to be; it is solely reality which is reflected in its concepts, reality as it is. It cannot

direct itself critically against this, but only against the abstractions which push themselves between reason become objective and our subjective consciousness. Philosophy can level its critique against Fries and the Student Associations [*Burschenschaften*], but not against the institutions of the state. It does not present any guideline for revolutionizing praxis, but only a lesson to those who falsely employ philosophy as an inspiration for political action. The dictum on the *ex post facto* character of theory determines its relation to praxis. Political theory cannot aim at "instructing the state what it should be like, but rather instead how the state—the moral universal—should be known." [18]

The political writings show that Hegel had not always taken this position. This deviation is not the least of what makes these occasional writings, so wholly unconcerned with system-relatedness, so attractive in relation to the system.

"Instruction" of those who engage in political action is the common purpose of the published as well as the unpublished writings on politics. But in each of these writings this intention is understood by Hegel in a different way. The didactic purpose with which he translates Cart's letter is enunciated epigrammatically in the motto that heads it: "*Discite justiciam moniti*, but the deaf will be hard hit by their destiny," which betrays a rather conventional attitude. In the classical doctrine of Politics, as well as in political historiography from Thucydides to Machiavelli, the consideration of the exemplary is the rule which, in terms of a typical event, presents the disastrous consequences of politically imprudent or practically reprehensible conduct. It is this model which Hegel has before him; he only spares himself the trouble of giving "a lot of practical applications" because the most recent events have themselves written in the book of history the moral of this didactic drama, the deserved downfall of a decadent aristocracy. The victorious government of Bern of 1792, which had triumphed after putting down the rebellion, had in the meantime been overthrown, and its true character revealed for all to see.

During the Frankfurt period, in his work on the municipal constitution and in the introductory fragment to the German Constitution, the instruction departs from the traditional framework of classical Politics. Now Hegel would grant philosophy the critical role, almost in the sense which the Young Hegelians—and Marx more sharply than all the others—claim for critique as preparation for a revolutionizing praxis. Hegel departs from the positive character [*Positivität*] of existing reality. "Positive" he calls a society from whose historically petrified forms the spirit has fled, a society whose institutions, laws, and constitution no longer correspond to interests, opinions, and sentiments. This state of division Hegel had investigated in his early theological works, in terms of the decay and disintegration of substantial morality in an idealized Antiquity. Now he comprehends the state of his homeland's constitution in terms of the same concepts, and soon thereafter also that of the German Reich. The impotent timidity of those who feel the necessity of change and yet stubbornly hold onto that which exists, Hegel confronts with the courage of enlightened men who examine with calm eyes what is no longer tenable. Hegel sees as unavoidable alternatives, on the one side violent overthrow "in which revenge joins with the needs for amelioration," and on the other, a prudent praxis of reform "which can completely, peacefully, and honorably remove what is tottering and produce a secure condition." A changing of reality which destroys the positivity of extinct life is unavoidable; but in the revolutionary overthrow blind fate drives compulsive fear before it while the anticipatory courage of a reform which carries out justice carries out the same fate consciously and divests the force of this destiny of its violent character.

In the large treatise on *The Spirit of Christianity and Its Destiny*, which Hegel wrote in Frankfurt, the confrontation between the punishment of law and punishment as destiny serves as the first unfolding of the historical dialectic.[19] The movement of concrete moral life is subject to the lawfulness of a context of guilt, which springs from a division of the moral totality. Hegel calls a social condition, in which all members attain their rights and satisfy their needs, moral. A criminal, who violates moral conditions, by oppressing the life of others, experiences the power of this alienated life as hostile destiny. But the historical necessity of destiny is only the reactive power of this repressed and defunct life, which makes the guilty one suffer until he has experienced the deficiencies of his own life in the destruction of others' lives, and in the turning away from the life of others the alienation of his own. At work in the causality of destiny is the power of denied life, which can be reconciled only when the experience of the negativity of divided life gives rise to the longing for the life that has been lost and necessarily brings one to identify in the other's existence one's own denied existence. Then both parties recognize their hardened posture toward each other as the result of the separation, the abstraction from their common interconnection of life—and in this, recognize the basis of their existence. The positivity of the conditions under the old municipal constitution of Württemberg and that of the Reich also bears the marks of such a division, so that Hegel believes he discerns in the palpable negativity the punishing power of reprimanded life. The upheaval which must set in is a just destiny. In the revolution it is carried out on the contending parties—and beyond them—as its agents and its victims at the same time. To be sure, at that period, in Frankfurt, Hegel saw still other possibilities of a preventive reflection on the destiny which was drawing near, as the introductory fragment to the *German Constitution* also shows. This task Hegel assigns to a critique, which measures what exists against the concrete justice of destiny, divests it of its mask of merely pretended universality, and gives legitimation "to that part of life which is demanded." The philosopher who reflects destiny can induce a reform which does justice, in order not to suffer the terrible justice of blind revolutionary violence. In the prerevolutionary situation, the interest of the masses, who only sense the contradiction between the life that is allowed and that which is unconsciously desired, supports the intellectuals, who have raised the nature of this idea to clarity within them. But the latter cannot simply stop at the contradiction between subjectivity and the reified world [20] and enjoy it with a feeling of melancholy; they must comprehend it historically. That is the viewpoint of critique, which confronts limited life with this life's own concept. Addressing itself to the rulers, a philosophy which comprehends history as destiny can articulate the contradiction by which the unreflecting masses are obscurely driven, and unmask the decadence of the particular by confronting it with the mirror of the universal interests to which it still presumes. The critique is not to attain practical power, as Marx expects it to, by stirring the masses; it is to attain practical influence by changing the consciousness of the rulers. It can instruct the politicians about the justice of a destiny which will be visited upon them objectively, if they do not muster the courage to will this destiny.

When Hegel once more corrected the already revised introduction to his work on the constitution several years later, and wrote a clean copy, he had relinquished this position. Those who comprehend historical events as destiny and can learn from history do not have the power to intervene in the historical process; while those who are politically active can derive no benefit from the mistakes they have made. That division between the philosophers and the ones who conduct the business of the world spirit, for which the reasons are presented in the *Logic,* already begins to delineate itself, a division of labor by which, in his lectures on the Philosophy of History, Hegel wants to exclude a feedback effect of theory on praxis. The reflection on destiny is condemned to an *ex post facto* existence; it can no longer break destiny's objective power. Already in 1802, formulations are to be found in this work, as recopied, which reappear in the preface of 1821; the philosophy which comprehends the contemporary situation in terms of the concrete connections of world-historical justice is directed critically solely against those who interject between the events and their immanent necessity a host of subjective concepts and purposes. The work on the constitution only seeks to understand what *is.* The instruction which it can impart is now only of use to those who suffer: it makes it easier for them to bear their fate; for "not that which is makes us restless and makes us suffer, but only that it is not as it should be; once we recognize, however, that it is as it must be . . . then we also know that it ought to be thus."

Now the polemical form of a treatise, which is an unmistakably politically contentious piece of writing and which ends with programmatic proposals, contrasts most oddly with this wholly unpolitical intention of educating malcontents and world reformers to Stoicism and a world-historically enlightened quietism. The original Jena manuscript was not initially composed in this spirit. To be sure, it does conclude with the conviction that no matter how much the reform of the German Reich may correspond to a deeply and definitely felt objective need, it could never be accomplished by means of a critique, but only by force: "the insight into the necessity is too weak to have an effect on action." Hegel relinquishes the hope that critical insight could prepare the praxis of a prudent reform and, in the medium of enlightened courage, could render the force of destiny more supple. But the naked force of the conqueror, the magnanimous Theseus, once he had subjugated the particularism of the local princes, is still supposed to lead to that very renovation which once had been directly attributed to the readiness on the part of the rulers to undertake reforms. But that is how it is—"to the concept and the insight something so suspicious adheres, that they have to be justified by force; then men will submit to them." However, here too Hegel could still claim for the philosophical concept the same critical prevision; it is only that for its actualization despotic power is required.

The new affirmative evaluation of power is related to the fact that in the interim Hegel has acquired from Machiavelli and Hobbes the modern concept of the state. Through his historical-political studies of the Frankfurt period, and especially through his discovery of the Oriental world, Hegel has gained a perspective of historical development in which the Greek world represents only a stage and not the model of what the modern world must aim to restore. The overcoming of the historically superseded forms of a condition petrified in positivity is therefore no longer conceived, as in the theological writings of Hegel's youth, as the renewal of Ancient morality. It is seen instead as the transformation of the Reich into a modern bureaucratic state, based on a centralized administration of taxation and on a tautly organized professional army, a state which as such remains external to the sphere of laissez-faire bourgeois private intercourse. And, indeed, those attributes of morality which Hegel had initially gathered from the classical concept of the *polis* are now transferred to this state.[21] The determination of sovereignty is therefore linked with the establishment of a power which assures effective military assertion externally by means of the obligation of the citizens to sacrifice the freedom of their personal existence and their lives for the defense of the whole.

From now on the category of war attains a dominant position. War is the medium through which the world-historical destiny of the nations is fulfilled. In war the health of the sovereign state and the political morality of its citizens must stand the test. The causality of destiny is no longer comprehended as the ironical punishment by which our own deed strikes back at us. Now it springs from a tragedy in the moral sphere which begins with a voluntary sacrifice, the self-alienation of the absolute to its Other.[22] On the basis of the fetishized sacrifice, Hegel can attach the reality of the moral idea to the self-assertion of the modern bourgeois state and its brusque apparatus of domination. If, however, the sacrifice of the citizens, who relinquish their private existence in order to defend the totality of their property, is not to be solely the ashes out of which the state arises into the magnificence of its external power, if it is rather the internally based power of the state which is the only altar upon which the citizens can make their sacrifice, then the renewal of a Reich, which has ceased to exist as a state, can be possible only by external force, by the triumph of a conqueror—and not from the outset by the peaceful reform of internal conditions.

The triumph of a victor, who is as yet only expected, could not, however, be celebrated; at the time it could only be anticipated by the political writer. Thus in Hegel's critique, the concept of the new state already appears before weapons have gained objective assertion for it. We know that Hegel's concept of the German Reich was not made into a reality on the Napoleonic battlefields. It was only at the end of the Jena period, after Austerlitz, that Hegel attained the position from which philosophy could finally divest itself of its role of a critique of the world, and confine itself to contemplation: now the concept justifies a reality which has completed itself; the concept no longer requires a justification by external force. Hegel concludes his course of lectures on September 18, 1806, with the words:

> We find ourselves in an important epoch of time, a fermentation in which the spirit has lurched forward, has gone

beyond the shape it had assumed till now and has attained a new shape. The whole mass of conceptions and concepts held until now, the bonds of the world, are dissolved and collapse like the image of a dream. A new emanation [*Hervorgang*] of the spirit is preparing itself. Philosophy, especially, has to acclaim its appearance and to recognize it, while the others, resisting impotently, remain glued to past things and the majority of men unconsciously constitute the mass of its manifestation. Philosophy, however, recognizing this new spirit as the eternal, must show it honor.[23]

Hegel can relieve philosophy of its critical efforts to confront the complacent existence of social and political life with its own concept after he has recognized, with a sigh of relief that the spirit has lurched forward, that the principle of reason has entered into reality and has become objective. Now it is only a question of time and contingent circumstances before the new epoch will stride over the resistance of those who oppose it impotently and gain universal recognition for its principle. Only now can Hegel content himself with recognizing the spirit which has become objective, call it by its name, and turn critically against those who have not yet comprehended the lesson of world history. That is the tenor of the polemic against the Württemberg estates. "They seem to have slept through these last twenty-five years," Hegel writes in 1817, "probably the richest which world history has ever enjoyed, and for us the most instructive, because our world and our conceptions belong to them."

Abstract right and the revolution celebrated

The point of time at which this perspective opened up for Hegel, that is, 1806, seems to make the assumption likely that it was only with Napoleon's victory over Europe that the spirit had made its "lurch" forward. But that is not the case. It was rather the case that not until that point, at the end of the Jena period, had Hegel fully developed the theoretical standpoint, from which he could comprehend one result of the French Revolution, namely, the assertion of abstract right, as that which was essentially new and revolutionizing.

During the Frankfurt period Hegel had pursued the study of economics, and had written a commentary to the German translation of Steuart's *Political Economy,* which has not been preserved. Then, as the *System of Morality,* composed in 1802, and above all, the lectures of 1803–1806, show, in Jena Hegel had worked out for the first time an adequate concept of modern bourgeois society, in terms of a critical examination of the economic theory of his time. In the context of this "system of needs," abstract Right also attains a new role within the system.

Until now Hegel had conceived abstract right on the same level with the positivity of universal laws and the limited character of the Kantian ethic, thus as a product of the decay of absolute morality. As early as his Bern period, the distinction between the Greek religion of imagination [*Phantasiereligion*] and positive Christianity presented the occasion for deriving the genesis of formal bourgeois private right from the downfall of the *polis* and the rise of the Roman universal empire.[24] In the Jena essay on the scientific treatment of Natural Law, the "loss of absolute morality," depicted with a coloration furnished by Gibbon, again constitutes the genesis of formal right:

> With universal private life, and for the condition in which the people consist only of a second estate (namely of those engaged in trade), the formal relationship of right, which confirms property, is immediately at hand; and from such depravity and universal degradation the most complete elaboration of legislation relating to this right did indeed develop and evolve. This system of property and right which for the sake of the confirmation of solitary individuality [*Einzelnheit*] exists in nothing absolute and eternal, but wholly in the finite and formal, must . . . constitute itself within a social stratum of its own, and from there be able to extend itself throughout its whole length and breadth.[25]

Hegel sees the necessity that this system of the commerce of privatized citizens must be accorded a relative right and a realm "within which it can establish itself and in its confusion, and the sublation of one confusion by means of the other, develop its full activity" [26]—for that is the other side, the inverse, of the tragedy in the moral domain. But in the contemporary work, on the Constitution of the Reich, the sphere of bourgeois society is still only negatively specified and is excluded from the philosophical concept. Only by way of the economic studies does social labor gain weight within the system; then bourgeois society, instead of remaining the sphere of divided morality, becomes the arena for the species' active emancipation from the state of nature.

Subjective spirit forms its solitary existence in processes of labor. In *labor* consciousness makes itself into a thing in order to subjugate things. In the *tool* domination over nature becomes just as objective as does the drive satisfaction rendered permanent in *possession,* as the product of labor become universal. But subjective spirit goes over into the sphere of actual spirit only after the struggle for recognition has led to a system of social labor and to emancipation from the state of nature. Only when the *division of labor* has produced abstract labor, and the *commercial exchange* has produced abstract enjoyment, when both make possible the labor of all for the satisfaction of the needs of all, does the *contract* become the principle of bourgeois commerce. Then fortuitous possession is transformed into *property,* guaranteed by universal recognition, and through property subjective spirit forms itself into the person.[27] From that point on Hegel never again lost sight of "the moment of emancipation which lies in labor" (*Philosophy of Right,* §194).[28]

Later, of course, in the *Philosophy of Right,* he obscured the materialistic path along which he had come by all his knowledge of the dignity of abstract right, until it became unrecognizable. Under the title of jurisprudence, bourgeois private right enters into modern bourgeois society, as it were, from outside, although it is to this society alone that it owes its formation and existence. But still, just as before, Hegel ties the existence of freedom to the principles of abstract Right. The French Revolution is a world-historical watershed only because it has as its result the realization of these principles. In Jena Hegel acclaims Napoleon, also—and above all—because he is the patron of the new

bourgeois legal code. With the Revolution, and the great Bona-
parte as the executor of its testament, the principle of reason has
become reality in the form of the legally guaranteed freedom of
all human beings as persons. That is the basis for his critique of
the Württemberg estates:

> One must regard the beginning of the French Revolution
> as the struggle which rational constitutional law undertook
> with the mass of positive right and the privileges by which
> the former had been suppressed; in the debates of the estates
> of Württemberg we see the same struggle between these
> principles, only that the positions have been reversed here.
> . . . Thus in Württemberg the king has established his con-
> stitution within the realm of rational constitutional law;
> the estates oppose this, as defenders of positive rights and
> privileges; indeed, they present the perverted spectacle of
> doing this in the name of the people, against whose interests
> these privileges are directed, much more than against those
> of the prince.

The substantial state and the revolution feared

When he wrote the work on the estates in 1817, Hegel the
political writer for the first time is in agreement with Hegel
the logician and the philosopher of right, as far as the relationship of his theory to his praxis is concerned—and that means, in
agreement with the self-understanding of his system. After theory
had comprehended the self-formative process of spirit, it could turn
critically against those who stood beneath the level of world-
history. The critique was no longer turned against a reality, but
against the bondage of an abstraction, which had to be liberated
to become the concept of reality.

Yet in the work on the estates, too, that critical viewpoint
appears which later induces Hegel to attack the English Reform
Bill. The constitution proposed by the king solely limits active
voting rights by the qualifications of age and income. Against
this Hegel argues for a scale of the citizens' political rights, according to their civil status within the society. He sees state power

threatened in its very substance if social interests are translated directly onto the level of political decision. The filter of voting rights according to professional status is to prejudice the choice of representatives in such a way that the political opinion that prevails in the Assembly of the Estates will not undermine the independence of the state authority from the social conflicts it is supposed to control and will keep it from being merely an expression of such conflicts. To "mistake the state for civil society" and thereby define the state solely as "for the protection of property and personal liberty and for security" (*Philosophy of Right,* §257) is a danger which again becomes acute as a result of the July Revolution. In France voting rights were democratized, and an electoral reform was impending in England. So Hegel concluded his pamphlet against the English Reform Bill with an entreaty, warning of the power of the people and of an opposition which could be misled into "seeking its strength in the people and bringing about a revolution instead of a reform."

It hardly seems convincing to me to interpret purely psychologically the insensitivity of the old Hegel and his Cassandra-like warnings, which seem to correspond so little with the self-assurance of a system of the self-conscious spirit, in which reality has formed itself into reason. And if it is only, as Rosenzweig feels, pure fear of revolution by which Hegel was driven at this time, still there is no reason for suddenly separating this attitude toward current political issues from his systematic conceptions. Is not Hegel's pessimism, which intensified into a feeling of insecurity toward the end of his life, perhaps a symptom of a deeper uneasiness, a perturbation which is not limited to his private concerns, but instead derives from the first stirring of doubt concerning theory itself, doubt of which Hegel is as yet hardly conscious?

For comparison we can turn to a passage from the somewhat earlier lectures on the Philosophy of Religion. At the end of the course Hegel undertook to define his views with respect to that delicate question of the "sublation" of religion in philosophy, which gained such momentous significance after Hegel's death, through the controversies among his pupils. Hegel sets the task for philosophy of justifying the contents of religion, especially of Christianity, before the higher authority of reason, by divesting these contents of the form of faith. In any case, reflection had broken in upon religion during the course of the Enlightenment: "Thinking, which has begun in this way, has no place to rest anymore, pushes on to its conclusion, empties the psyche [*Gemüt*], the heaven, and the knowing spirit, and religious content then takes refuge in the concept. Here it must receive its justification. . . ." [29] Now because of its philosophical nature, this religious knowledge which replaces faith cannot be universally disseminated. For Hegel, regressing in this behind the intentions of the Enlightenment, has never departed from the soil of the basic Parmenidean prejudice, which has lived on in Western philosophy: that the many are excluded from participation in the Being [*im Seienden*—"that which is"]. Therefore the truth of religion, as soon as it takes refuge in the concept, must emigrate from the community of the faithful to make its abode with the philosopher, and thus lose its universal recognition. The public atheism of so-called cultivated people will also seize hold of the poor, who until that time have lived in a state of ingenuous religiosity. Even the power of the state can do nothing against this decline of faith. The consequences of demythologization cannot be arrested. The fulfillment of the epoch, whose sign is the need for justification by means of the concept, is accompanied precisely by a demoralization of the people:

> When the gospel is no longer preached to the poor, when the salt has become dumb, and all the fundamental rites [*Grundfeste*] are accepted in silence, then the people, for whose permanently limited reason truth can only exist in the representational image, no longer know how to find aid for their inner needs [*Drange seines Innern*].[30]

In the context of our present concern, the Stoical placidity and composure with which Hegel anticipates this development are remarkable. He speaks coolly of a "false note" that is present in reality. This disharmony is resolved for and by philosophy, for it recognizes that the "Idea" is inherent in Revelation. But this reconciliation is only a partial one; it has validity only for the "isolated priesthood of the philosophers." The reaction which the transition from one stage of absolute spirit to the next effects in the world of objective spirit, this tremor which shakes the moral totality, cannot be alleviated by philosophy: "How the temporal, empirical present can find a way out of this dilemma, how it is to form itself, that must be left to this world and is not the immediate practical task, is not the business of philosophy." [31]

This continence of theory, which mirrors its superiority, and at the same time its impotence, in the face of a danger so full of practical consequences, is consistent with the meaning of the system's compelling presuppositions. But a short time later Hegel loses the equanimity, required by philosophy, when confronted with that other danger, emanating for a second time from Paris, and he seeks to exert an influence on praxis, again in the role of political journalist. He thereby enters into contradiction with his own system.

As his various views of the estates show, from the Jena period on, beginning with the System of Morality, and the essay on Natural Law, for Hegel the relation between the state and society had always been a problem. In the Philosophy of Right he finally found a solution. It permitted him to comprehend modern bourgeois society as an antagonistic interrelationship of compulsions, and at the same time, as the work on the German Constitution has already shown, to allow the modern state a posture of substantial power in the face of this society. The state is not determined by the functions of that societal structure as a utilitarian and calculating enterprise; instead, political power re-establishes the absolute morality of an Aristotelian order aiming at the Good Life, which is only mediated by the social system of needs. But Hegel can mediate between the modern concept of bourgeois society, developed in terms of rational Natural Law and Political Economy, and the classical concept of Political Rule only by means of entities which are interposed between state and society. Looking to the past, Hegel finds these in a corporative articulation of society, and in an assembly of the estates that has an organic composition. Measured against this status-stratified [*ständesstaatlich*] constitutional construction, the contemporary elements of the liberal constitutional state, as evolving, each in their own way, in France and England, had to seem backward to

Hegel. And Hegel did in fact denounce them as elements of a reality which lagged behind the principle that had already gained world-historical validation, and thus behind Prussia.

But if this was indeed the case, then why could Hegel not reassure himself with the thought, for which he had been able to present so many examples from world-history, that spirit requires a long time to obtain universality for a principle which has been enunciated and rendered objective in one place? Instead Hegel, the Prussian university professor in Berlin, composed a political polemic against a law proposed by the government in London.

Hegel's easy-going pessimism, which recognized in the demise of a historical period its perfect completion [*Vollendung*], as he did in the lectures on the Philosophy of Religion, gave way to the anxious pessimism of his last political writings because the doubt arose in him whether it was not really France and England, rather than Prussia, which represented reality and in which the dominant principle of history had incorporated itself most profoundly. Perhaps Hegel had already had some intimation of Marx's objection against his political philosophy a decade later: that those political estates of prebourgeois society, in whose residues Hegel anchors the authority of his state, have dissolved to become "social" estates—classes. To still assign to these the function of mediation between state and society would then be an impotent attempt at restoration, "to throw man within the political sphere itself back into the limitations of his private sphere." [32] Then Hegel's critique of the July Revolution and the Reform Bill would recoil against him. He would be the one who had denied the separation between state and society, which had taken place in reality, by the abstraction of a new rank-structured constitution, by hypostatizing backward Prussian conditions, by a "reminiscence," as Marx put it.

Hegel seems to have felt that his critique was now no longer directed against a subjectivism made obsolete by the course of world-history, as it had been in 1817, but against the consequences of the same revolution which he had acclaimed, as long as the principles of abstract Right remained confined within the limits of bourgeois private law and did not extend to the right of political equality. For the last time the critique into which philosophy had been translated in the hands of Hegel the journalist changes its position: again it turns, as it had in the days of his youth, against the objectivity of actual conditions, but this time not, as formerly, against the state of a world petrified in positivity, but against the living spirit of the revolution continuing to propagate itself. The wind which Hegel feels no longer is at his back.

Hegel became a political journalist for one more time at the end of his life, because he saw not only his person, but the theory itself, attacked by the course of events. And, indeed the current events which the journalist confronts can only challenge philosophy at all because philosophy, which is the dialectic, claims to comprehend the permanent in the passing of the eternally transitory.

Hegel's political philosophy today

Hegel's political philosophy cannot simply be projected without difficulty onto the plane of the twentieth century. The Nazis have sought to reclaim Hegel for the total state.[33] No more cautious is the procedure of the innocent apologists for the open society, who in an abstract inversion once more confirm the old legend.[34] Both interpretations are but variations on the same melody and have already been effectively refuted by Marcuse and Ritter. The Hegel who opposed the terroristic manner in which the Revolution was carried out but never opposed its ideals, and who defended the historically progressive principles of rational Natural Law as vehemently against the new reactionaries as against the Old-Frankish traditionalists, can hardly be refashioned as the precursor of Carl Schmitt or of Binder, Larenz, and others. Not quite so wrongheaded, but just as unconvincing, is the tendency, on the other hand, to adapt Hegel for incorporation into the *juste milieu* of Western democracy, and to confer upon him the title of honorary liberal.[35] Two aspects distinguish Hegel most strikingly from contemporary liberals and from the comfortable views of his liberal pupils: on the one hand, the ruthlessly radical character of the recognition he accords to the dynamics of historical development (*Philosophy of Right*, §§243–248), and on the other, the peculiar narrowness of his view, limited by the tradition of Protestant officialdom and then politicized and confined to the Prussian sphere.

Hegel places us before a task which cannot do him dishonor: to comprehend the discrepancy between the all-embracing power of the *Enzyklopädie,* which once more devoured the whole world into philosophy, and the secret limits of his horizon, betraying the parochialism of a tradition which was not fully open to his insight. Hegel too was not able to transcend his time and his circumstances.[36] And these were, as Marx remarked, the circumstances of a country which took part in the restorations of the modern nations, without participating in their revolutions. Hegel, too, in spite of his own claims, continues a particularism to which German philosophy owes its estrangement from the Western spirit. To overcome this was necessarily easier for a Rhenish Jew in exile in London, than for a Tübingen seminarian and Prussian official in Restoration Berlin.[37]

6

Between Philosophy and Science:
Marxism as Critique

(1) The "separation" of the state from society which is typical of the liberal phase of capitalist development has been superseded by a reciprocal interlocking of the two in the stage of organized capitalism. The sphere of commodity exchange and social labor requires so much centralized organization and administration that bourgeois society, once left to private initiative operating according to the rules of the free market, is forced to resort to political mediation of its commerce for many of its branches. However, if it is no longer autonomously constituted as that sphere which serves as presupposition and basis for the state, then state and society no longer stand in the classical relationship of superstructure and base. An approach which in its method isolates at the outset the laws of motion of the society can only claim to comprehend accurately the interrelationships of life of this society in its essential categories as long as politics is dependent on the economic base and is not to be comprehended the other way around, as a function of conflicts which are pursued and resolved with political self-consciousness.[1]

(2) Furthermore, in advanced capitalist countries the standard of living has, in any case, risen to such an extent, at least among broad strata of the population, that the interest in the emancipation of society can no longer be articulated directly in economic terms. "Alienation" has been deprived of its palpable economic form as misery. At most, the pauperism of alienated

labor finds its remote reflection in a poverty of alienated leisure—scurvy and rickets are preserved today in the form of psychosomatic disturbances, hunger and drudgery in the wasteland of externally manipulated motivation, in the satisfaction of needs which no longer are "one's own"—the more sublime form of deprivation is no longer even specific to one class. The "deprivations" have become more secret, even if as consuming as ever.[2] In the same manner, domination, as the other side of alienation, has divested itself of its undisguised expression, as a relation of power embodied in the wage labor contract. In the same measure as the economic and political status of those "in service" is made secure, relations of personal power retreat behind the anonymous compulsion of indirect manipulation—in ever more extensive domains of social life, directives lose their form of commands and are translated by means of sociotechnical manipulation in such a manner that those forced to obey, now well integrated, are allowed to do, in the consciousness of their freedom, what do they must.

(3) Under these conditions, the designated executor of a future socialist revolution, the proletariat *as* proletariat, has been dissolved. To be sure, the mass of the population, judging by their objective role in the process of production, is "proletarian"; they have no actual powers of control over the means of production. So-called "people's capitalism" can change none of this; at the present level of the concentration and centralization of capital anything approaching democratic control in a nonpolitical form, namely, on a continuing basis of private property, can hardly be considered likely.[3] But on the other hand, the exclusion from control over the means of production is no longer bound up to such an extent with deprivation of social rewards (income, security, education, and so forth) that this objective situation would still in any way be experienced subjectively as proletarian. And any class consciousness, especially a revolutionary class consciousness, is not to be found in the main strata of the working class today.[4] Every revolutionary theory, under these circumstances, lacks those to whom it is addressed; therefore arguments can no longer be translated into slogans. Even if there still were the critical mind, its heart is lacking; and thus today Marx would have

to abandon his hope that theory can become a material force, once it has taken hold of the masses. To be sure, the class struggle which has been pacified within the nations now is reproduced on the international level in the struggle between the capitalistic and the socialistic "camps."

(4) Finally, the Russian Revolution and the establishment of the Soviet system are *the* historical facts by which the systematic discussion of Marxism, and with Marxism, has been paralyzed to the greatest extent. Initiated by a weak proletariat and supported by petty bourgeois and prebourgeois peasant masses, the anti-feudal movement which liquidated the dual power of Parliament and Soviets in October 1917 under the direction of Leninistically schooled professional revolutionaries had no immediate socialist aims. But it established a rule of functionaries and Party cadres, on the basis of which, a decade later, Stalin was able to initiate the socialist revolution bureaucratically from above, by the collectivization of agriculture. Emerging from the war against Fascism as a world power, Soviet Marxism forced the leadership strata of the West, organized on a capitalistic basis, to exercise the greatest vigilance over the stability of their system. The enforced control over broad social domains has produced, in the West, organizational forms for securing social positions and the more equal adjustment of social compensation, thus a kind of permanent institutionalized reform, so that a self-regulation of capitalism by the force of "self-discipline" appears to be possible; the catch-word for this development has been coined in the United States: the "new capitalism." [5] In the face of this, the Soviet path to socialism only recommends itself as a method for shortening the process of industrialization in developing countries, one which is far removed from the realization of a truly emancipated society, and indeed at times has regressed again from the constitutional rights attained under capitalism to the legal terror of Party dictatorship. To be sure, the Soviet Union succeeds in raising the productive forces at a rate which permits it to enter into a peaceful competition to achieve the highest standard of living, under the slogan of "overtaking and outstripping" the capitalist world. In the long run, the social structure and the apparatus of domination are also affected by this, in such a manner that a convergence of

the two systems on the middle ground of a controlled mass democracy within the welfare state is not to be excluded. To be sure, in that case, the danger of a society which feels "content in alienation," indeed the artificially stimulated well-being in a hygienically perfected alienation—dangers which are mirrored in the cautionary images of negative Utopias such as the "Brave New World"—would not be laid to rest by such a development. If indeed the old Utopias of the best possible social order and eternal peace, the highest degree of freedom and perfect happiness, contain the underlying rational themes of a theory, no matter how distorted into a derivative myth, as their implicit basis; and if praxis must legitimate itself in terms of this theory, because it has now been invested with the mantle of a state ideology—then one may cautiously raise the consideration, as Herbert Marcuse does, whether ultimately such a system does not have a corrective for such dangers at its disposal.[6] But before that, of course, the other dangers, which grow daily out of the tensions of a global civil war, only patched over in the most fragile manner by the atomic stalemate, are so overwhelming that hardly anyone can dare to speculate beyond the primary question: whether the peaceful coexistence between the two camps can be made secure institutionally at all, and, if so, how this is to be done.[7]

The confrontation with Marxism—forms of typical reaction

Together the four historical facts indicated above form an insuperable barrier to any theoretical acceptance of Marxism, especially in the form codified by Stalin—"Diamat" [the official version of Dialectical Materialism], and (until the middle of the sixties) congealed into a basic view of the world. And the theoretical forms of the reaction to Marxism were also shaped by the tacit force of these historical facts; even today they are marked by the dominant compulsion exercised by the relationship of friend and foe that holds between the parties of a class struggle transposed onto the international plane.[8] We can distinguish a series of typical forms which this reaction takes:

(1) The political and ideological configuration of Soviet Marxism can be made the object of a scientific analysis, without

regard for what it itself would like to be. In this category there are, on the one hand, several investigations of value, in the field of political science, of the Soviet system as a typical example of totalitarian rule. On Fascism there have been works by authors of the Marxist school (Franz Neumann) in which the relationship between the constellations of economic interests and the political institutions was kept in view; but a corresponding Marxist analysis of Soviet Marxism has hardly been undertaken as yet.[9] This confinement of vision to the political structure, methodically isolated, becomes especially problematical when applied to an object which immanently contains the claim to substantially changing political relations as the consequence of rationally reorganizing the processes of social reproduction, namely, to dissolve them thereby *as* political relations.

On the other hand, in the same category there are valuable investigations, from the cultural science viewpoint, of Soviet ideology. Aside from the attempt to assign it its place in the history of religion, as derived from gnosis (Vögelin) or Judeo-Christian eschatology (Löwith), the derivation, within the history of philosophy, from the speculations of German Idealism is also customary: from an appropriation, foreshortened in the Young Hegelian manner, of the Hegelian dialectic, flows the consequence of a total knowledge which is no longer rationally demonstrable, and which forms the basis for a total planning with inhuman consequences. Marxism is presented as the secularization of a religious or philosophic faith which, however, cannot be rationally resolved. This analysis remains content with the useful indication of the affinities in intellectual history, and wholly refuses to consider the immanent claims of the theory that it is in possession of the knowledge of society's laws of motion.

For the rest, Marxism is offered as an example of a dialectics of an excessive presumption, which then reacts on its own intentions. Thus Carl Schmitt seeks to prove that the political substance will take revenge on any attempt to resolve politics into rational administration, due to a fatality contained in the revolutionary initiative, by terminating in just that totalitarian rule which is to be abolished. Analogously, Karl Jaspers develops the supposition that transcendence, whether interpreted mythically, religiously, or philosophically, will avenge itself on any attempt to extend it into a total science, due to a fatality contained in the critical concept, by becoming precisely that ideology whose bonds it intends to burst.

(2) On another level, a theological and philosophical discussion with Marxism is being carried on, which is ready to deal with its intentions, and which at times approaches the threshold of a partial acceptance. This is especially true of a part of the Protestant churches, as well as of that philosophy which has Protestantism as its inspiration. In these circles[10] two characteristic positions of acceptance have formed: one under the aspect of a philosophical theology (Landgrebe), the other under that of philosophical anthropology (Metzke, Thier, and others).

Marx's Naturalism is understood from the perspective of his revolutionary Humanism and sharply differentiated historically from the metaphysical Materialism of the epigones, Engels and Kautsky, Lenin and Stalin. Marx's position is specified in terms of his relation to Hegel. Against the background of Occidental metaphysics, viewed as ontological history, where Plato, Descartes, and Hegel mark off the epochs, Hegel appears as the successful and yet unsuccessful [*glücklich-unglücklich*] fulfillment of modern consciousness. This is, above all, because, with the full elaboration of his system of absolute reason, he had only fallen back under the confining spell from which he had already apparently freed himself, in the theological works of his youth, with the bold anticipation of a dialectic of lovingly comprehending reason. To this buried point of departure, namely, the problem of restoring to life all the extinct relations between man and nature and human beings with each other, Marx, to be sure, without being conscious of it, returns again. His dialectic of self-alienation unfolds within a scope, which only was created by the fact that in the *Enzyklopädie* the dialectic does not solve the problem that Hegel himself once had unraveled so promisingly, with his critique of "positivity." To be sure, if this "restoring to life" of the world, and of nature within it, is to be conceived in terms of a concept of life which can only flourish on the soil of the Christian revelation—as it does in Hegel's youthful works—then the atheistic attempt of Marx's early writings must collapse into a bottomless abyss. Landgrebe's interesting version seeks to place Marx within the historico-ontological [*seingeschichtlich*] perspective of the late works of Heidegger. To be sure, he prejudices the case by taking the position that truth can be confronted as present only in the mode of contemplating the sacred [*Heilige*], and not produced in a praxis guided by critique; but within this—if you like—idealistic prejudice, the radical claims of Marx and the authenticity of his attempt can at least be discussed, no matter how peculiar this transposition into the dimension of faith and contemplation may seem.[11]

The other path of philosophical acceptance is by way of the "image of man" presented in Marx's early works. For in these, above all in the *Paris Manuscripts,* the structure of alienated labor is analyzed, employing several central categories of Hegel's *Phenomenology of Mind,* which are translated into the language of Feuerbach's Anthropology. Thus the appearance arises, as though Marx was concerned only with the "objective essence" of man, who, as a being of nature, produces himself by working. Externalization of his essential capacities, realization of the human being, but also his nature in its essence, at the same time produced and liberated by the rational reproduction of social life: this complex can be interpreted anthropologically or even in terms of fundamental ontology, as a constant structure. Actually, however, it was developed as a specific analysis of a concrete situation, namely that of the "condition of the working classes" produced by the dialectic of wage labor and capital.[12]

Both forms of Marx's influence have their limitation in not being willing to relinquish the "presuppositions of philosophy"—presuppositions which are suspended by the materialistic critique; for the critical achievement of the latter consists, to begin with, in forcing philosophy to recognize the poverty of its self-consciousness and to accept the insight that it can neither furnish the rational grounds for its own origin, nor can it realize its own fulfillment by itself.

(3) Now there are a number of scholars who break through this limitation by means of a critique of philosophy, as philosophy of origins [*Ursprungsphilosophie*].[13] They make their own the approach of a philosophy of history with practical intentions, and

see through the misunderstanding of an ontological interpretation of Marxism, of whatever variety. They know that Marx never
sought the essence of man or of society as such, and never asked
how the meaning of being or even of social existence [*soziales
Sein*] is constituted, asking questions such as, why is there Being
and beings [*Seiendes*] and not instead, nothing? On the contrary,
Marx limited himself, again and again, to confront only one, the
initial question, driven to this by the spur of a palpably experienced alienation: why does this specific historical and social situation exist, under the objective compulsion of which I myself
have to preserve, arrange, and conduct my life—why is this existent [*Seiende*] thus and not otherwise?

The philosophers and sociologists who are still animated by
a similar cognitive interest no longer turn the effort of their
conceptualization directly toward the sphere of the reproduction
of social life, as Marx did—since Hilferding there hardly have
been any Marxist economists of comparable rank.[14] Instead, they
are concerned with those derivative phenomena, which Marx included in the superstructure. It is not the fact alone that with the
intensification of the state of global civil war the sanctions too
have been intensified which is mirrored here. To this negative
aspect corresponds the positive fact that the critique of ideology
attains greater urgency to the degree that the forms of alienation
grow in refinement. Wherever the system of organized capitalism
has attained relative stability—without having to silence the economic conflicts by means of the institutionalized force of an
authoritarian regime, or by diverting these conflicts into military
expansion—and maintains itself at a high level of production and
employment, there a critique of the satisfaction of need denied or
inhibited must instead seek out the sphere of "culture" rather
than the so-called basic needs. In so doing it is only following in
the footsteps of the repressive forces themselves, which in their
tendency have already been transferred from the economic mechanisms of the labor market to the sociopsychological mechanisms
of the leisure market—the manipulated consumption of culture
perhaps confirms the old relations of power in a new and certainly
more acceptable form.[15]

Among the older scholars, still bound to the Marxist tradition, efforts of this sort frequently take on the form of a *hidden orthodoxy:* the categories of the Marxist labor theory of value are revealed in their applications to cultural critique, without being explicitly named as such. In the esoteric fabric of aesthetic reflections lingers something like the echo of a Critique of Political Economy. The less these are explicitly stated, the more their canon can, tacitly and intangibly, be made the underlying basis. Just the intangible character of this underlying basis of course permits one to doubt whether it still is there at all—and the longer this doubt remains, the stronger it becomes. A complementary phenomenon among the younger scholars, who have only gained acquaintance with the Marxist tradition from the perspective of the breakdown of Fascism, is the historical recourse to the original Marx, contrasted emphatically to the "history of Marxism's decay," which already sets in with Engels. Often they prefer to call themselves Marxologists, in distinction to Marxists, and in the guise of history of philosophy conduct highly specialized investigations, above all of the concept of ideology, of the materialistic dialectic, and of revolutionary strategy—a sort of *free-floating* orthodoxy, which cannot attain any clarity as to its own systematic cogency as long as, in its efforts, the problems of political economy are assiduously avoided.

(4) To this peculiar pendulum motion between a hidden or tacit Marxist orthodoxy and a quite open and outspoken Marxist historicism also belongs an intellectual and political enterprise, in which the academic economic and sociological debate with Marxism has practically been at a standstill for decades. From the official viewpoint of the positive sciences such a debate is considered "obsolete," while Marxist economics and sociology themselves have hardly developed since World War I. Only a handful of Anglo-American authors, among them Paul M. Sweezy and Paul A. Baran in the United States, Maurice Dobb and his pupil Ronald L. Meek in England, have made the effort of keeping pace with contemporary research. They have produced works which rise far above the general level, that of sectarian autodidacts, characteristic for this field.[16]

In sociology the development was able to take a different course, because, in any case, it was not confronted with the labor theory of value as the systematic point of departure, but only with its specific theoretical derivations. Within the viewpoint of its specialization it could allow decisions as to fundamental questions to remain undecided, and fruitfully appropriate certain components, isolated from the system, for its own scholarly apparatus. In the twenties the doctrine of ideology was assimilated in the form of the Sociology of Knowledge (Mannheim). Later, above all the analyses of the famous chapter 13 of volume I of *Capital* were incorporated into the sociology of labor (G. Friedmann); and the central component of Marxism, the theory of classes, too, was finally formalized in the doctrine of social classes, to be incorporated into that structural-functional theory which enjoys such authority today.[17] All these instances of acceptance have, of course, taken place under the premises of a division of labor in the social sciences, premises pronounced by Schumpeter (on the occasion of his own very arbitrary incorporation of the theory of the total societal development from capitalism to socialism):

> We must now do something which is very offensive to the faithful. . . . What they resent most is when one takes Marx's work apart, into pieces, and discusses each of these in succession. They will say that this action in itself shows the incapacity of the bourgeois to comprehend the magnificent total structure, the essential parts of which are complementary and explain each other reciprocally, so that the correct meaning can no longer be recognized as soon as any one part or one aspect is considered by itself. However, for the present we have no other choice.[18]

Why Schumpeter had no other choice he does not explain; and he could only have done so by pointing to the institutionalized enterprise of science as his reason for departmentalizing Marxist doctrine into two scientific disciplines and two disciplines outside of science. He investigates the economic and the sociological elements, each by itself, and carefully disengages them from the "philosophical" framework and from the aim of exercising a political, pedagogic influence on the reader. Thereby three basic themes are from the outset excluded from rational examination: namely, the prior integration of the economic and sociological aspects, separated analytically, to form the unity of one single object, the society as totality; second, the dialectical conception of society as a historical process is also excised, a process which in the conflict of specifiable tendencies drives forward to produce one situation out of the other; and finally, a relation between theory and praxis which Marxism explicitly incorporates into reflection. For Marxism's structure, from the perspective of the philosophy of science, corresponds to that of a philosophy of history with political intentions. By the elimination of these three elements, which are constitutive for the entire Marxist approach, Marxism is reduced to "pure" science, as it was previously reduced to "pure" philosophy. When, in accord with a linguistic usage clarified by Logical Positivism, scientific statements can only be extracted from hypothetic deductive systems, or at least their derivations, which can be empirically tested, that is, can be falsified by basic statements, then Marxist doctrine, according to its own claims, cannot as a whole be subsumed under science. To be sure, it wants to subject its insight to the control of scientific statements of this type; but in order to comprehend society as a totality which has come to be historically, and to do so for the purposes of a critical genesis of political praxis, it requires, in addition—and, indeed, from the outset—the rationalization of those steps which otherwise would be left to the pragmatics of common sense or to the irrationality of its prejudices. For the rationalization of these steps cannot be accomplished by means of the calculus and the experiments of objectified science. Still, science is to remain in force as a falsifying control. Once one really takes this claim seriously, then what Schumpeter dismisses with such ironical superiority actually does become plausible: that an isolation of the "components" of Marxism, in keeping with the viewpoint of the social sciences' division of labor, only ends up with *disjecta membra,* torn out of the context of a dialectical understanding that comprehends the meaning of a theory envisaging society as a totality and related to praxis.[19]

The positivistic dissolution of the claimed unity of theory and praxis

Within the concept of society as a historical totality Marx could still hold together what later fell apart into the specific subjects of the separate social sciences. The consoling promise of a "synthesis" *post festum* cannot restore what must be lost in the gaps between the various sectors of economics, sociology, political science, and jurisprudence: the system of human social life as such. In the days of Lorenz von Stein the general political sciences [*Gesamten Staatswissenschaften*] still retained this in view—thus it is not solely the privilege of Marxism.

Certainly, on the basis of their division of labor, several of the social sciences have meanwhile made the proud advance in knowledge that enables them to draw abreast of the natural sciences. However, this progress has exacted a price which is imposed on the natural sciences to a lesser degree than on the sciences of society, especially when they themselves are no longer in any way aware of this cost. In terms of one single example we should like to demonstrate how a science, in this case modern sociology, has to constrict the range of its possible insights more severely, the more rigorous the criteria to which it subjects its specific results.

(1) Today sociology views human beings as the bearers of social roles. With the operational introduction of this category it opens up domains of social behavior to exact analysis. Insofar as role, defined as the behavioral expectation of a reference group, represents a historical magnitude, its variations during the course of the historical development of mankind must remain closed to sociological investigation. This imposes a limit even on dynamic theories, which seek to do justice to the process and conflictual character of social events. In this respect the experience which they represent is in no way historical. Only in an advanced stage of industrial society, with what Max Weber called the rationalization of social relations, has the functional interdependence of institutions grown to such an extent that the subjects, claimed for their part by an increasing and varying multiplicity of social functions, can be interpreted as the points of intersection of social obligations. It is only the multiplication, the grow-

ing independence, and the accelerated interchangeability of dissociated behavior patterns that endow the "roles" with a quasi-reified existence with respect to the persons who "externalize" themselves in these roles, and develop the demands for inwardness within this externalization, as it comes to their consciousness—as the history of bourgeois consciousness, especially during the eighteenth century, has shown. Marx was convinced that the reification of modes of conduct could be traced back to the expansion of the relations of exchange and, ultimately, to the capitalistic mode of production. Be that as it may, this much is certain in any case: the analytical fruitfulness of the category "role" is not independent of the stage of development of the society, in terms of the relations of which society must first prove itself. If, however, it is generalized to apply to social relations as such and thus becomes a universal historical category, then role analysis, with its historical dependency, must ignore social evolution as a historical process altogether—as though it were wholly external to the individuals whether they are subsumed under a few natural roles, like the medieval serfs, or whether, like the employees in an industrially advanced civilization, they are subsumed under multiple, rapidly changing, and somewhat dissociated roles. In this dimension of development, there is a growing opportunity to relate to the roles as roles. This brings about increased freedom of scope for mobility in accepting and exchanging roles as well as of a new sort or lack of freedom, insofar as one sees oneself forced to take on externally assigned roles; and perhaps the more external these roles become, the more deeply they have to be internalized.

A sociology committed to role analysis will ignore this dimension, and will therefore be forced to reduce historical development to a social modification of basic relations which remain eternally the same. The roles as such are posited as constant in their relationship to their bearers, as though the complex of social life were as external to the life of the human beings themselves, as in Kant's relation of the empirical character to the intelligible character.[20]

(2) But the price which sociology pays for the advancement of knowledge is not only a methodological blindness with respect to the historical character of society. Together with its methodo-

logical abstinence with respect to the practical consequences of its own activity, it must also accept a limitation which not only obstructs its view of its object but even of the discipline itself. This can be demonstrated by the same example. To separate rigidly the scientific construction of the role bearer from the dimension of moral decision, when confronting the real human beings (as in Kant's distinction between the phenomenal and the noumenal domains), is intended to help clarify the conflicting positions into which the sociologist gets, as scientist and politician in one person. According to the well-known resolution of the controversy about value judgment, he must strictly separate the two: on the one side, keep the answers to technical questions which he has discovered by empirical, theoretical means, in pursuing explanatory problems; and on the other side, keep those answers to ethical and political questions which he has attained by traditional or philosophical means in pursuing normative problems. Today, however, sociology, to a growing degree, is becoming an applied science in the service of administration. The technical translation of research results is not applied to analytic schemata, but instead to a social reality which has already been schematized. Therefore the isolation between the two domains remains a fiction. With a view to its sociopolitical consequences, sociology, in spite of its methodical distance from its object, still deals with actual human beings, with the living interrelationships of society.

Only when role theory is referred back to the activity of the sociologists themselves do its fundamental problematics begin to emerge: how can a mediation of the construction of phenomena, on the one hand, and of social existence, on the other, be incorporated in this reflection itself? And how can the relation of theory to praxis be dealt with adequately in theory, and if possible, incorporated into theory itself? Some have sought to do justice to this problem, on the basis of value-free method, with the postulate that the sociologist must select his problems from the viewpoint of their relevance to the freedom of the individuals:

> There can be no danger to the purity of scientific activity, if sociology prefers such verifiable theories, which take into account the right and the fullest value [*Fülle*] of the individual. Not to lose sight of the thought about the possible

application of the results, for the uses and the well-being of the free individual, when pursuing scientific activity that has society as its subject matter is completely above suspicion.[21]

However, how can these specific goals be rationally applied to concrete situations? And indeed, beyond that, are the interests which guide inquiry determining only for the selection of the problems, or do they also impinge on the selection of the fundamental categories of the system? Does not a prior understanding of intelligible character always necessarily enter into the sociological construction of empirical character, in the sense in which this Kantian distinction has been subjected to Hegel's general critique? For the latter quite correctly points out that Kant cannot wholly eradicate the substantial elements from his functional concept of truth (defined by the transcendental conditions of the possibility of knowledge), that he must also presuppose a prior correspondence of reason and nature, subject and object.[22] Of course, Marx removes the idealistic basis for the dialectical relation between the two. The self-movement of the spirit in which subject and object are interwoven, he interprets as the self-generation of man by means of social labor. Man does not have in his possession the "unity of subject and object" from the outset [*von Haus aus*], neither as spirit nor as a being of nature; only in the exchange, by labor, with nature as the reciprocal self-formative process of nature is this unity practically constituted. All possible experience is confined within the horizon of this praxis; at its root it is structured by specific interests.

Though indeed the unity of subject and object, given in interested experience, is formalized by the separation between subject and object which science brings about methodologically, it is never wholly suspended. The kinds of experience and the degree of their scientific character are distinguished only by the degree to which their links to interest can be formalized. Now the interest in acquiring control over real processes is indeed susceptible to a high degree of formalization: it is fundamental and powerfully active in all historical and social situations. And beyond that, the interest is confirmed to the degree to which it actually leads to domination, of nature, to begin with, and is thus confirmed retroactively by its successes; it is stabilized through positive feedback. Therefore this interest can become so self-evident that, once it has been fully invested in the initiative toward knowledge, it "disappears." Still, in the domain of the social sciences it must become problematic. We have no experience of what happens within nature "itself" as it comes under the control of the categorial apparatus of the sciences (physics) and the technical apparatus of the applied sciences (technology), nor do we need to, as we are not "practically" interested in the "fate" of nature as such. But we are practically interested in society. For even if we place ourselves (fictitiously) outside the social interrelationships of life in order to confront them, we still remain part of them, even in the act of insight, as subject and object in one. The interest in attaining control over society initially invested in the cognitive initiative of scientific theories interferes with the simultaneous interest in society "in itself." Therefore a prior understanding originating in interested experience always infiltrates the fundamental concepts of the theoretical system.

But if experiences dependent on the situation must necessarily also enter into the strictly scientific approach, then the interests which direct knowledge must be brought under control, they must be legitimized as objective interests, unless one wants to arbitrarily break off the process of rationalization. Whether the theory of social integration (arising out of the experience of the insecurity produced by social crises) seeks to understand the social system as a structure of a harmoniously equalized and enduring order, or whether the theory of social conflict (arising out of the experience of how deceptive the security of compulsive political integration can be) seeks to understand that same system as an association of domination [*Herrschaftsverband*] kept open and in flux by internal oppositions—no matter which approach is chosen, an anticipatory interpretation of society as a whole always enters into the selection of the fundamental categories. Significantly, this is a prior understanding of how the society is and, at the same time, of how it ought to be—for the interested experience of a situation in which one lives separates the "is" from the "ought" just as little as it dissects what it experiences into facts, on the one hand, and norms, on the other.

The dialectical interpretation comprehends the knowing

subject in terms of the relations of social praxis, in terms of its position, both within the process of social labor and the process of enlightening the political forces about their goals. According to Horkheimer, this twofold reflection distinguishes "critical theory" from "traditional theory":

> The traditional conception of theory is abstracted from the scientific enterprise, as this is carried on within the division of labor at a given level. This conception corresponds to the activity of scholars, as it is carried out side by side with all the other activities in society, without any direct insight into the connections between these separate activities being attained. In this conception, therefore, the real social function of science does not appear, thus, not what the theory means for human existence, but only what it means within the detached sphere in which it is being produced under historical conditions. . . . The professional scholar, as scientist, views social reality, with all its products, as external to him, and, as citizen, perceives his interest in this society in terms of political articles [he may write], membership in parties or benevolent organizations, and participation in elections, without connecting these two, as well as several other modes of conduct, in any way, except, at most, by psychological interpretations; while critical thinking is motivated by the actual attempt to overcome this tension, to resolve [sublate] the opposition between the consciousness of goal, the spontaneity, the rationality immanent within the individuals, and the relations to the labor process which are fundamental for society.[23]

For Marx the problem of such a "materialistic" self-consciousness on the part of critique did not arise out of the immanent difficulties of the positive sciences, but out of the consideration of the political consequences that flowed from the philosophy of his time—or rather, its lack of consequences. At that time the social sciences had by no means achieved a status in which they could have held up before dialectical theory the mirror of the inheritance salvaged from the bankruptcy of philosophy.[24] So much philosophical substance had been incorporated into the approach of economic theory of the eighteenth and the early nineteenth centuries that the critique of political economy met it on its own scientific ground and from there delivered its judgment on the false scientific claims of philosophy. The ideological self-understanding of the phenomenological experience of spirit was to be condemned by means of the critical experience of the social interrelations of life; philosophy was to be superseded *as* philosophy. Today, on the contrary, the positive sciences are at one with the philosophy of that time in the "idealistic" aspect, by which traditional theory in general is distinguished from critical theory.[25] The latter occupies its distinctive position between philosophy and positivism in such a manner that a critical self-enlightenment of positivism leads into the same dimension at which Marx arrived, so to speak, from the opposite direction.

> *Critique and crisis: mythological origins and scientific structure of an empirical philosophy of history with practical intent*

With its position "between" philosophy and positive science only a formal designation of Marxist theory has been established. Nothing has been ascertained thereby about its distinctive status from the perspective of the philosophy of science. We want to assure ourselves clearly of its structure as a philosophy of history, explicitly undertaken with political aims, and yet scientifically falsifiable without feeling any embarrassment at exploiting the advantage of those born later: of understanding Marx better than he understood himself.

Marx gave his theory the name of critique—an inconspicuous name, if one comprehends the critique of political economy as the completion of that undertaking which began with the philological criticism of the Humanists, continued in aesthetic literary criticism, and which finally learned to understand itself *as* critique in the theoretical and practical critique of the philosophers. At that time critique became practically synonymous with reason, defining good taste and penetrating judgment. It was the medium for ascertaining the right, insofar as it corresponded to the just in accord with the laws of nature—just as it was the energy, which restlessly drives argument forward, and finally turns it against itself. The participants in this great enterprise were called "Les Philosophes," and Kant proudly called himself a philosopher, even in the practical pedagogic sense of a "free teacher of the Law" [*freie Rechtslehrer*]. In the face of this it appears strange that Marx no longer calls his critique philosophy, but rather, its supersession. In the nineteenth century, even as early as certain allusions in Rousseau, critique again begins to relate explicitly to crisis, both words deriving from the same root, and not only etymologically.[26]

(1) In Greek usage the critical judgment referred to the crisis, as the dispute over right which presses on to a decision; critique itself was an element within the objective context of the crisis. In Latin the word is limited to medical usage. The Gospel of St. John finally transfers crisis to the process of salvation, the separation of good from evil. The critical decision, which condemns or frees from guilt, is thus raised into the dimension of damnation and salvation, a theological anticipation of the categories which the eighteenth century then learned to apply in developing the philosophy of history. When, at this time, critique altogether takes on a scientific form, it emancipates itself not only from domains of application in the pragmatic disciplines, such as jurisprudence and medicine, but also from the objective crisis context which is still retained in the story of salvation—critique becomes a subjective faculty. And in that discipline which undertakes to subject the world-historical development of mankind to critique, in the philosophy of history, critique no longer understands itself in its correspondence to crisis. The process of civilization is not recognized as a self-critical process, but at best as progress toward critique.

The material of world-history, regarded at the outset from the perspective of nascent bourgeois society, seemed to offer so little resistance to the goal of emancipation from the "naturally" developed feudal relations that critique deemed it sufficient to dissolve theoretically what in practice had long been in dissolution: the separation of the new from the old, of bourgeois freedom from the bonds of feudal hierarchy, of the capitalistic mode of production from the feudal relations of production. All this was borne forward by such powerful motive forces at that time that this process no longer had to be comprehended as a crisis. A critical decision with respect to uncertain or even ambiguous consequences did not seem to be required. Condorcet and his contemporaries understood history as linear progress and were able to understand it thus, and not as the separation of ambivalent forces. The first shock, which was registered by Voltaire, Lessing, and Goethe, was sustained by this consciousness as the result of the Lisbon earthquake, a natural event. But when such natural events first erupted from the soil of society itself, when the birth pains of industrial capitalism pushed the Lisbon earthquake back into forgetfulness—that is, with the economic crises of the nineteenth century—then subjective critique was confronted by crisis as an objective complex, now, to be sure, emerging from history. The eschatological consciousness of crisis attained a historical consciousness of itself.

Now, critique is set in motion by the practical interest in deciding the process of crisis toward a favorable issue, the good. Thus it cannot find its theoretical foundation within itself. Indeed, because the crisis complex, universalized to become the world as crisis, leaves no transmundane locus on which pure knowledge can take its stand outside of itself, because man as judge is involved in this crisis as litigation to the same degree that man as physician is afflicted by it as disease, critique becomes conscious of its own peculiar involvement in the object of its criticism. The objective complex of relations, which critique, although also encompassed within it, reflects as a totality and, which, just by means of this, it wants to drive to the conclusion of the crisis, is obdurate. Consequently all efforts are equally condemned to remain without consequences, if they do not go beyond critique and intervene in the crisis, employing the means of the crisis itself, namely, practically: *nemo contra Deum nisi Deus ipsi*. Because the crisis, become world-historical, overpowers every merely subjective critique, the decision is shifted over into praxis, so that only by the success of this praxis can the critique itself become valid.

(2) In certain traditions, above all in Jewish and Protestant

mysticism (as represented by Isaak Luria and Jakob Böhme), the weight of the radicalized problem of the theodicy pressed on toward a Gnostically inspired version of the story of salvation, namely, to that remarkable conception of theogony and cosmogony, according to which the God of Origin, a quite candid and playful God, becomes external to Himself, not by stepping outside, by manifesting, externalizing Himself and become externalized, but rather by going into exile within Himself, by encapsulating Himself egotistically, so to speak, emigrating into the darkness of His own bottomless foundations [*grundlosen Grundes*], and, in the highest intensification of Himself, becoming His Other: nature, understood as nature within God. By this involvement within Himself, an original self-dethronement, God surrenders and loses control over Himself to such an extent that at the end of his painful creature-like process of restitution, Adam can thrust Him from His throne a second time. Therefore, under this mythical repetition compulsion, man, left to himself alone in history to confront the work of his redemption, must simultaneously carry out the redemption of nature with his own powers, and even the redemption of the overthrown God, a Christ in the Promethean role of Lucifer. In him, God, while still God, has ceased to be divine in the strict sense. He has surrendered Himself completely to the risks of an irretrievable catastrophe; it is only at this cost that He has initiated the world process as history.[27]

We let this sophisticated myth stand without further comment; we have only mentioned it because from the dialectical metaphor of divine self-abasement Hegel has extracted a metaphysical calculus, with the aid of which he can compute [*durchkalkulieren*] the whole of world-history as a crisis complex. At every stage of development, the evil, contrary, destructive element unfolds its distinctive obstinacy, toughness, and power—the negative; indeed negation itself attains such positivity as only God within the anti-Godly can bring about. The outcome of the crisis is then put seriously into question anew in every phase, if the forces which become divided are of equally primal origin, are of equal rank as they wrestle with each other, are, in Schelling's word, "equipollent." God's unreserved surrender to history renders the crisis complex perfect as a totality. Yet a transcendence within the immanence still is preserved, because, after all, the lost God once was God; thus, with this extinguished past, God is prior to the residue submerged in the historical present. In the crisis He is prior to the crisis; He is the one who, at first returning to Himself as stranger, still recovers Himself and recognizes Himself. Thus Hegel rationalizes the mythic schema into the dialectical logic of world-history as crisis; indeed, its supple course is the course of the supple dialectic itself. But still in the end the God, liberated by man in the absolute spirit, to be restored to Himself [*zu sich selbst befreit*], still knows that He anticipated everything from the beginning, and even *in* history still retained His mastery *over* history. With the science of logic philosophy therefore spoils the point it plagiarized from the myth, of an atheistic God who dies to become history and therefore truly exposes Himself to the risk of a birth brought about by man historically, which therefore cannot be merely a *re*birth.

In its dialectic this philosophy of the world as crisis has still retained much of the myth's contemplative substance: For it does not comprehend itself as subject to the crisis and delivered up to it; rather, philosophy understands itself as the resolution of the crisis. The philosophic God, who, in spite of all appearances, did not surrender Himself entirely to history, is restored to Himself in the philosophic reflection of absolute spirit, which, unaffected by the crisis and superior to it, therefore also does not have to comprehend itself as critique, nor as the judgment in a life-and-death struggle—nor as the advocate of life, who has as yet to be confirmed by life itself. Instead, philosophy forms itself into its own totality; it is not critique but synthesis.

It is precisely of this that Marx finds the Hegelian system to be guilty, as early as in his dissertation, when he says that "philosophy has closed itself off to form a complete and total world." It is confronted by the unresolved character of a world torn apart, as another totality, and as the existent counterevidence to its pretended resolution—a relation in which

the system is degraded to an abstract totality. . . . Inspired by the urge to actualize itself, it comes into tension

against the other. . . . Thus the consequence results that
the becoming philosophical of the world at the same time
is a becoming worldly of philosophy, that its actualization
is at the same time its loss.[28]

And yet such a critique still presupposes the logic of this
philosophy, namely Hegel's dialectic. As is well known, Lenin
recommended reading the *Logic* as an aid to the study of *Capital*.
The presupposition of Hegelian logic in Marxism is a widely
pursued topic of the more recent critique of Marxism. Actually,
Marx takes as his systematic point of departure the categories of
the objective spirit; he premises the idea of morality, as the concept of society as a whole, in such a way that the realization of
society must be measured by it, and thus recognized as the immoral condition of a world torn asunder. As far as objective
spirit is concerned, Marxist sociology shows that, as a deceptive
mirror image of anticipated reconciliation, it can only be arrived at
from the existing contradictions of established society through
determinate negation, but as no more than a determinate negation
of that society. Only if the dialectic is presupposed as a dialectic
of the social conditions themselves can these be recognized. What
"allows" Marx to do this? How can he justify this basic presupposition without this entailing a secret adoption of the idealistic
premises he has explicitly rejected? The initial interest in the
resolution of the crisis, by which critical knowledge allows itself
to be guided, is only a form of "subjective spirit" to begin with.
The urgency evoked by experience of an evil and the passionate
urge to counteract it, Hegel calls a "practical feeling" for the
"inappropriateness of being to ought." [29] Marx must therefore
show his practical interest to be an objective one—that his critical
impulses are rooted in the objective tendencies of the crises themselves. And because these are manifested in economic crises, Marx
attempts to furnish this proof by way of an analysis of social labor,
precisely that labor which is alienated under the conditions of
private ownership of the means of production during the first
phase of industrialization. In our context, it is important above
all that he began to undertake this analysis without the presuppositions of Hegelian logic. It was only while he was carrying

out this task, that he discovered in the relationship of wage labor and capital the distinctive domination of dead labor over living labor, which can be deciphered materialistically as the "rational core" of the idealistic dialectic. Marx sets down this insight in a sentence in the *Paris Manuscripts* which has since become famous: what is great in the *Phenomenology of Mind*

> is that Hegel comprehends the self-generation of man as a process, the objectivization as the generation of a confronting object [*Entgegenständlichung*], as alienation [*Entäusserung*] and the resolution [sublation] of this alienation; that he thus comprehends the essence of labor and objective man, understands true, actual man as the result of his own labor.

Marx seeks out the fundamental basis of that motif of the God who debases Himself and confines Himself within Himself, the theme which has already been divested of its mythological form in Hegel's dialectic, but still remains obscured by the idealistic self-understanding of philosophy: through the multiple effort to preserve their life by the labor of their own hands, men make themselves the authors of their own historical development, without however recognizing themselves as the subjects of that development. The experience of alienated labor is the materialistic verification of the dialectical experience: in relating to what befalls them men are confronting the sediment of their own history; in the forces which gather over their heads they encounter only their own powers and in the appropriation of objects only take back the objectification of their own essential capacities [*Wesenskräfte*]. But if the domain of social labor can be interpreted thus as the experiential basis of the dialectics of history, then one of the guarantees still contained in the idealistic version is dropped, that at every stage mankind will ultimately recognize itself rationally in that which confronts it—and will actually resolve [that is, sublate] alienation. Thus it remains uncertain whether mere critical insight into the dialectic of alienated labor will arise out of the objective crisis complex, or whether this insight will also attain practical efficacy. The point of the myth of an atheistic God, which Hegel's idealistic dialectic had spoiled, is restored as justified by making atheism true and by recognizing that mankind whose intimation of its own power over history always slipped away from it had encoded this intimation in the image of God. For a God who in truth has become historical not only cannot be a God any longer, but can never in seriousness have been one. Mankind is left alone to itself and with its work of salvation, and so long as it has not freed itself from its state of dependency [*Unmündigkeit*] it must represent as salvation what, after all, it can only rationally bring about by itself, by way of its self-generation. Only against this background can the effect, so difficult to reconstruct today, of Feuerbach's not particularly profound critique of religion on Marx and Engels, be understood.[30]

(3) Marx comprehends the crisis complex materialistically in terms of the dialectics of social labor. The categories of the latter were developed in the Political Economy of his time, but not recognized in their completely historical character. Therefore Marx's investigation of the capitalist system takes the form of a critique of Political Economy. With this unpretentious title, the "critique," to begin with, claims that term's meaning of a critical examination of the extant literature; but beyond this it also claims the associated meaning of a theory developed with the practical intention of overcoming the crisis. Thus the critique of Political Economy is a theory of crisis in the genuine sense. The analysis of alienated labor has the propaedeutic character of an introduction to the materialistic dialectic; the critique itself then can be conducted from the viewpoint of this dialectic: it demonstrates to human beings who make their history without explicitly knowing this, that the superior power of "natural"—fortuitously or spontaneously arising—conditions is actually the work of their own hands. Marx begins with the proof of the fetishistic character of commodities:

> Thus the mystery of the commodity form is simply this, that it mirrors for men the social character of their own labor, mirrors it as an objective character attaching to the labor products themselves, mirrors it as the social natural

property of these things. Consequently the social relation of the producers to the sum total of their own labor, presents itself to them as a social relation, not between themselves, but between the products of their labor. Thanks to this transference of qualities, the labor products become commodities, sensuously transcendental or social things. . . . Inasmuch as the producers do not come into social contact until they exchange their labor products, the specifically social character of their individual labor does not manifest itself until exchange takes place. [In other words, the labor of individuals becomes an effective part of the aggregate of social labor solely in virtue of the relation which the process of exchange establishes between the labor products and consequently between the producers.] That is why the social relations connecting the labor of one private individual (or group) with the labor of another, seem to the producers, not direct social relations between individuals, but what they really are: material relations between persons and social relations between things.[31]

But it is not only those who participate directly in the process of production and distribution to whom the social relations appear, with objective irony, as that which they are, but actually are not; even the science which makes these relations its object of investigation falls victim to the semblance which reality itself produces:

Man's thought about the forms of social life, his scientific analysis of these forms, runs counter to the actual course of social evolution. He begins with an examination of the finished product, the extant result of the evolutionary process. The characters which stamp labor products as commodities, the characters which they must possess before they can circulate as commodities, have already acquired the fixity of the natural forms of social life, when economists begin to study, not indeed their history (for they are regarded as immutable), but their meaning." [32]

It is for this reason that Marx can carry out his critique of the objective complex of crisis in the form of a critique of Political Economy.

Of course, the commodity form can only be generalized to embrace all possible products of labor once labor itself has assumed the form of a commodity, once the mode of production has become capitalistic. Only with the appearance of the free wage laborer, who sells his labor power as his sole commodity, has the historical condition been established under which the labor process confronts man in its independence, as a process of exploitation [*Verwertungsprozess*], in such a manner that the production of use values seems to disappear entirely within a kind of self-movement, an automatism, of capital. The critique of this objective semblance—as the theoretical presupposition for the practical appropriation of man's essential powers, which have been capitalistically alienated—identifies wage labor as the source of surplus value.

The theory of surplus value takes its departure from a simple consideration. If the transformation of money into capital is to be possible under the conditions of the exchange of equivalents, then the owner of the money must be able to buy commodities at their true value and sell them at their true value, and still be able to extract more value at the end of the process than he put into it at the beginning. Therefore there must be a specific commodity which is exchanged at its true value, like all the others, but the use value of which is of such a nature that from the utilization of this commodity value is produced: "But if value is to be derived from the consumption of a commodity, our possessor of money must be lucky enough to find somewhere within the sphere of circulation, on the market, a commodity whose use-value has the peculiar quality of being a source of value; a commodity whose actual consumption is the process whereby labor is embodied [*Vergegenständlichung*], and whereby therefore value is created. Our friend does actually find in the market such a specific commodity. He finds it in the capacity for labor, or labor power." [33] The value of labor power is measured by the socially necessary labor time which the production of the means for its subsistence requires; for its part, the labor power purchased by the capitalist is put to work for a longer time than the labor time that would be required for its reproduction. This surplus labor is considered to be the source of surplus value.

The analysis of this relationship does not, as the term "exploitation" might suggest, have the character of a moral judgment. (The behavior of capitalists is not in any way to be attributed to individual persons, but is objectively determined by their position in the process of production.) Instead, Marx is critically interested in the opposition of wage labor and capital, with a view to a practical resolution of the crisis complex that presents itself to him, because in this opposition he believes to have discovered the origin of that dialectic of self-concealment which prevents human beings from recognizing themselves as the subjects of their history, which they are after all, and from securing their rightful place.

Marx asserts now that the crises of the capitalist system arise necessarily from the process of utilization [investment] of capital, thus from that fundamental relationship which is established with the appropriation of surplus value. This thesis presupposes another one, namely, that the basis of the world as a crisis complex is exclusively the economy, that is, it is inextricably involved in these economic crises and is resolvable together with them. This first thesis is developed in the Political Economy into the theory of crises, the other in Historical Materialism into the doctrine of ideology.

Establishing the economic basis of the world as a crisis complex

(1) The crises within the capitalist system devalue existing capital, in order thereby to set the process of the investment of capital as a whole into accelerated motion again; investment periodically comes to a standstill, whether due directly to a fall in the rate of profit or indirectly to the decrease of profitable opportunities for capital investment. This process will always fall back into the same contradictions, of which every crisis promises to cure it, for:

The *real barrier* to capitalist production is *capital itself*. It is that capital and its self-expansion [*Selbstverwertung*] appear as the starting point and the closing point, the motive and the purpose of production; that production is only production for *capital* and not vice versa, the means of production are not mere means for a constant expansion of the living process of the *society* of producers. The limits within which the preservation and self-expansion of the value of capital resting on the expropriation and pauperization of the great mass of producers can alone move—these limits come continually into conflict with the methods of production employed by capital for its purposes, which drive towards unlimited extension of production, towards production as an end in itself, towards unconditional development of the social productivity of labor. The means—unconditional development of the productive forces of society—comes continually into conflict with the limited purpose, the self-expansion of the existing capital. The capitalist mode of production is, for this reason, a historical means of developing the material forces of production and creating an appropriate world-market and is, at the same time, a continual conflict between this its historical task and its own corresponding relations of social production.[34]

The contradiction presses toward two typical forms of crisis. The one is directly linked to the fall in the rate of profit and is initiated by a situation in which a heightened rate of accumulation inflates the volume of employment and drives up the level of wages. The limitation of the opportunities to maximize profit within the usual volume interrupts the process of accumulation until the mechanism of the so-called industrial reserve army again intervenes and pushes down wages to the value of labor power, or even below this value.

There is, however, a way out for the capitalists which permits them to exhaust the reservoir of the labor force only to such an extent—in spite of the rising rate of accumulation—that the "natural" rate of surplus value is no longer endangered. They introduce labor-saving machines, in order to preserve the pressure which the industrial reserve army exerts on the active work force, by means of a technologically conditioned layoff of labor power. For this reason the accumulation of capital is accompanied by a progressive mechanization of the production process. Of course, this leads, as Marx believed he had shown in his most famous and controversial "law," the law of the tendential fall of the rate of profit, to a renewed cause of precisely the sort of crisis which it was intended to prevent.[35] To the degree that the process of production is mechanized, the proportion of variable capital decreases in relation to constant capital; thus the organic composition of the total capital rises, so that the rate of profit sinks:

> Since the mass of employed living labor is continually on the decline as compared to the mass of materialized labor set in motion by it, i.e., to the productively consumed means of production, it follows that the portion of living labor, unpaid and congealed in surplus value, must also be continually on the decrease compared to the amount of value represented by the invested total capital. Since the ratio of the mass of surplus value to the value of the invested total capital forms the rate of profit, this rate must constantly fall.[36]

In connection with the derivation of this law Marx analyzes a number of factors that affect the rate of profit in the opposite direction, and that if they do not arrest its fall, at least inhibit it.

The controversy around this law has continued for generations, and within Marxism too (L. von Bortkiewicz, Natalie Moszkowska, Paul M. Sweezy). A serious objection is directed against the alleged fact that Marx conceives this law under the presupposition of a constant rate of surplus value and only subsequently introduces an isolated connection between the rising productivity of labor and the rising rate of surplus value, as one of the counteracting causes. Roman Rosdolsky has been able to deprive this objection of its force, for the time being, by pointing to a number of passages in the text.[37] Marx always takes into account the functional interconnection of the rising productivity of labor with *both* factors, the falling rate of profit (as consequence of the changing composition of capital) as well as the rising rate of surplus value (as consequence of the cheapening of goods received in compensation, in general a retroactive devaluation of variable capital). In response to this the critics can emphasize all the more that from such an interrelationship no historical prognosis of the fall of the rate of profit can be derived:

> The law of the tendential fall of the rate of profit is not a historical, but instead a dynamical law, which solely formulates the dependency between two magnitudes, namely: when the rate of surplus value remains the same, the rate of profit falls; when the rate of profit remains the same, the rate of surplus value rises.[38]

Marx certainly sought to prove that the factor which lowers the rate of profit asserts itself more powerfully than the factors counteracting it; but (with the exception of one single consideration, to which we will return below) his arguments do not go so far as to incorporate the predominance of the tendential fall in the rate of profit over the tendential rise in the rate of surplus value into the formulation of the law itself.[39]

The controversy over the law of the tendential fall in the rate of profit is most instructive, because it leads directly into the value-theoretical range of problems of the productivity of labor. Marx takes into consideration the introduction of labor-saving machines from the viewpoint of a saving in variable capital relative to the stored-up portion of constant capital. But by subsuming the introduction of machinery under the expression of the value of constant capital, he neglects the specific aspect of such an introduction, which is exhibited in the remarkable phenomenon accompanying this: a rising rate of surplus value. With mechanization the organic composition of capital changes not only quantitatively, but qualitatively, that is in the specific mode that enables capitalists to retain a greater portion of surplus labor from the given quantity of labor power (now applied to machines or to better machines). To be sure, the formulation of the law certainly permits a change in the magnitudes, the relation of which is designated by the rate of surplus value; but it excludes the necessary relation which holds between this kind of constant capital and the rate of surplus value; it does not include this as a lawlike relation. Usually a rise in the productivity of labor is associated with a growing organic composition of capital; however, every corresponding change in the expression of value is not, inversely, accompanied by a rise in productivity; constant capital does not have imprinted on its forehead whether it covers the value of labor-saving machines or other costs. It is not sufficient simply to throw in labor-saving machines with the other items of constant capital without any further characterization. Joan Robinson observes "that periods of falling profits may occur, when capital per man increases very rapidly relatively to the rate of advance in technical knowledge." [40] Thus, the law of the tendential fall in the rate of profit could only take into account specifically the introduction of labor-saving machines if the expression of value for stored-up constant capital explicitly incorporated the advance in technical knowledge contained in it. Then, of course, one could no longer ignore in the theory of value that type of labor which, although not productive itself, is applied in order to increase the level of productivity of labor.

In the *Grundrisse* for the *Critique of Political Economy* a very interesting consideration is to be found, from which it appears that Marx himself once viewed the scientific development of the technical forces of production as a possible source of value. For here Marx limits the presupposition of the labor theory of value, that the "quantum of applied labor is the decisive factor in the production of wealth," by the following:

> But as heavy industry [*die grosse Industrie* = large-scale industry] develops the creation of real wealth depends less on labor time and on the quantity of labor utilized than on the power of mechanized agents which are set in motion during the labor time. The powerful effectiveness of these agents, in its turn, bears no relation to the immediate labor time that their labor cost. It depends rather on the general state of science and on technological progress, or the application of this science to production.[41]

Marx, of course, finally dropped this "revisionist" notion: it was not incorporated in his final formulation of the labor theory of value.[42]

As the term "degree of exploitation of labor" itself shows, Marx, in considering the historical changes in the rate of surplus value, first thinks of that physical exploitation which presses an ever increasing portion of surplus labor from the available labor force, with the kind of labor remaining the same: speedup of the work and lengthening of the labor time. Naturally, he then also takes other methods into consideration: the intensification of the productivity of labor by means of a rationalization of how the work is organized, and mechanization of the process of production. But even these appropriations of surplus labor he still conceives according to the crude model of such exploitation: here, just as there, the rate of surplus value is considered to be a magnitude on which the computation of value must be based as on a datum of natural history. As little as, say, the physical compulsion under which the pace of labor may once have been accelerated finds expression in the law of value other than as a rise in the rate of surplus value which cannot be derived further economically, so just as little does that labor which develops the methods for the rationalization of labor find an adequate value expression. The value expression of total capital changes only when the methods applied require capital—as, to be sure, is the case with a progressive mechanization of production.

(2) The specific influence which the labor of preparation and development has on the process of formation of value slips through between the categories of Marx's labor theory of value. This indifference of the value-theoretical instrument with respect to the increase of productivity is an inadequacy. There are plausible reasons, indeed, which make it important also to incorporate an index of this increment itself into the expression of value of the product, especially of the gross national product. An important empirical question arises especially in relation to the law of the tendential fall in the rate of profit. Marx did give at least *one* sound argument claiming that in the course of the mechanization of production and a corresponding increase in the productivity of labor the tendency of the falling rate of profit would, in the

long run, still prevail over the tendency of a rising rate of surplus
value. It is stated as follows:

> The value can never be equal to the entire workday; that
> means, a certain part of the workday must always be ex-
> changed for the labor embodied in the worker. Altogether
> the surplus value is only the ratio of the living labor to that
> embodied in the worker; the one member of the relationship
> must therefore always remain. Because the ratio is constant
> as a ratio, although its factors change, a definite relation be-
> tween the increase in the forces of production and the in-
> crease in value is given . . . the greater the surplus value
> of capital before the increase in the power of production
> . . . or the smaller the fraction of the working day which
> forms the equivalent of the worker already is, the smaller
> the increment in the surplus value which capital receives
> back from the increase in the power of production. Thus
> the more developed capital is already . . . the more fruit-
> fully must it develop the productive power, in order to ex-
> pand itself at merely a small rate, that means, in order to
> add to the surplus value—because its barrier always remains
> that ratio between that fraction of the day which expresses
> the necessary labor and the entire workday.[43]

But if we do assume that this argument is sound, then the
law, which is supposed to support it, is inadequate to explain the
fact that in advanced capitalist countries the rate of profit has
shown no unambiguous tendency toward long-range change during the last eighty years, in spite of the rising level of wages.
Under the classical presuppositions of the labor theory of value,
the actual growth of value obviously cannot be satisfactorily explained. Therefore empirical grounds also suggest that we consider whether the work incorporated in rationalization must not
be understood and evaluated as second-order productive labor—
as an additional source of the formation of value, though not an
independent one, because it depends on productive labor of the
first order. On the other hand, this work is not productive in
the sense of the direct production of goods; still, it changes the

preconditions for production in such a way that not only more surplus value results, but also more exchange value altogether. Then, the conditions of equilibrium of the law of value would only be valid for a given level of the technological forces of production.

As his unorthodox reflections in the *Grundrisse* show, Marx even interpreted the conditions of thoroughly automated production in such a way that the production of value would be transferred from directly productive labor to science and technology:

> Labor does not seem any more to be an essential part of the process of production. The human factor is restricted to watching and supervising the production process. . . . He [the worker] is no longer the principal agent of the production process: he exists alongside it. In this transformation, what appears as the mainstay of production and wealth is neither the immediate labor performed by the worker nor the time that he works—but the appropriation by man of his own general productive force, his understanding of nature . . . which appears as the great foundation of production and wealth. . . . As soon as labor as labor, in its direct form, has ceased to be the main source of wealth, then labor time ceases, and must cease to be its standard of measurement.[44]

What Marx exemplifies here in terms of an advanced stage of technical development must of course also be taken into consideration for every stage: "the understanding of nature and the mastery of it" gain weight as a further "factor in the production of wealth" to the degree to which they increase the productivity of direct labor technically. The law of value in its classical form would then be valid only for a given level of the technical forces of production. Also to comprehend the development and growth of these forces would require supplementing the functional relationship between the rate of surplus value and the rate of profit by including an expression of value which varies according to the degree of productivity of labor.[45]

With the introduction of a corresponding corrective factor

the rate of surplus value would not cease to be a prior given as a "natural magnitude"; and the value of labor power, too, could be recognized and taken into consideration in its historical character. Marx certainly noted that the cost of reproducing labor power depends on the cultural standard of life, which is given only "for a specific country at a specific period":

> . . . The amount of the means of subsistence must be sufficient to maintain the working individual as a working individual in his normal state of life. But the natural wants, such as food, clothing, shelter, fuel, etc., differ from country to country in accordance with variations in climatic and other natural conditions. On the other hand, the comprehensiveness of what are called "needs," and the method of their satisfaction, are likewise historical products, depending in large measure upon the stage of civilization a country has reached; and depending, moreover, to a very considerable extent, upon what conditions, and therefore with what habits and claims, the class of free workers has come into existence. Thus the value of labor power includes, in contradistinction to the value of other commodities, a historical and a moral factor. Still, for any specific country, in any specific epoch, the average comprehensiveness of the necessities of life may be regarded as a fixed quantity.[46]

Marx, however, did not systematically take into consideration that capitalism itself could revolutionize the "historical and moral element" that enters into determining the value of labor power; that in the course of the accumulation of capital, together with the total level of culture, the "extent of so-called necessary needs," "the customary requirements of life" would also be expanded and basically changed. Meanwhile capital has reproduced itself at a vertiginously high level of escalation and has yielded a continually multiplying mass of use values, for the class of wage laborers, too. Therefore it would be ridiculous still to measure the value of labor power in accordance with the standard of living enjoyed by English workers around the middle of the previous century; to be sure, it would be no less ridiculous to measure it by the average cultural standard in the advanced capitalist countries, without introducing the dimension of the "historical and moral element" explicitly into the method of determining the value of labor power. But that is again only possible when the rise of productivity as such is incorporated into the computation of value.[47]

(3) But it is not only for that type of crisis which is directly related to the fall in the rate of profit, but also for the theory of crises of realization, that a revision of the foundations furnished by the labor theory of value would have the most far-reaching consequences. Marx himself presents the following determinations:

> As soon as all the surplus-labor it was possible to squeeze out has been embodied in the commodities, surplus-value has been produced. But this production of surplus-value completes but the first act of the capitalist process of production—the direct production process. Capital has absorbed so and so much unpaid labor. With the development of the process, which expresses itself in a drop in the rate of profit, the mass of surplus-value thus produced swells to immense proportions. Now comes the second act of the process. The entire mass of commodities, i.e., the total product, including the portion which replaces the constant and variable capital, and that representing surplus-value, must be sold. If this is not done, or done only in part, or only at prices below the price of production, the laborer has been indeed exploited, but his exploitation is not realized as such for the capitalist. . . . The conditions of direct exploitation, and those of realizing it, are not identical. They diverge not only in time and place, but also logically [*begrifflich*]. The first are only limited by the productive power of society, the latter by the proportional relation of the various branches of production and the consumer power of society. But this last-named is not determined either by the absolute productive power, or by the absolute consumer power, but by the consumer power based on the antagonistic conditions of distribution, which reduce the consumption of the bulk of society to a minimum

varying within more or less narrow limits. It is furthermore restricted by the tendency to accumulate, the drive to expand capital and produce surplus-value on an extended scale. This is law for capitalist production, imposed by incessant revolutions in the methods of production themselves, by the depreciation of existing capital always bound up with them, by the general competitive struggle and the need to improve production and expand its scale merely as a means of self-preservation and under penalty of ruin.[48]

If, on the contrary, one proceeds from the assumption that value arises from an increase in productivity per se, then it can be shown that within an expanding capitalist system the surplus value nourished by a twofold source can, under certain conditions, be sufficient to assure an appropriate rate of profit *and,* at the same time, a rising level of real wages. Certainly, at all times the system produces of itself the tendency to restrict, on the basis of antagonistic relations of production, the power of consumption available to the great mass of the population; but a political regulation of the relation of distribution would not be irreconcilable, under the presuppositions of a revised labor theory of value, with the conditions of a production oriented toward the maximization of profits. The possibility and the success of a conscious policy of crisis management then depend on whether the forces pressing toward a democratization of society succeed in penetrating the total complex of production, insofar as it "exercises its compulsion, as blind law, on the agents of production," and to subject it, "as a law comprehended by the joint [*assoziiert*] understanding and thus a law that is mastered . . . to their collective [*gemeinsamen*] control." [49] The "democratic factor" itself would thus be introduced into the critique of political economy.

John Strachey, especially, analyzes the economic consequences of democracy, continually neglected by Marxists:

There is no mystery about what caused the standard of life of the wage earners in Britain to rise roughly in step with the national income. Many other factors, such as the rise of productivity, have been a necessary condition; nevertheless the operative factor, without which the rise would not in fact have taken place, has been the growing power of the people. And by "the people" I mean that 90% of the British population who have usually received (as we have seen) about half the national income. It is this which has prevented the innate tendencies of the capitalist system from working themselves out in the ever-increasing misery of the wage earners. . . .

We reach the paradoxical conclusion that it has been, precisely, the struggle of the democratic forces *against* capitalism which has saved the system. It has done so not only by making tolerable the conditions of life of the wage earners, but also by keeping open that indispensable market for the final product which the self-destructive drive of capitalism to a more and more inequitable distribution of the national income would otherwise have closed. Thus democracy has had far-reaching economic consequences. It has determined, within limits sufficiently wide to be profoundly significant, the actual distribution of goods and services between persons and classes of persons. It has gone far to determine, in plain English, who shall be rich and who shall be poor, and how rich and how poor they shall be.[50]

Strachey is of the opinion that with the tools for crisis management developed by Keynes the tendencies which Marx diagnosed correctly can be controlled operatively and the antagonisms within the system can thus be resolved. From this perspective the class conflict loses its revolutionary guise, a progressive democratization of society is not excluded from the outset, even within the economic order of capitalism. This is a version of democratic socialism, which, to be sure, has learned and also retained enough from Marx not to lose sight, for the sake of developing and securing a constitutional welfare state, of those refractory tendencies which recurrently arise in the process of capital investment and which represent an increasing danger for the young and vulnerable form of government which the mass democracy of the welfare state represents.[51]

(4) If indeed the development of the forces of production has reached a level on which the mass of the use values produced is not only capable of satisfying "necessary" as well as "superfluous" needs, but, within the scope of an ever expanded purchasing power, actually does satisfy them, then a continuation of the process of accumulation would only be necessary as required by the growth of population and scientific technological progress; in general and on the whole, accumulation could then be halted and the spiral of expanding reproduction could be directed back into the cycle of simple reproduction.

This situation would provide the objective possibility of emancipation, which would grant to individuals the affluence of a life relieved to a large degree of the burdens of labor as well as of manipulated consumption. As long as the self-expansion of capital determines the outcome and the ends of production, as long as production is for the sake, not of use values, but primarily exchange values, thus not for the wealth that is to satisfy the needs of society but, on the contrary, for a wealth whose needs society must satisfy, the process of labor will remain subjected to the process of capital investment. A self-conscious decision on the part of the associated producers to limit accumulation will not be possible under such circumstances. Marx saw the limits of the capitalistic mode of production

> in that the expansion or contraction of production is determined by the appropriation of unpaid labor and the proportion of this unpaid labor to materialized labor in general, or, to speak the language of the capitalists, by profit and the proportion of this profit to the employed capital, thus by a definite rate of profit, rather than the relation of production to social requirements, i.e., to the requirements of socially developed human beings.[52]

A democratization of society which would seek to come to grips with this contradiction, instead of allowing itself to become entangled in the false consciousness of an evil infinity of material progress, would ultimately not be able to avoid creating the conditions under which the decisions to make investments and the decisions to refrain from investments could be divorced from the motive of maximizing profits.

To be sure, there are also indications that for wholly different reasons the economic motives for accumulation are to an ever greater extent becoming embedded in political motives. Certainly the subjective motive forces are still primarily reinforced by interests in the maximizing of profits; to this extent the economic motives are not simply replaced by political ones. But they are "superseded" in the sense that into such subjective motives enter in also those social motive forces which arise primarily from the interest in strengthening the national position with respect to competition among the world powers. And the process of accumulation can indeed be switched over from economic to political mechanisms to the degree to which, in any case, state intervention is forced to regulate and stabilize the total economic cycle.

Under these conditions, the dependence of political actions on economic interests, as this is presupposed by Marxism, becomes problematic. Thus, too, the weakness of the theory of imperialism, especially its contemporary application to the export of capital to developing countries, is connected with a blind spot. For it is a fact that due to the increasing self-mediation of organized capitalism by means of political intervention and conventions, the structure of economic compulsion can no longer be construed as a closed system. It appears instead that precisely for the preservation of the system on the basis of the private ownership of the means of production—no matter how this may be modified—political instrumentalities have to be erected which attain a certain independence from the economic interests of the proprietors of capital.[53]

Critique of ideology and the critical appropriation of traditional ideas

To use the words of Schelling, here taking up links to the mystical traditions, the distorted world and a humanity that is concealed from itself [*verstellt*] manifest their curse and their flaw in the peculiar domination of the external over the internal, of the lower over the higher, of anger over love, of the force of the dark sediments over purity and clarity [*Lauterkeit*]. On this same experience is based the prejudgment of Historical Materialism, which grants priority to the base over the superstructure. The barbaric power with which the economic conditions, in a certain manner, hold a determinate sway over all that is more sublime, is of course not accepted by this materialism triumphantly as the sign of the ontological structure of the world for all time, say, in the sense of Nicolai Hartmann's ontology, according to which the categories of the lower levels of Being hold in dependency the higher ones, even where the former are reshaped by the latter. Instead, this power of the material is considered to be the sign of a governance of nature over society that still reigns even within society emancipating itself from natural forces; this governance is historical and therefore to be overthrown in the course of history. This natural condition, generated out of itself, subjects the system of social life to the yoke of the process of reproduction in its naked economic form. Just as that God, in a mythical act of unfathomable egoism, alienated Himself from His essence by withdrawing within Himself, so the "egoistic" relationship which is established together with private property is interpreted by Marx as the "encapsulation" within which the essential human forces are concentrated and estranged from the human beings themselves. Private property is considered to be the dark focal point at which the eclipsing of the world is concentrated, the knots in which all the threads of compulsive social relationships are drawn together and fastened. Certainly images can only have a scientific bearing insofar as concepts can be developed out of them; but their coloration preserves the wealth of meaning for the conceptual distinctions. It is not otherwise with the concept of ideology: of course interests as well as ideas are but dialectical moments of the same totality; but this, as totality, is held together by the categories of a process of reproduction, which constitutes itself as a closed system (and therefore can be reconstructed as such), as long as subjects do not recognize as their own the praxis that is severed from them within this context.

(1) Before any critique of ideology can be possible in the fields of religion, art, and philosophy, this anticipatory conception must prove itself in terms of the relation between politics

and economics; political actions and institutions have to be derivable from conflicts of interests, which, in turn, necessarily have to emerge from the capitalistic process of production. This Marx sought to show empirically, especially in the example provided by the "Civil War in France." In so doing he already presupposes, of course, that the movements in the sphere of reproduction itself can be comprehended as a systematically coherent complex. The proof for this must be furnished by political economy carried out as a critique, in that it derives all economic phenomena from the process of the accumulative utilization [*Verwertung*] of capital, without any recourse to phenomena outside of this sphere. Political economy cannot be permitted to transfer the real problems to the data; that which modern economics allows as given in the form of data series, it must also comprehend economically.

The social conditions under which Marx undertook this attempt were favorable to his aims. The fictions of the model of unlimited competition found a certain *fundamentum in re* during the liberal phase of capitalism as did the model of "bourgeois society" as a sphere of autonomy prior to the state and upon which the state was based, namely, an autonomy founded on the free disposition of property. The process which Marx himself prognosticated, of the concentration and centralization of capital (and corresponding to this, the oligopolistic transformation of trade and commerce), has, on the one hand, quickly and to a growing degree forced the weaker parties on the market to assert their claims in a political form, and on the other hand, induced the organs of the state to intervene in the domain of commodity exchange and social labor. But in the same measure, this domain ceases to develop according to its immanent economic laws. Due to the introduction of elements of the superstructure into the base itself, the classical dependency relationship of politics to the economy was disrupted. In his systematic conception, Marx did not count on such a shift under capitalism: "He failed to see that essentially political forces would arise in the advanced capitalist societies, which would balance, and in the end, even begin to outweigh, the inherent tendencies of the system." [54]

But it is not only by virtue of this that the foundations of the doctrine of ideology become problematic; its orthodox formulation was already influenced by the misunderstanding of itself as a science, under which critical thought suffered.[55] Before the authority of scientific consciousness, the dialectical relation of an idea alienated from its interest, and therefore subjected to it, was transformed only too readily into the dependence of spirit on nature as a causal relationship, the dependence of consciousness on its historical existence [*Sein*]; one can see this as early as the famous preface of 1859 to the *Critique of Political Economy*. And later Marx never explicitly rejected the naturalistic version of the doctrine of ideology which Engels supplied. In this version the complex of relations which only lurk in the background in Marx emerge quite clearly. As long as historical materialism no longer saw itself as involved in the objective crisis complex, as soon as it understood its critique exclusively as a positive science and the dialectic objectively as the law of the world, then the ideological character of consciousness had to take on a metaphysical quality. Spirit then was considered simply and always as ideology, and this included socialism. Within this superficial understanding, the correct ideology was distinguished from the false solely according to the criteria of a realistic theory of knowledge. The socialist *Weltanschauung* was the only correct one, because it correctly "depicts" [*abbildet*] the cosmic law in nature and in history.[56]

Certainly Marx understood the dialectical method well enough not to misuse it crudely in this manner. But that this misunderstanding could arise, under his eyes and provided with the blessings of Engels, and thus become the foundation of an "orthodox" tradition, can be traced back to the failure to reflect on critique as such: namely, not only to justify the scientific elements against philosophy, but also to justify those elements which critique owes to its philosophical origins, against the positivistic limitations of science. Just as Maimon and Fichte, first, and then later the representatives of objective idealism were able to sharpen their argument against Kant's subjective idealism— that in pursuing the enterprise of a critique of knowledge, the latter had forgotten to account for transcendental knowledge itself. In the same way those who came after Marx could employ an analogous argument against him: that the critique of political economy did not become aware of its own specific capacity as a critique, in distinction to the positive sciences, among which it counted itself.

(2) Because Ernst Bloch, in returning to Marx's *Theses on Feuerbach*, explicitly re-establishes the practical significance of critique, he can go beyond the critique of ideology which is summarized in these theses. In the Fourth Thesis it is stated:

> Feuerbach proceeds from the fact of religious self-alienation, the duplication of the world in a religious and a worldly one. His work consists in resolving the religious world back into its worldly basis. But that this worldly basis elevates itself above itself and establishes itself as an independent realm in the clouds can be explained only as a result of the internal rupture and self-contradiction of this worldly basis. The latter must thus be both understood in its contradictions and revolutionized practically.[57]

But if the religious world is so intimately a part of its earthly basis that the idea is debased, distorted, and made use of as ideology by the inner conflict that sunders the world, yet without wholly being dissolved into this ideology (indeed emerging as a product of the earthly contradiction, yet at the same time also transcending it)—then the false consciousness of a false world is not nothing. For as the negation of the negative, though not consciously as such, it is still full of encoded experiences. Within the ideological shell Bloch discovers the Utopian core, within the as yet false consciousness the true consciousness.[58] Certainly, the transparency of a better world is refracted by hidden interests, even in those aspects which point beyond the existing state; but still, the hopes which it awakens, the longings which it satisfies, contain energies that at the same time, once instructed about themselves, become critical impulses. The initial experience of evil, classified and declassed by Hegel as "practical" feeling, at one with the aggressive interest in overcoming this evil, Bloch comprehends as the point of departure for a materialistic phenomenology of a spirit which, however, develops into critique. He reflects on what critique must have that goes beyond science, in order to force the latter to discuss, with practical intent, what transcends the merely technical application of its results, and because he no longer confuses critique with science, Bloch comprehends in that first critical impulse that chained productive force of hope which must be set free and provided with an understanding of its own history. This hope awakens the sense, freed from the narrowness of consciousness, of the objective possibilities within the established reality; it stimulates awareness of the superfluity of productive forces pressing beyond the institutionalized relations of production. The latter, where they are not blindly swept away by the material forces of production, require just that "productive force" of the critical impulse, in order to be resolved and raised to a new level [sublated] by the will and consciousness of human beings.

But what is remarkable is that in his attempt to preserve within the critique of ideology the tradition that is criticized, Bloch confines himself to the deciphering of myth and religion, literature and music; what arouses his interest is not the state, but fiction about the state, not the norms of law which are in force, but theories of justice. For obviously ideas will reveal their Utopian excess, that goes beyond ideology, all the more readily the more indirect the mediations that relate them to social conflicts. The formations of the spirit which are claimed by the ruling interests *directly* for the purposes of legitimation, or even as elements of organization in the exercise of their rule, and thus *incorporated* into the economic sphere itself, appear to lose their power of transcendence to the degree of their instrumentalization. Of Utopian excess there remains only the false consciousness of absoluteness, of a divorce from praxis, which behind their back delivers the ideas all the more blindly up to interests, to be held captive as mere ideology. On the lowest rungs of the ideological ladder, as in the case of the fetishism of commodities, the estrangement of the theoretical elements from the practical marks, as it were, only the "estrangement" of praxis from itself, the "worldly foundation torn in conflict with itself"—here ideology itself becomes practical, while its ideal claims, contained in the idea of an exchange of equivalents, have departed almost entirely.

Bloch's search for Utopia not only confines itself entirely to the sphere which Hegel reserves for absolute spirit; even within this sphere he stops before he gets to the formations of modern consciousness. Especially the most recent developments in art, literature, and music must seem peculiarly unfruitful for his quest, because experimental art incorporates its reflections on itself into its works; and in representing its own ways and means it formalizes, its apparently "realistic" relevance to the world for the sake of stylistic variations remote from the world. Like Hegel, Bloch still adheres to the classicist aesthetics and to its central concept of the symbolic; the manifestation of the Idea is only supplanted by the epiphany of matter. Walter Benjamin has countered this with the concept of the allegorical, which, employed with virtuosity by Adorno, has proved its singular appropriateness especially for modern art, though it had first been formed in terms of the baroque. For this no longer conserves the conciliatory experiences of the anticipated moment in beautiful illusion [*Schein*], whether it be of a symbolically manifested or naturalistically projected world of mastered contradictions. Instead, it incorporates the cracks and crevices of a world torn apart mercilessly into its representations. But artistic representation does not imitate the contingency of these fragments in realistic duplication. Instead, through creating an artificial distance, it lays bare the world constructed as crisis.

Adorno[59] understands modern art as a legitimate source of critical insight, even if its mode of knowledge is distinct from that of science. With this at least one formation of absolute spirit is preserved for our contemporary period; it is not merely protected in Bloch's manner from being reduced by the sociology of knowledge, as though under the ideologically petrified crust a burgeoning Utopian seed were to be laid bare, but rather it is taken altogether out of the sphere of ideology, and placed beside critical theory on an equal footing. This attempt corresponds more clearly than any other to the embarrassment into which critique falls due to the loss of innocence of its consciousness as science. For to what sources of experience can critique appeal, if in the materialist manner it renounces philosophy as First Philosophy and yet cannot be reduced to a positive science? Must it not open itself to the historically variable source of experience provided by the socially concrete life-world, prior to all methodological objectivations, in order to legitimize the critical initiative as such? And do not, on the other hand, quantities of experience from this source flow into those forms of absolute consciousness, into art, religion, and philosophy, which have been devalued by the critique of ideology? [60] Art, religion, and philosophy are, each in its own way, capable of presenting the concept of morality as manifestation [*eines Hervorscheinenden*] (Marx recognized this of Hegel's philosophy). Only when they misuse this power as a magical incantation, which presents the mirage of moral relations as presently existing, do they fall prey to the particular interests of a world torn apart and become ideological; however, as long as they render the presently existing world in the mirror of moral relations as a world torn apart—as, say, modern art does—then they preserve their intention toward the concrete universal and are critical. A restoration of value to the spirit which has been devalued by the critique of ideology seems possible—indeed, seems already to be real—in such a manner that the heritage of the absolute spirit (in its Utopian contents) can be appropriated and carried further (for the demonstration of that which is unreconciled in all its unreconcilable character).

Marx would never have conceded that critique has a propaedeutic need for this, additional, literary source of knowledge. Though he never trusted a logic of history which in the gathering darkness presents its epilogue, subsequently, in a two-volume *Logik;* but he still trusted to a logic of history which would complete itself practically and thus also permit its own resolution [sublation], as was anticipated by a theory of revolution built up from the dialectical anatomy of bourgeois society. Marx never explicitly posed for himself the epistemological question concerning the conditions of the possibility of a philosophy of history with political intent. [61]

The presuppositions of a materialist philosophy of history

In a certain way, the philosophy of history begins early in the eighteenth century with Vico's famous explication of the *topos verum et factum convertuntur:*

According to our first indubitable principle the historical world [has] quite certainly been made by men. . . . And therefore its essence is to be found in the modifications of our own spirit . . . for there can nowhere be greater certainty than where he who also creates the things also gives an account of them. Thus this science (the philosophy of history) proceeds exactly as does geometry, which creates the world of magnitudes itself while it constructs it according to its principles and contemplates it; but does so with so much greater reality, as the laws of human affairs have more reality than those of points, lines, planes, and figures. And this, O reader, must provide you with a divine pleasure, for in God to know and to do is the same thing.[62]

The allusion in the last sentence, which so flatteringly compares historical reason with divine intelligence, indicates the complex of problems which from the very beginning accompanies the claim to knowledge made by philosophy of history; the *intellectus originarius* creates the world by thinking it; but even in the best case Vico can only give man the hope of knowing his history after he has made it—he is supposed to be able to think it as his own creation. He is supposed to be able to comprehend his spirit as the product of history and, within it, history as his own product. Even a historical reason which succeeded in accomplishing this would still be separated by a hiatus from the divine intellect. While for the latter the conception of the natural world is sufficient in order to create it, man creates his historical world, only afterwards to be able perhaps to conceive what it is. The philosophy of history cannot claim affinity with the *intellectus originarius* by the same right as geometry.

(1) It is not accidental that the epistemological question is posed in a theological form. For the historical theology of the Church Fathers anticipated in its thought what the philosophy of history elevates to the theme of what is intended to be a scientific concern. This theology had already conceived the unity of the historical world as world-history; it construed the beginning and the end as the origin and the goal, and the extension between the two as the occurrence of perdition and redemption [*Unheil*

und Heil]. With the unity of world-history and with the character
of destiny conferred upon its coherence, history was laid out as a
totality and a crisis process in one. From the viewpoint of eschatology—the salvation from origin sin—history does, to be sure,
retain a dual basis as both the history of the world and of redemption; for theism painstakingly preserves the distinction between
the subject of history and the subject who acts historically, between the lord of history and those who are merely subjected to
it. In this construction there is only one single philosopher of
history; and for him Vico's definitions are indeed appropriate:
God Himself. The *Scienza Nuova,* however, would like to make
everyone a legitimate participant in providence. The philosophy
of history now lays claim only to the natural source of historical
reason.

Vico still ignored the concept of progress, which was to
dominate the century. He based the claim to knowledge of the
New Science on men's ability, above all, to know what they have
made; in consequence, the philosophy of history from now on is
to do without the hypothesis of God as the subject of history; but
in His place Vico retained the human race. Mankind is recognized
as the author of history, yet it lacks the qualities which would
make it history's subject: it is not all-powerful and provident;
men make their history, yet they do not make it with consciousness. History remains ambiguous: the free act and the event,
action and occurrence. Therefore Vico does not eliminate Divine
Providence wholly from the theory of history; the law of providence still appears to him to be so "natural" and acts in such a
"simple manner" that it coincides with the empirical laws of
historical development. Providence is absorbed into the nature of
things in such a way that from the latter's own development the
Divine Plan shines forth—recognizable to the naked eye of reason.
Vico stretches providence as though it were a net under the
trapeze of history, so that the nations are always caught by it
again, as long as they still do not control history with their will
and consciousness, even though, in themselves, they are the subjects of history. After each aborted initiative, which, had it succeeded, would have fulfilled history in the Christian *mondo civile,*

mankind is subject to the repetition compulsion: from the degenerate barbarity of reflection it is led back into the healing barbarity of primitivism. The periodicity of *corso* and *ricorso* makes plain the role played in the system by the hidden providence. Only it can guarantee that the disintegration of civilization on its highest level will not exhaust itself in mere regression; only it opens up the horizon, within which, in the depths of the catastrophe, the catharsis becomes yet visible, the Redemption in the devastation.

The chance for gaining knowledge of such a dialectical interpretation is lost as soon as historical reason relinquishes this compensatory function of a naturalistically conceived providence. Then the progression from beginning to end can only be conceived unambiguously as progress from origin to goal. Beyond this, a proof is required that in the succession of phenomena a continual progression toward an essentially better state can be ascertained. Every regression that is empirically noted in the development of civilization would, because now it would stand by itself and be nothing but a naked regression, force reason to simply despair of the progress of mankind. To this is added a further problem.

Vico's philosophy of history remains retrospective. The spirit comes to know history after it has made it; and indeed it is capable of comprehending it as a whole and as lawful—in spite of the fact that it is not closed, not yet concluded—only insofar as its processes recur cyclically. The ultimate breakthrough of the circle of *corso* and *ricorso,* the fulfillment of time, strictly speaking is no longer covered by the laws of the New Science.[63] Even this epistemological justification of the philosophy of history's retrospective view, no longer holds if the cyclical schema is replaced by a linear one. The philosophy of history now has the precarious task of construing future states in which the past ones are not simply reproduced, thus of construing them according to laws of progress; it becomes prospective, and requires a justification, in the critique of knowledge, for its prognostic achievements. Neither problem was really solved in the eighteenth century. Turgot and Condorcet went back before Vico to the Cartesian tradition, with their conception that it would only require a Newton of history in order to comprehend the law of history's progress as a natural law. Subjected to the critical distinctions of Kantian philosophy, however, every attempt to subsume the laws of history under the universal laws of nature soon revealed the equivocal character of its presuppositions. That reason which made these presuppositions, as nature, the basis of the development of mankind, now was painstakingly distinguished from *the* reason, which a human race grown to adult autonomy [*mündig*] was itself only as yet to realize historically in the future.

With the conception of linear progress, which he retains, Kant returns to the foundations of Vico's problem and measures the latter's maxim of knowledge: *verum et factum convertuntur* against the requirements of a prospective philosophy of history. The predictability of historical development is only possible when "the prophet makes the events himself which he has prophesied." Insofar as the historical subjects, as mature and responsible [*mündig*] individuals, are in essence the subject of history, a permanent peace within an order of world-citizenship is prescribed as goal for their moral activity and only predictable in relation to whether they actually fulfill their duty; however, insofar as the reflective capacity of judgment constructs the progress of history toward its goal as the necessary connection of the phenomena, it must presuppose a purpose of nature, or a providence, as though there were a subject in history which actualizes that goal in a purposeful manner. Divine teleology, even if only presupposed hypothetically, does of course again reduce mankind to a natural species subject to the laws of causality. The historical subjects are, as it were, split up into their noumenal and their phenomenal aspects; they are the authors of their history, but still they have not yet constituted themselves as its subject—they are at once a causally determined species of nature and morally free individuals. But if mankind itself is to bring the unity of this contradiction to a conclusive outcome in the course of its history, then the contradiction jutting into the epistemological foundation of the philosophy of history must be comprehended as belonging to history, indeed as its actual motive force. In this manner Kant (pursuing his question about the possible agreement of politics with morality) still conceives this problem within his own philosophy of history, without of course having been able to solve it within that framework.[64]

It remained for Hegel to accomplish this. Because human beings are also that which comes to them from history as something alien, from the outside, therefore at each stage the appropriation of something previously alienated is repeated. The concept penetrates the object and awakens to a new life what has died in prior objectivations. Because mankind is the subject of history and yet is not subject as such, the philosophy of history from Vico to Kant believed, on the one hand, that it based its claim to knowledge on the premise that history was "makable," and still, on the other hand, could not wholly give up providence, be it only for heuristic purposes. Philosophy of history was only able to do this when Hegel first discovered, in just that contradiction, the driving force of a humanity which continually extricates itself from its conceptions [*Vorstellungen*] and so creates itself, thus the dialectic of a history that is self-moving.

To be sure, with that only one of the two problems which are posed anew once Vico's cyclical schema is abandoned is resolved. The other problem, that of a justification of prediction in the critique of knowledge, also escaped Hegel's grasp. True, he dialectically incorporates the philosophy of history into history itself. Still he does so in such a way that history for its part, is recapitulated as the history of the spirit in the absolute self-consciousness of philosophy. To be sure, implicit in the perspective of the philosophy of history is its own effort as that philosophy which finally frees mankind from the imprisoning spell of its world-historical disguises [*Verstellung*]; still, just like Vico's philosophy of history, on this higher level it remains retrospective. The philosophy of history only divests itself of this absolute point of view, from which history is reflected philosophically as a totality, with the transformation of its dialectic into a materialistic one. As we saw, Marx discovered in the domination of dead labor over living labor the actual reason for the impotence of historical subjects compared with *the* subject of history, which men nevertheless are, without, however, as yet being subjects as such. That is why it is labor, conceived as alienated, which moves history, and

not the labor of the concept in the Hegelian sense. Not the consciousness which finds itself again, but active appropriation will
"penetrate" the objectified relations. This praxis is mediated by
theoretical acts, but theory as such, even that last theory which
sees through history's laws of motion dialectically in its philosophy of history, still remains the penultimate step prior to a
praxis that is only initiated and guided by theory. The Marxist
philosophy of history too—and it especially—has implicit within
it its own efforts; retrospective and prospective at the same time,
relating to the social praxis beneath it (production) and the
revolutionary praxis before it, it transforms contemplation into
critique, nonetheless.

In his critique Marx reconciles Vico, who is preserved [sub-
lated] in Hegel, with Kant. Like the latter, Marx makes the
Viconean maxims of knowledge the basis of a philosophy of
history which is prospective. The meaning of a still unconcluded
history can, as both believe, only be foreseen when mankind, as a
species, makes its history with will and consciousness; as long as
that does not happen, this meaning will have to be based on
practical reason. But while for Kant practical reason proffers
solely regulative ideas for moral action, so that the meaning of
history can only be delineated as an idea without relevance for
the theory of history in any way, Marx establishes just this relevance with his thesis that the meaning of history can be recognized
theoretically to the degree that human beings undertake to make
it true practically.[65] Marx declares the will to *make* to be the
precondition for the ability to *know,* because he has learned from
Hegel to comprehend the "meaning" of history as emancipation
from the contradiction of humanity with itself, which extends
even into the cognitive approach of the philosophy of history. The
meaning of history as a whole is revealed theoretically to the
degree to which mankind practically undertakes to make with
will and with consciousness that history which it has always made
anyhow. In so doing, critique must comprehend itself as a moment
within the situation which it is seeking to supersede [sublate].
For in the end a philosophy of history, with this materialistic
self-involvement in history, finds the legitimations for its presup-

positions after the fact, presuppositions as a consequence of which it substitutes the contradiction in history itself.

(2) As is well known, Marx did not merely address his critique to the proletariat; he goes beyond this to derive the epistemological justification of the viewpoint taken by this critique from the history of the proletariat's development. Alienated labor, the domination of dead labor over the living, as expressed in the pauperized existence of this class, developed into a commanding need for its own abolition as a class—a need that was "the practical expression of necessity." Therefore, so Marx argues, at the same time as this class has occupied the objective position of the proletariat within the process of production it has also achieved a point of view outside this process, from which the system as a whole can be comprehended critically and convicted of its obsolescence. Here we will not go into the extent to which this argument was appropriate for laying the foundation of a philosophy of history with practical intent, in a materialistic version, and thus also was able to base the transformation of theory into critique materialistically on the comprehended process of history itself. But it was not sufficient for an extrapolation from the class struggle situation of that day to the structure of history as a whole. In this the rationale cannot be found for the acceptance of the theological framework, within which alone the history of the world presents itself as a history—a story—with a beginning and an end, in such a way that Marx can summarily comprehend it as a history of class struggle. In short, Marx's argument does not of itself validate the anticipatory conception which enters into the way the philosophy of history poses its question as such, and which universalizes the contemporary phenomena of crisis into the totality of a world-historical crisis structure.

The theological framework given by the event of Redemption could only be rendered functional for a philosophic consideration of world-history to the degree to which a consciousness of the unity of the world, of mankind and its development, had formed itself—only in that way did an empirical subject of history become conceivable. The philosophy of history therefore presupposes the consciousness of global unity which arose in the eighteenth century. The great discoveries of the period of colonization, the missionary enterprise in China, and finally the beginnings of independence for the North American territories, forced European civilization to relativize its conception of itself: it learned to view itself from the outside (Voltaire's Philosophy of History begins with China) as well as in terms of prehistoric origins (to see itself in contrast to the "savages," who preoccupied many minds). At the same time it experienced itself within the context of a historical continuity and within the framework of a growing global unity, which seemed to be secured more by the social intercourse of men with each other than by the historically fortuitous fact of a salvation through Christian revelation.

The unity of the world is one of the presuppositions for the philosophy of history; that history can be made, the other. Human beings can only rationally appropriate their history insofar as it it of their handiwork. As the capitalistic mode of production established its predominance, ever more extensive spheres of social intercourse were dissolved into relations of exchange. With the development of the material forces of production, more and more institutions of social life lost their "natural," spontaneous force. Beyond that, the revolutionizing of the feudal relations of production and the establishment of bourgeois society as a sphere of private autonomy coincided with a rationalizing of further domains, no matter how particular. The ability to make history grows in direct proportion to the growth of the self-consciousness of the Enlightenment, of learning how to exercise rational control over history.

Thus these two subjective motives for the way the problem of the philosophy of history is posed are linked to objective tendencies of the historical development: their origins can be localized in the general field of a bourgeois society developing during the course of centuries and finally, between the English Revolution of the seventeenth century and the French Revolution of the eighteenth, attaining consciousness of itself.

Two final conclusions suggest themselves. On the one hand, the tendencies described here have grown stronger. On the basis of industrial society and its technically mediated commerce, the interdependence of political events and the integration of social relations have progressed so far beyond what was even conceivable two centuries ago that within this overall complex of communication particular histories have coalesced into the history of *one* world. Yet at the same time, mankind has never before been confronted so sharply by the irony of a capacity to make its own history, yet still deprived of control over it, as is the case now that the means of self-assertion by force have developed to such a degree that their deployment for attaining specific political ends has become highly problematical. Thus the immanent presuppositions of the philosophy of history have not by any means become invalid; on the contrary, it is only today that they have become true.[66] That is why all the counterideologies, which allege that the way the philosophy of history poses the question is now outdated, must arouse a suspicion of escapism.

On the other hand, and this is the second final conclusion, the framework which philosophy has taken over from theology, of history as totality, becomes questionable.

If the loose threads of the historical development can be tied together into a network of world-historical interconnections only at a relatively late stage, this network cannot then retrospectively be made to cover history as a whole; the fact that the global unity itself has only come to be historically contradicts an approach which makes the totality of history from the very beginning its premise. If, in addition, social conditions become accessible to rational planning on the part of human beings only at a relatively late stage of their development, then the possibility of its being *made* can also not be asserted for history as a whole; the fact that the capacity for rationalization itself has only come to be historically, is in contradiction to a viewpoint which presumes a subject for history from the beginning.

Especially the materialistic philosophy of history should comprehend its presuppositions in terms of the context of the epoch in which it emerged historically. It should incorporate critically into its self-consciousness the fact that the two categories —the unity of the world, and that history can be made—have only acquired their truth in history itself at a specific phase.

Just as the extension of contemporary conflict back to the beginnings of history retains a merely heuristic character, so too the anticipatory presupposition of history's end remains hypothetical. The philosophy of history creates the fiction of historical subjects as the possible subject of history, as though objective tendencies of development, which actually are equivocal, were comprehended with will and consciousness by those who act politically and were decided by them for their own benefit. From the lofty observation post of this fiction the situation is revealed in its ambivalences, which are susceptible to practical intervention, so that an enlightened mankind can elevate itself then to become what up to that point it was only fictitiously.[67]

7

Dogmatism, Reason, and Decision: On Theory and Praxis in Our Scientific Civilization

In the major tradition of philosophy, the relation of theory and praxis always referred to the good and the righteous—as well as the "true"—and to the life, both private and collective, of individuals as well as of citizens. In the eighteenth century this dimension of a theoretically guided praxis of life was extended by the philosophy of history. Since then, theory, directed toward praxis and at the same time dependent on it, no longer embraces the natural, authentic, or essential actions and institutions of a human race constant in its essential nature; instead, theory now deals with the objective, overall complex of development of a human species which produces itself, which is as yet only destined to attain its essence: humanity. What has remained is theory's claim of providing orientation in right action, but the realization of the good, happy, and rational life has been stretched out along the vertical axis of world-history; praxis has been extended to cover stages of emancipation. For this rational praxis is now interpreted as liberation from an externally imposed compulsion, just as the theory which is guided by this interest of liberation is interpreted as enlightenment. The cognitive interest of this enlightenment theory is declaredly critical; it presupposes a specific experience, which is set down in Hegel's *Phenomenology of Mind*, just as it is in Freud's psychoanalysis—the experience of an emancipation by means of critical insight into relationships of power, the objectivity of which has as its source solely that the relationships have not been seen through. Critical reason gains power analytically over dogmatic inhibition.[1]

Reason takes up a partisan position in the controversy between critique and dogmatism, and with each new stage of emancipation it wins a further victory. In this kind of practical reason, insight and the explicit interest in liberation by means of reflection converge. The higher level of reflection coincides with a step forward in the progress toward the autonomy of the individual, with the elimination of suffering and the furthering of concrete happiness. Reason involved in the argument against dogmatism has definitely taken up this interest as its own—it does not define the moment of decision as external to its sphere. Rather, the decisions of the subjects are measured rationally against that one objective decision, which is required by the interest of reason itself. Reason has not as yet renounced the will to the rational.

Now this constellation of dogmatism, reason, and decision has changed profoundly since the eighteenth century, and exactly to the degree to which the positive sciences have become productive forces in social development. For as our civilization has become increasingly scientific, the dimension within which theory was once directed toward praxis has become correspondingly constructed. The laws of self-reproduction demand of an industrially advanced society that it look after its survival on the escalating scale of a continually expanded technical control over nature and a continually refined administration of human beings and their relations to each other by means of social organization. In this system, science, technology, industry, and administration interlock in a circular process. In this process the relationship of theory to praxis can now only assert itself as the purposive-rational application of techniques assured by empirical science. The social potential of science is reduced to the powers of technical control— its potential for enlightened action is no longer considered. The empirical, analytical sciences produce technical recommendations, but they furnish no answer to practical questions. The claim by which theory was once related to praxis has become dubious. Emancipation by means of enlightenment is replaced by instruction in control over objective or objectified processes. Socially effective theory is no longer directed toward the consciousness of human beings who live together and discuss matters with each other, but to the behavior of human beings who manipulate. As a productive force of industrial development, it changes the basis of human life, but it no longer reaches out critically beyond this basis to raise life itself, for the sake of life, to another level.

But, of course, the real difficulty in the relation of theory to praxis does not arise from this new function of science as a technological force, but rather from the fact that we are no longer able to distinguish between practical and technical power.[2] Yet even a civilization that has been rendered scientific is not granted dispensation from practical questions; therefore a peculiar danger arises when the process of scientification transgresses the limit of technical questions, without, however, departing from the level of reflection of a rationality confined to the technological horizon. For then no attempt at all is made to attain a rational consensus on the part of citizens concerning the practical control of their destiny. Its place is taken by the attempt to attain technical control over history by perfecting the administration of society, an attempt that is just as impractical as it is unhistorical. When theory was still related to praxis in a genuine sense, it conceived of society as a system of action by human beings, who communicate through speech and thus must realize social intercourse within the context of conscious communication. Through this communication they must form themselves into a collective subject of the whole, that is capable of action—otherwise, the fortunes of a society ever more rigidly rationalized in its particular parts must slip away as a whole from that rational cultivation, which they require all the more urgently. On the other hand, a theory which confuses control with action is no longer capable of such a perspective. It understands society as a nexus of behavioral modes, for which rationality is mediated solely by the understanding of sociotechnical controls, but not by a coherent total consciousness—not by precisely that interested reason which can only attain practical power through the minds of politically enlightened citizens.

In industrially advanced society, research, technology, production, and administration have coalesced into a system which cannot be surveyed as a whole, but in which they are functionally interdependent. This has literally become the basis of our life. We are related to it in a peculiar manner, at the same time intimate and yet estranged. On the one hand, we are bound externally to this basis by a network of organizations and a chain of consumer goods; on the other hand, this basis is shut off from our knowledge, and even more from our reflection. The paradox of this state of affairs will, of course, only be recognized by a theory oriented toward praxis, even though this parodox is so evident: the more the growth and change of society are determined by the most extreme rationality of processes of research, subject to a division of labor, the less rooted is this civilization, now rendered scientific, in the knowledge and conscience of its citizens. In this discrepancy, scientifically guided techniques and those of decision theory—and ultimately even cybernetically controlled techniques —encounter a limitation which they cannot overcome; this can only be altered by a change in the state of consciousness itself, by the practical effect of a theory which does not improve the manipulation of things and of reifications, but which instead advances the interest of reason in human adulthood, in the autonomy of action and in the liberation from dogmatism. This it achieves by means of the penetrating ideas of a persistent critique.

Committed reason and the interest of the Enlightenment: Holbach, Fichte, and Marx

These categories, in general the constellation of dogmatism, reason, and decision, on which the unity of theory with praxis is founded, originate in the eighteenth century. In the preface to his *System of Nature,* Paul Thiry d'Holbach speaks of the contamination of the mind by prejudices: the mind has become so fused with the veil of opinions with which it has been covered from childhood on that it can only extricate itself with the greatest effort.[3] Here dogmatism still bears the name of prejudice; it is confronted by reason guided by experience. It induces men to study nature, while the misfortune of dogmatism has arisen from the attempts to transcend this sphere of the visible world. Critical reason will confine men to the role of physicists; man has become entangled in the chimeras of his prejudices because he tried to be a metaphysician before he was a physicist. Thus here that distinction is already made with complete clarity, for which the principles of positivism merely form the refrain. And still, in its confrontation of dogmatism with reason, the intention of the Enlightenment was in no way positivistic.

For the term prejudice covered more than the epitome of subjective opinions. The constraint of dogmatism is not simply an error which can readily be resolved by means of analysis. Rather, the error with which the Enlightenment endeavored to deal was the false consciousness of an epoch, anchored in the institutions of a false society, a consciousness which in turn secured the dominant interests. The massive objectivity of this prejudice, for which the metaphor of prison walls would be more appropriate than that of figments of fantasy, became tangible in the repressions and denials of an adult autonomy withheld: "To error we owe the oppressive chains, which despots and priests everywhere forge for the people. To error we owe the slavery in which the people languish in almost all countries. To error we owe the religious terrors which freeze human beings in fear and make them slaughter each other for the sake of figments of the mind. To error we owe the deep rooted enmity, the barbarous persecutions, the continual bloodshed and horrifying tragedies. . . ." [4] Ignorance coincides with suffering and happiness denied, uncertainty with slavery and the incapacity to act correctly.

But because the prejudices derive their own peculiar objectivity from this link between withheld autonomy and the denial of freedom and satisfaction, the critical dissolution of the existing untruth, of error as substance, requires, conversely, even more than rational insight. Above all, it requires the cardinal virtue of courage. More precisely, reason itself draws its life from the courage to be rational, the *sapere aude* that Kant elevated to the motto of his reply to the question: what is Enlightenment? Reason will attain power over dogmatism incarnate only because it has incorporated the will to reason in its own interest. Therefore it cannot address itself to corrupted human beings—of this Holbach is convinced:

Her voice can only be heard by generous souls accustomed
to reflection, whose sensibilities make them lament the num-
berless calamities showered on the earth by political and
religious tyranny—whose enlightened minds contemplate
with horror the immensity, the ponderosity of that series of
misfortunes with which error has in all ages overwhelmed
mankind.[5]

Reason is equated unquestioningly with the talent for adult
autonomy and with sensibility to the evils of this world. It has always made its decision in favor of justice, general welfare, and
peace; the reason which defends itself against dogmatism is a
committed reason.

Now this commitment could still be considered the undisputed basis of all rational endeavor, because, at that time, man
and nature were still conceived as one, precisely what was separated by a later enlightenment. For does not Holbach's preface
begin with the classical avowal, "Man is unhappy because he has
an erroneous view of nature"? Insight into the laws of nature is
believed to be capable of providing, at the same time, instruction
for the just life. It is no accident that in the subtitle of the work
the *loix du monde physique et du monde morale* are reduced to
a common denominator. As in Hobbes, the study of nature appears to lead to both knowledge of what nature is and instruction
on how man is to conduct himself in accordance with nature.
However, as soon as nature is objectivated in empirical science,
the hope of at the same time drawing from the knowledge of
causal laws any certainty with respect to normative laws must be
abandoned. The positivistic enlightenment, which, for that reason, calls itself a radical enlightenment, has seen through the
ambiguities contained in the concept of nature, has dissolved
the convergence of truth and happiness, of error and suffering,
and has reduced reason to a potential for knowledge that has lost,
together with its critical sting, its commitment, its moral de-
cisiveness, and has been separated from such a decision as from
an alien element.

This consequence could be avoided for a time; reason could
still have been salvaged as a category of the Enlightenment and

turned even more pointedly against dogmatism, when at the close of the eighteenth century Fichte substituted for the System of Nature a transcendental Doctrine of Science [*Wissenschaftslehre*]. Kant had already removed from nature the source of the laws governing both the causally determined realm of phenomena and the realm of freedom under self-imposed norms; he located this source in the synthetic achievements of the subject. Fichte made practical reason autonomous and reduced nature so that it became the material of action produced by freedom. Under these changed premises of idealism, dogmatism could no longer be overcome by a reason which studies nature and is verified by sense experience. Indeed, on these premises, dogmatism itself has gained still more power and impenetrability; it becomes all-pervasive and universal, because dogmatic constraint does not first have to establish itself in the form of prejudice institutionalized by tyrants and priests—a consciousness that comprehends itself as a product of the things around us, as a product of nature, is already dogmatic: "The principle of the dogmatists is represented by faith in things for their own sake: thus an indirect faith in their own self which is dispersed and supported only borne by objects." [6] Fichte conceives of dogmatism in a more elementary manner than Holbach. In German Idealism the prejudice of the French Encyclopaedists appears under the title of "dispersal," a fixation of a weak ego or immature consciousness on the external props provided by existing things; what it means is the reification of the subject.

However, when reason constitutes itself in terms of a critique of reified consciousness, then its viewpoint, namely idealism, cannot be compelled by means of arguments according to the rules of logic alone. In order to divest oneself rationally of the limitations of dogmatism, one must first have made the interest of reason one's own: "The ultimate basis of the difference between the idealist and the dogmatist is thus the difference of interest." [7] The desire for emancipation and an original act of freedom are presupposed, in order that man may work his way up to the viewpoint of adult autonomy, from which viewpoint alone the critical insight into the hidden mechanism of the genesis of the world and of consciousness first becomes possible.

The young Schelling enunciates Fichte's thought as follows: that we can make no other beginning in reason "than by means of an anticipation of practical decision." [8] Reason is so little conceived as knowledge detached from volition [*Wollen*] that it is reason itself which first creates the level on which it can then reflect on a consciousness adhering to objects and recognize it as a false consciousness. The developed system of reason is "necessarily either an artifice, a game played in thought . . . or reality must be *conferred* on it, not by means of a theoretical capacity, but by a practical one, not by a cognitive capacity, but by a *productive one which actualizes,* not by knowledge but by action." [9] In precisely this sense Fichte's famous dictum must also be understood: what sort of a philosophy one chooses depends on what sort of a human being one is.[10] For Holbach the rationality of the subject —a certain degree of autonomy and a certain kind of sensibility— was the precondition for the capacity for critical insight; for Fichte reason is even more closely intertwined with the complexity of the human spirit at an advanced stage of its historical evolution. The freedom achieved in the world-historical process of the species' self-formation—freedom to accept the interest of reason as one's own—distinguishes those human beings who have surmounted dogmatism: to them not primarily a theoretical, but a practical merit must be attributed:

> A few, who have not yet raised themselves to the full feeling of their freedom and absolute independence, find themselves only in the conceiving [*vorstellen*] of things; they only have that dispersed self-consciousness which adheres to objects and can be reconstructed from the manifold of objects. Their image is only reflected to them by things as by a mirror; for their own sake they are not able to give up the belief in the independence of these things; for only with these do they themselves subsist. . . . But whoever becomes conscious of his independence and autonomy of all that is external to him—and this one can become only by making oneself into something, independently of all things, by means of one's own self [*durch sich selbst*]—he does not re-

quire things as a support for his self, and can have no use for them, because they abolish that independence and transform it into empty semblance [*Schein*].[11]

The price which Fichte paid for the unity of reason and moral decision, for the sake of a critical concept of reason, was of course too high, as the last sentence of the passage especially shows. And indeed, Schelling and Hegel soon discovered that the spontaneity of an absolute "I," which posits the world and itself, remains abstract; they showed that nature cannot be reduced to indeterminate material for acting subjects—lest a human world that is itself divested of qualities shrinks down to the blind point of action for action's sake.[12] Therefore, on the level of discussion which Hegel had prepared, Marx—after Holbach and Fichte representing the third generation of committed spokesmen for enlightenment—showed how the inner content of reason and the partisanship of thought against dogmatism also arose historically from a self-formative process. In confrontation with and on the basis of nature, which has its own structure, the laboring subjects strive toward a form of social intercourse which ultimately is freed from the compulsion and domination of nature—and thereby achieves the political autonomy of adult maturity. Against Fichte, Marx shows that reified consciousness must be criticized practically at the level of things themselves—instead of merely epistemologically by a withdrawal into the autonomous subject, by a denial of the realism of healthy common sense. Compared with its role in Fichte's philosophy, dogmatism in Marx's theory has become weightier, just as it was weightier in Fichte than in Holbach. It gains in the impenetrability of substance, in the naturally given character of objective deception. The two "main subspecies of man" which Fichte distinguishes as the dogmatists and the idealists are divested of the opposition of their interest and of the purely subjective guise of a moral specification. Instead, those interests which bind consciousness to the yoke imposed by the domination of things and reified relations are, as material interests, anchored in historically specific configurations of alienated labor, denied satisfactions, and suppressed freedom. This historical determination applies equally to the interests which, throughout the real contradictions of a world torn apart, seek to bring about the unity of life-processes as the rationality that is immanent in social conditions. From institutionalized prejudice, then passing through the mediation of the form of transcendental dispersion, dogmatism now assumes the form of ideology. Reason committed against dogmatism from now on is active as the critique of ideology. But its partisanship claims the same objectivity as that which is attributed to the illusion it criticizes. The interest directing knowledge is legitimized by virtue of the objective context in which it is embedded.

In the concept of reason active as critique of ideology, knowledge and commitment are related dialectically: on the one hand, it is only possible to see through the dogmatism of a congealed society to the degree to which knowledge has committed itself to being guided by the anticipation of an emancipated society and actualized adult autonomy for all human beings; at the same time, on the other hand, this interest demands that insight into the processes of social development be already attained, because only in these processes can such insight be constituted as objective. On the level of the historical self-reflection of a science with critical intent, Marx for the last time identifies reason with a commitment to rationality in its thrust against dogmatism.

In the second half of the nineteenth century, during the course of the reduction of science to a productive force in industrial society, positivism, historicism, and pragmatism, each in turn, isolate one part of this all-encompassing concept of rationality.[13] The hitherto undisputed attempt of the great theories, to reflect the complex of life as a whole is henceforth itself discredited as dogmatic. Reason, once it is particularized, is assigned to the level of subjective consciousness, whether as the capacity for the empirical verification of hypotheses, for historical understanding, or for the pragmatic control of behavior. At the same time, interest and inclination are banished from the court of knowledge as subjective factors. The spontaneity of hope, the act of taking a position, the experience of relevance or indifference, and above all, the response to suffering and oppression, the desire for adult autonomy, the will to emancipation, and the happiness of discovering one's identity—all these are dismissed for all time from the obligating interest of reason. A disinfected reason is purged of all moments of enlightened volition; external to itself, it has externalized—alienated—its own life. And life deprived of spirit leads an existence of arbitrariness that is a ghostly spirit indeed—all under the name of "decision."

The positivistic isolation of reason and decision [Entscheidung]

Prior to positivism, critical knowledge referred to a scientific orientation in action. Even the knowledge of nature (physics in the classical sense) had its role to play with respect to praxis (to ethics and politics). However, after the empirical sciences of the new type, so successful since the time of Galileo, had attained a consciousness of themselves in positivism, and after analytic philosophy, inspired by the Vienna circle as well as by Peirce and Dewey, had explicated this self-understanding in terms of the philosophy of science, especially in the work of Carnap, Popper, and Morris,[14] the two cognitive functions were distinctly separated—and both deprived of their power of orientation for action.

The *affirmative* achievement of the modern sciences consists in statements about empirical uniformities. The hypothetical laws, gained from a deductive connection among statements and tested by controlled experiments, refer to regular covariances of empirical variables in all the domains accessible intersubjectively to experience. Under given individual initial conditions, universal laws of this kind serve as explanations. The theoretical statements which permit the causal explanation of effects, in the same way make possible the prediction of effects, given the causes. This predictive application of the theories of experimental science reveals the interest of knowledge which guides these generalizing sciences. As artisans were formerly guided, in working on their materials, by rules of experience which had been proven in the tradition of their trade, so in the same way engineers in all sectors can rely on such scientifically tested predictions in the choice of the means they employ, of their instruments and operations. To be sure, the reliability of the rules distinguished the exercise of technique [*techne*] in the old sense from what we call technique [technology] today. The function of the knowledge of modern science must therefore be understood in connection with the system of social labor: it extends and rationalizes our power of technical control over the objects or—which comes to the same thing—objectified processes of nature and society.

From this affirmative achievement of knowledge reduced to empirical science derives also its other function, its *critical achievement*. For when this type of science attains a monopoly in the guidance of rational action, then all competing claims to a scientific orientation for action must be rejected. This activity is now reserved for a positivistically circumscribed critique of ideology. It is directed against dogmatism in a new guise. Any theory that relates to praxis in any way other than by strengthening and perfecting the possibilities for purposive-rational action must now appear dogmatic. The methodology of the empirical sciences is tacitly but effectively rooted in a technical cognitive interest that excludes all other interests; consequently all other relations to life-praxis can be blocked out under the slogan of ethical neutrality or value-freedom. The economy in the selection of purposive-rational means which is guaranteed by conditional predictions in the form of technical recommendations is the sole admissible "value," [15] and it too is not seen explicitly as a value, because it simply seems to coincide with rationality as such. In fact, we have here the formalization of one sole relevance to life, namely, the experience of success as feedback control, built into the systems of social labor and already realized in every successful elementary performance of labor.

According to the principles of an analytic philosophy of science, empirical questions which cannot be posed and solved in the form of technical tasks cannot therefore expect to receive a cogent theoretical answer. From the outset, all practical questions, which cannot be answered adequately by technical prescriptions, but which instead also require a self-understanding within their concrete situation, go beyond the cognitive interest invested in empirical science. The only type of science admitted by the positivistic approach is one that is not capable of investigating such questions rationally. And theories which in spite of that offer such solutions can be convicted of dogmatism by these criteria. The goal of a critique of ideology abbreviated in this manner is to respond to every dogmatic assertion with the decisionistic [*dezisionistisch*] thesis that practical questions (in our sense) cannot be discussed cogently and in the final instance must be simply decided upon, one way or another. The magic word for release from the spell of dogmatism is "decision," decision that has been painfully isolated from reason: practical questions are not "capable of truth" [*wahrheitsfähig*].

At this point in the positivistic confrontation with the new lineaments of dogmatism,[16] the inverse side of such a critique of ideology is revealed. It is correct in removing the veil of a false rationalization of what has been derationalized in value ethics [*Wertethik*] such as Scheler's and Hartmann's philosophy and in referring ideal objects back to the subjectivity of needs and inclinations, value judgments and commitments. But the result of its labors is monstrous enough: from the mainstream of rationality the pollutants, the sewage of emotionality, are filtered off and locked away hygienically in a storage basin—an imposing mass of subjective value qualities. Every single value appears as a meaningless agglomeration of meaning, stamped solely with the stigma of irrationality, so that the priority of one value over the other—thus the persuasiveness which a value claims with respect to action—simply cannot be rationally justified. Thus on this level the critique of ideology involuntarily furnishes the proof that progress of a rationalization limited in terms of empirical science to technical control is paid for with the corresponding growth of a mass of irrationality in the domain of praxis itself. For action still demands an orientation, as it did before. But now it is dissected into a rational implementation of techniques and strategies and an irrational choice of so-called value systems. The price paid for economy in the selection of means is a decisionism set wholly free in the selection of the highest-level goals.

The positivistically cleansed demarcation set between knowing and evaluating of course represents less a result than a problem. For the detached domain of values, norms, and decisions is now seized upon anew by philosophic interpretations, precisely on the basis of that division of labor shared with a reduced science.

The *subjective philosophy of value* is no longer as assured of the reference to meaning split off from the context of life, and hypostatized, as the objective value ethics was, which had immediately made of this a domain of ideal Being, transcending sense experiençe. It too sought to reclaim the existence of orders of value (Max Weber) and of forces of faith [*Glaubensmächte*] (Jaspers) in a sphere elevated above history. But scientifically controlled knowledge cannot simply be complemented by intuitive knowledge. The philosophic belief that remains midway between pure commitment and rational comprehension must pledge itself to one of the competing orders, without, however, revoking the pluralism of these orders, and without being able wholly to resolve the dogmatic core which is the source of its own life. Polemic, responsible although in principle undecidable, between philosophers, as the intellectually honest and existentially committed representatives of spiritual forces, appears as the only permissible form of discussion in this domain of practical questions. *Decisionism* as a worldview today no longer is ashamed to reduce norms to decisions. In noncognitive Ethics, in the form of linguistic analysis, the decisionistic complement to a positivistically limited science is itself still conceived positivistically (R. M. Hare). As soon as certain fundamental value judgments are posited as axioms, a deductive chain of statements can be analyzed cogently for each; at the same time, such principles themselves are not accessible to rational comprehension: their acceptance is based solely on a decision, a commitment. Such decisions can then be interpreted either in an existential-personal sense (Sartre) or in a public, political sense (Carl Schmitt) or institutionally from anthropological presuppositions (Gehlen), but the thesis remains the same: that decisions relevant to the praxis of life, whether they consist in the acceptance of values, in the selection of biographical [*lebensgeschichtlich*] design, or in the choice of an enemy, are not accessible to rational consideration and cannot form a rationally substantiated consensus. But if practical questions, eliminated from knowledge that has been reduced to empirical science, are dismissed in this way entirely from the controlling powers of rational investigation, if decisions on questions touching on the praxis of life must be pronounced as beyond any and every authority committed to rationality, then we cannot be astonished by the ultimate desperate attempt to secure socially binding precommitments on practical questions institutionally by a return to the closed world of mythical images and powers (Walter Bröcker). As Adorno and Horkheimer have shown, this complementing of positivism by *mythology* is not devoid of its logically compelling character, whose abysmal irony can be turned to laughter only by dialectics.

Sincere positivists, in whom such perspectives choke off laughter—thus, positivists who recoil before the half-concealed metaphysics of an objective value ethics and a subjective philosophy of value, as they do before the proclaimed irrationality of decisionism and the resurrection of mythology—seek their foothold in a reified critique of ideology with self-understanding, which, however, in the primitive form of nullifying projections, as developed from the time of Feuerbach down to Pareto, has itself congealed into the program of a *Weltanschauung*. For the one thing that remains unclarified in all this radicalism is the root: the motive of the critique of ideology itself. If the goal of the latter consists only in differentiating in principle the scientifically rationalized shaping of reality from the "value-laden forms of a world-view seeking interpretation of the world and self-interpretation of man" [17]—where such attempts at "enlightening consciousness" cannot make a claim to demonstrable rationality—then the critique of ideology closes off for itself the possibility of justifying its own endeavors theoretically. For as critique, it too is making an attempt to enlighten consciousness, and certainly not to shape reality; it does not produce new techniques; at best it could prevent given techniques from being misapplied in the name of a merely alleged theory. But from what source does this critique draw its power, if reason divorced from commitment must be wholly devoid of any interest in an emancipation of consciousness from dogmatic constraint?

Certainly science must be allowed to exercise its affirmative function as knowledge—it is, so to speak, itself recognized as a

value. This is served by the separation, performed by the critique
of ideology, of knowing from commitment, and such a separation,
once carried out, would have abolished dogmatism. But even so,
science in its critical function of knowledge, the combating of
dogmatism on a positivistic level, is possible only in the form of
a science which reflects on itself and wills itself as an end—thus
again a kind of committed reason, the *justified* possibility of
which is precisely what the critique of ideology denies. If, on the
other hand, it renounces a rational justification, then the dispute
of reason with dogmatism itself remains a matter of dogmatic
opinion: the impossibility of resolving dogmatism would be admitted at the outset. Behind this dilemma there lies, it seems to
me, the problem that the critique of ideology must tacitly presuppose as its own motivation just what it attacks as dogmatic,
namely, the convergence of reason and commitment—thus precisely an encompassing concept of rationality. To be sure, this
hidden concept of a substantial rationality is conceived differently depending on whether the motivating reflection is per-
suaded solely of the value of scientific techniques, or also of the
significance of a scientific emancipation for adult autonomy; thus
whether the critique of ideology is motivated on the level of understanding by an interest in the empirical sciences' increase in
technical knowledge, or is motivated on the level of reason by an
interest in enlightenment as such. Positivism is as little capable
of distinguishing between these two concepts of rationality as it
is capable, altogether, of being conscious that it itself implies just
what it seeks to oppose externally—committed reason. But on this,
or the proper distinction between these two forms, depends the
relation of theory and praxis in a scientific civilization.

The partisanship of the critique of ideology in favor of technological rationality

No matter how much it insists on a separation of theory and
commitment in its opposition to dogmatism, positivism's critique
of ideology itself remains a form of committed reason: *nolens
volens* it takes a partisan position in favor of progressive rationalization. In the case which we will analyze to begin with, its

concern, without reservation, is for the extension and dissemination of technical knowledge. In its conflict with dogmatism, as understood by positivism, this critique removes traditionalistic barriers, and ideological barriers of any sort, which can inhibit the progress of the analytic-empirical sciences and the unlimited process of their utilization. This critique is not a value-neutral analysis; its underlying premise is the value of empirical science theories, and this not simply hypothetically, but normatively. For with its first analytic step it already presupposes, normatively, that behaving in accordance with technical recommendations is not only desirable, but also "rational." This implicit concept of reason can, of course, not be clarified by means of the conceptual resources of positivism itself, even though this concept expresses its intention. By positivistic criteria, rationality of conduct is a value which we simply decide to accept or reject. At the same time, according to these same criteria, it can be demonstrated quite compellingly that rationality is a means for the realization of values, and therefore cannot itself be placed on the *same* level with all the other values. Indeed, the critique of ideology's preparation for rational conduct recommends rationality as the preferred—if not exclusive—means for the realization of values, because it guarantees the "efficiency" or "economy" of procedures. Both of these terms betray the interest of knowledge guiding the empirical sciences to be a technical one. They reveal that from the outset rationalization is confined within the limits posed by the system of social labor, that what it refers to is exactly the making available of objective and objectified processes. And in this the power of technical control remains wholly indifferent with respect to the possible value systems, in the service of which it is to be exercised. Efficiency and economy, which are the definition of this rationality, cannot, in turn, be themselves conceived as values, and yet, within the framework of positivism's understanding of itself, they can only be justified as though they were values. A critique of ideology whose sole goal is to make technological rationality prevail, cannot escape from this dilemma: it desires rationality as a value, because it has the advantage over all the other values of being implicit in the rational modes of procedure themselves. Because this value can be legitimized by pointing to the process of scientific investigation and its technical application, and does not have to be justified in terms of pure commitment alone, it has a preferential status as against all other values. The experience of the controlled success enjoyed by rational conduct exercises a rationally demonstrated compulsion toward the acceptance of such norms of conduct; thus even this limited rationality implies a decision in favor of rationality. In the critique of ideology, which at least tacitly realizes this, a particle of committed reason therefore remains active—in contradiction to the criteria by which it criticizes dogmatism. Because, no matter how perverted, it still remains of a piece with committed reason; it also entails consequences which violate its alleged neutrality toward any value systems whatsoever. On the contrary, the concept of rationality which it seeks to make prevail in its commitment ultimately implies an entire organization of society: one in which a technology become autonomous dictates a value system—namely, its own—to the domains of praxis it has usurped—and all in the name of value freedom.

I wish to distinguish four levels of rationalization, on which we extend our technical powers of control qualitatively. On the first two levels, technologies demand an exclusion of normative elements from the process of scientific argumentation; on the two subsequent levels, however, this elimination changes into its opposite in the subordination of values, which have first been pronounced irrational, to technological procedures, which then establish themselves as values.

The *first* level of rationalization depends on the methodological state of the empirical sciences. The mass of corroborated lawlike hypotheses determines the extent of possible rational conduct. In this is involved technological rationality in the strict sense: we employ techniques placed at our disposal by science for the realization of goals. If, however, there is a choice between actions of equal technical appropriateness, a rationalization on the *second* level is required. The translation of technical recommendations into praxis—thus the technical utilization of theories of the empirical sciences—is also to be subject to the conditions of technological rationality. But the information furnished by empirical science is not sufficient for a rational choice between means which are functionally equivalent, given concrete goals, and which are to be realized within the framework of a value system. Thus instead, this relation between alternative techniques and given goals, on the one hand, and value systems and maxims for reaching decisions, on the other, is clarified by decision theory.[18] It analyzes the possible decisions normatively in accordance with a rationality of choice defined as "economical" or "efficient." But in so doing, rationality refers solely to the form of the decisions, and not to objective situations and actual results.[19]

On the first two levels, the rationality of conduct enforces an isolation of values, which are removed from any and every cogent discussion, and can only be related to given techniques and concrete goals in the form of hypothetically entertained imperatives; these relations are accessible to rational calculation, because they remain external to the values rendered irrational as such. "What is designated as a value system here is thus a system of rules which prescribe how the consequences described by the information system are to be evaluated *on the basis of the value perceptions* [*Wertempfindungen*] of the actor."[20] The subjectivistic reduction of the interests which are decisive in the orientation for action to "sentiments" or "perceptions," which cannot be rationalized beyond that, is a precise expression for the fact that the value freedom central to the technological concept of rationality functions within the system of social labor, and that all the other interests of the praxis of life are subordinated for the benefit of the sole interest in efficiency and economy in the utilization of means. The competing perspectives of interest, hypostatized to values, are excluded from discussion. Revealingly enough, according to the criteria of technological rationality, agreement on a collective value system can never be achieved by means of enlightened discussion carried on in public politics, thus by way of a consensus rationally arrived at, but only by summation or compromise—values are in principle beyond discussion.[21] Naturally, the decision-theoretical assumption of "autonomous" value systems is not tenable in practice. The institution of formal rationality of choice, thus an extension of technological thinking to the selection of scientific techniques, changes the previously given value systems themselves. By this I mean not only the systematization of value conceptions required by this decision-theoretical analysis; I mean above all the reformulation or even total devaluation of traditional norms, which fail to function as principles of orientation for a technical realization of concrete goals. The dialectical relation between values which originate in specific configurations of interest and techniques for the satisfaction of value-oriented needs is evident: just as values become depreciated as ideological and then become extinct, when they have lost their connection with a technically adequate satisfaction of real needs over a longer period, so inversely new techniques can form new value systems within changed configurations of interest. As is well known, Dewey was able to derive from the interconnection of values with technical knowledge the expectation that the deployment of continually multiplied and improved techniques would not remain bound solely to the [existing] orientation of values, but also would subject the values themselves indirectly to a pragmatic test of their viability. Only because this interrelationship between traditional values and scientific techniques, which decision theory neglects, exists, can Dewey ask: "How shall we employ what we know to direct our practical behavior so as to test these beliefs and make possible better ones? The question is seen as it has always been empirically: What shall we do to make objects having value more secure in existence?" [22] This question can be answered in the sense of a reason which is interested in enlightenment; in any case, that is the sense in which Dewey posed it. Meanwhile, we first have to deal with the alternative answer, which subjects even the formation of value systems to technological rationality. With that we reach the *third* level of rationalization.

The latter extends to strategic situations, in which rational conduct in the face of an opponent who also acts rationally is to be calculated. Both adversaries pursue competing interests; in the case of a strictly competitive situation, they evaluate the same consequences according to inverse series of preferences, no matter whether the value systems correspond or not. Such a situation demands a far-reaching rationalization. Those acting do not only wish to gain control technically over a specific field of events by means of scientific prediction, but also to gain the same control over situations of rational indeterminacy; they cannot inform themselves about the conduct of the opponent empirically in the same manner as about processes of nature, by means of lawlike hypotheses; their information remains incomplete, not merely to a degree but in principle, because the opponent also has a choice of alternative strategies and thus is not confined to unambiguously determined reactions. What interests us, however, is not the game-theoretical solution of the problem posed, but the peculiar technical compulsion which, in addition, such strategic situations exercise on value systems. A basic value also enters into the technical task itself, namely, successful self-assertion against an opponent, the securing of survival. The originally invested values, that is, those value systems with which decision theory initially is solely occupied, are then relativized in terms of this strategic value, by which the game or the conflict is given its orientation.

As soon as the game theory's assumption concerning strategic situations is generalized to cover all decision-making situations, decision-making processes can be analyzed under political conditions on all occasions—here I use "political" in the sense of the tradition from Hobbes to Carl Schmitt, in the sense of existential self-assertion. Then ultimately it is sufficient to reduce all value systems to an, as it were, biological basic value, and to pose the problem of decision-making generally, in the following form: How must the systems by which decisions are made—whether by individuals or groups, specific institutions or entire societies—be organized in order to meet the basic value of survival in a given situation and to avoid risks. The goal functions, which together with the initially invested values furnished the program, here disappear in favor of formalized goal variables, such as stability or adaptability, which are bound solely to a quasibiological basic requirement of the system, that of reproducing life. To be sure, this self-programming of feedback systems only becomes possible on the *fourth* level of rationalization, as soon as it becomes possible to turn over the decision-making effort to a machine. Even if today there is a large class of problems for which machines can be utilized successfully in order to simulate the real case, still this last stage of rationalization as yet remains largely a fiction. However, it does reveal for the first time in its entirety the intention of a technological rationality extended over all the domains of praxis, and thereby the substantial concept of rationality, which the positivistic critique presupposes as its premise, and yet at the same time suppresses. Learning machines as cybernetic mechanisms for social organization can in principle take over such decision-making processes under political conditions. As soon as this threshold had been passed, the value systems excluded from the process of rationalization at a lower level would themselves also be rendered interchangeable in accordance with the criteria of rational behavior; indeed, these values could only enter, as a liquid mass, into the adaptive procedures of a machine which stabilizes its own equilibrium and programs itself because the values had previously been rendered irrational qua values.[23]

In a manuscript on the scientific and political significance of decision theory, Horst Rittel has drawn unmistakable conclusions for the fourth level of rationalization:

> Value systems can no longer be regarded as stable over a longer period. What can be desired depends on what can be made possible, and what can be made possible depends on what one desires. Goals and utility functions are not independent variables. They are in reciprocal interaction with the scope of decision-making. Within broad limits conceptions of value can be directed. In the face of the uncertainty which marks the alternatives of future development, there is no prospect for seeking to set up rigid models of decision-making and to offer strategies for longer time periods. . . . It proves more meaningful to view the problem of decision-making in a more general way and to look into the suitability of decision-making systems. How must an organization be constituted so that it will be equal to the uncertainty introduced by innovation and political vicissitudes? . . . Instead of assuming a specific decision-making system and a value system as definitely given, the suitability of this system for fulfilling its tasks must be investigated. What feedback mechanisms to its object system are necessary? What data about the object system are needed and to

what degree of precision? What devices are necessary for the preparation of this data? Which value systems are at all consistent and guarantee chances for adaptation, and therefore for "survival"? [24]

The negative Utopia of technical control over history would be fulfilled if one were to set up a learning automaton as a central system of societal control which would answer these questions cybernetically, thus by "itself."

The critique of ideology, which for the sake of resolving dogmatism and asserting technologically rational behavior insistently separates reason from decisions of commitment, in the end automates the decisions according to the laws of the rationality thus made dominant. Critique, however, cannot maintain this separation and only finds its own rationality in its partisanship for rationality, no matter how restricted. That is why even the type of rationalization developed on these four levels is not tolerant, to say nothing of indifferent, toward values. For from this concept of rationality the ultimate decisions concerning the acceptance or rejection of norms are not excluded after all. Even these decisions ultimately are incorporated into the self-regulating process of adaptation of a learning automaton according to the laws of rational behavior—connected to a process of knowledge oriented toward technical control. The substantive rationality suppressed in the innocent partisanship for formal rationality reveals, in the anticipated concept of a cybernetically self-regulated organization of society, a tacit philosophy of history. This is based on the questionable thesis that human beings control their destinies rationally to the degree to which social techniques are applied, and that human destiny is capable of being rationally guided in proportion to the extent of cybernetic control and the application of these techniques. But such a rational administration of the world is not simply identical with the solution of the practical problems posed by history. There is no reason for assuming that a continuum of rationality exists extending from the capacity of technical control over objectified processes to the practical mastery of historical processes. The root of the irrationality of history is that we "make" it, without, however, having been able until now to make it consciously. A rationalization of history cannot therefore be furthered by an extended power of control on the part of manipulative human beings, but only by a higher stage of reflection, a consciousness of acting human beings moving forward in the direction of emancipation.

On the self-reflection of rationalistic "faith"

Now, even in its positivistic form the critique of ideology can pursue an interest in adult autonomy; as the example of Popper shows, it need not stop at an adherence to the technical interest of knowledge. Certainly, Popper was one of the first to insist on the demarcation rigidly drawn by the logic of science between knowing and valuing. He too identifies the knowledge of empirical science conforming to the rules of a cogent universal methodology with science as such; he too simply accepts the residual definition of thought, which is purged of the components of rational volition, and does not ask whether perhaps the monopolizing of all possible knowledge by a technical interest of knowledge does not itself create the norms, measured by which everything that does not comply takes on the fetishistic guise of valuing, commitment, or mere faith. But Popper's critique of the configurations of dogmatism, as positivistically defined, does not share the tacit metaphysics to which the partisans of technological rationality are committed. His motive is that of enlightenment, with the prior reservation, however, that he can only justify rationalism as his professed faith. If scientific insight purged of the interest of reason is devoid of all immanent reference to praxis, and if, inversely, every normative content is detached nominalistically from insights into its real relation to life—as Popper presupposes undialectically—then indeed the dilemma must be conceded: that I cannot rationally compel anyone to support his assumptions with arguments and evidence from experience. And just as little can I justify compellingly, with the aid of arguments and experiential evidence, why I should be resolved to pursue this conduct. I must simply decide to commit myself to a rationalistic attitude. Even here the problem consists "not in a choice between knowing and believing, but in the choice between two kinds of faith." [25] What is at issue here for Popper is not the recommendation to accept technological rationality as a value. Rather, the rationalism in which he believes desires to obligate society, by means of the enlightened consciousness of its citizens, to a sociotechnically correct behavior. These citizens will act rationally, in the sense which already points beyond technological rationality, when they establish or change social norms and institutions with a knowledge of the scientific information at their disposal. For precisely that dualism of facts and commitments, with the implicit assumption that history can have meaning just as little as nature can, appears as the premise for the practical effectiveness of a rationalism adopted as commitment. It presupposes that, in the dimension of historical facts, by virtue of commitment and due to our theoretical knowledge of factual laws of nature, we can realize a "meaning" sociotechnically which is inherently alien to history. Popper's concept of rationality, too, at first preserves the semblance of a purely formal concept, no matter how much his category of meaning otherwise exceeds the criteria of economy and efficiency required by the system of social labor; this meaning itself, for the realization of which specific procedures are provided, remains undefined and open to concretization in terms of the requirements of accepted value systems. The material shaping of given situations cannot already be prejudiced from the start by the obligation to apply rational procedures—for then even in this other case a substantial concept of rationality would be presupposed which would deprive the rationalistic faith of its character of pure decision.

Rationalism in Popper's positivistically delimited sense initially demands only that as many individuals as possible assume a rationalistic attitude. This attitude, no matter whether it determines comportment in the process of inquiry or in social praxis, conforms to the rules of scientific methodology. It accepts the customary norms of scientific discussion, is instructed especially concerning the duality of fact and commitment, and knows the limits of intersubjectively valid knowledge. Therefore it resists dogmatism, as the positivists understand it, and obligates itself in its judgment of value systems, and in general of social norms, to conform to critical principles which specify the relationship of theory to praxis. First, the absolute validity of all social norms is denied; instead, they are considered to be open to critical investigation and possible revision at any time. Second, norms are accepted only after their effects in given social life-contexts have been tested and evaluated on the basis of available scientific information. Finally, every politically relevant action will seek to exhaust the reserves of technical knowledge and will employ all means of prediction, in order to avoid uncontrolled secondary consequences. All levels of this rationalization always refer back to the communication of the citizens carrying on discussion with a rationalistic attitude—and this distinguishes them from the four levels of technology enumerated above. For Popper has fictitiously extended methodology to the principles of political discussion, and thus has also extended the forum of scientific researchers examining methods and discussing empirical-theoretical questions to embrace the political public sphere as a whole.

The sociopolitical extrapolation of methodology into social policy represents more than merely the form of a rational realization of meaning. Indeed, it unfolds a specific meaning, and even the intention of a specific order of society, namely, the liberal order of the "open society." From the formal assumption of a rationalistic attitude Popper draws maxims for the decision of practical questions, which, if they were followed on an order of magnitude which is politically relevant, would have to intervene profoundly in the "natural" structure of the existing society. That process of scientifically enlightened communication to be institutionalized in the political public sphere, would set into motion a sociotechnical dissolution of all substantial forms of domination— and would maintain this dissolution itself in the permanent reflection of the citizens, for the sake of their emancipation. It is not without reason, therefore, that Popper expects a reduction of repression from such a liberalism in the formation of political will, reconstituted on the level of the modern sciences, and as a consequence of this, the growing emancipation of human beings: the reduction of collective and individual suffering within the limits of a noncompulsive consensus concerning the bases of general welfare and peace. Just as in the Enlightenment of the eighteenth century, lack of rationality once again coincides with freedom denied and deprivation of happiness.

If, however, a well-founded interconnection actually existed between the canon of scientifically cogent communication, extrapolated into the sociopolitical domain, and such practical consequences, then a positivism which reflected on itself could no longer detach reason's interest in emancipation from its concept of rationality. Now, however, that interconnection exists because in rational discussion as such a tendency is inherent, irrevocably, which is precisely a decisive commitment entailed by rationality itself, and which therefore does not require the commitment [*Dezision*] of pure faith. But rationalism would revoke [sublate] itself to become the positivistic version of blind faith if the comprehensive rationality of unconstrained dialogue between communicating human beings—which Popper tacitly requires from the outset—were merely to be subjected once again to the limited rationality of social labor.[26]

Popper's discussion of methodological questions, as David Pole pointed out against him quite correctly,[27] presupposes the prior understanding of a rationality that is not as yet divested of its normative elements: methodological decisions can only be discussed on a rational basis if prior to that we have formed a concept of a "good" theory, a "satisfactory" argument, a "true" consensus, and a perspective that is hermeneutically "fruitful"; in such a concept, descriptive and normative contents are still not separated. Popper, on the other hand, must deny the rationality of such decisions, because it is they which determine to begin with the rules according to which the empirical analysis can be carried out in a value-free manner. And what is cut off especially is a discussion which would have to develop the objective implications of methodical decisions within the social context of the process of research, but which cannot do so owing to an undialectical separation of questions of genesis from those of validity.

This precarious inhibition of rationality is revealed still more distinctly in the discussion of practical questions as envisioned by Popper. Value systems, too, are to be subjected to rational tests of validity that are just as rigorous as those of scientific theory, even if they are conducted in a different manner. According to the criteria for this validity, just as in the sciences, decisions would have to be reached methodologically. By means of such criteria, the factual consequences that value systems have for social life could be tested in given situations on analogy with the information content of empirical science theories. In this connection, Hans Albert makes the utilitarian suggestion "to place in the foreground . . . in the establishment of a criterion for the validity of ethical systems, the satisfaction of human needs, the fulfillment of human desires, the avoidance of unnecessary human suffering. Such a criterion would have to be discovered and established, just as this is true for the criteria of scientific thought. The social rules of the game and also institutions, which to a certain degree are embodiments of ethical ideas that could be tested with the aid of such a criterion, are based on human invention. It is not to be expected that such a criterion would simply be accepted without further argument . . . but a rational discussion of a usable criterion is possible without any difficulties." [28] Now, however, the establishment of such criteria is withdrawn from empirical scientific control, in view of the methodologically presupposed dualism of matters of fact and of moral decision. Precisely the desire for a far-reaching rationalization involuntarily renders visible the positivistic limits: questions of fact are prejudged in the form of methodological decisions, and the practical consequences flowing from the application of such criteria are excluded from reflection. Instead, a hermeneutic clarification of the need and the need satisfaction historically appropriate to the developmental state of society would be required, as well as a concept of suffering and "unnecessary" suffering valid for the epoch. Above all, the criterion selected would have to be derived as such from the objective complex of underlying interests and justified in terms of these. That in turn already presupposes a comprehensive concept of rationality, and especially one that does not hesitate to reflect on its own interrelationship with the historical stage of development attained by the knowing subjects. As soon as argument with rational warrants is carried on at the methodological—the so-called metatheoretical and metaethical—level, the threshold to the dimension of comprehensive rationality has already been breached. The proponents of positivistic enlightenment, who have confidence in their rationalism only as an article of faith, cannot reflect on what they thus presuppose *as* reason, as an interest identical with that of reason, for although they themselves have only been infected with the dogmatism of the technologists, they cannot see through it.

Only a reason which is fully aware of the interest in the progress of reflection toward adult autonomy, which is indestructibly at work in every rational discussion, will be able to gain transcendent power from the awareness of its own materialistic involvements. It alone will be able to begin reflecting on the positivistic domination of the technical interest of knowledge, growing out of the interrelationships of an industrial society that integrates science within it as a productive force, and which thus protects itself as a whole from critical insight. It alone can dispense with sacrificing the attained dialectical rationality of language to the deeply irrational criteria of a technologically constrained rationality of labor. Only it can seriously intervene in the complex of compulsive interrelations of history, which remains dialectical as long as it is not liberated so that the dialogue of mature, autonomous human beings can take place. Today the convergence of reason and commitment, which the philosophy of the great tradition considered to be intimately linked, must be regained, reflected, and reasserted on the level of positive science, and that means carried on through the separation which is necessarily and correctly drawn on the level of technological rationality, the dichotomy of reason and commitment. Science as a productive force can work in a salutary way when it is suffused by science as an emancipatory force, to the same extent as it becomes disastrous as soon as it seeks to subject the domain of praxis, which is outside the sphere of technical disposition, to its *exclusive* control. The demythification which does not break the mythic spell but merely seeks to evade it will only bring forth new witch doctors. The enlightenment which does not break the spell dialectically, but instead winds the veil of a halfway rationalization only more tightly around us, makes the world divested of deities itself into a myth.

Schelling's romantic dictum about reason as controlled in-

sanity gains an oppressively acute sense under technological domination over a praxis, which for that reason alone is detached
from theory. The motive of reason was already central and
determining in myth, religion, and philosophy; there it had the
function of laying the foundation, within the manifold of shape-
less phenomena, for the unity and coherence of a world; this motive lives on in a perverted manner in insanity. When the sciences,
within the flux of phenomena in principle devoid of world,[29]
seek to wrest from contingency that which is empirically uniform,
they are positivistically purged of insanity. They control but they
do not control insanity; and therefore insanity must remain un-
governed and uncontrolled. Reason would have to rule in both
domains; but this way, reason falls between two stools. Accordingly, the danger of an exclusively technical civilization, which is
devoid of the interconnection between theory and praxis, can
be clearly grasped; it is threatened by the splitting of its consciousness, and by the splitting of human beings into two classes—
the social engineers and the inmates of closed institutions.

Notes

Introduction

1. See my essay "Wozu noch Philosophie" ["Why Still Do Philosophy?"], in *Philosophisch-politische Profile* (Frankfurt: 1971).
2. *Naturrecht*—see Translator's Notes.
3. *Willensbildung*—see Translator's Notes.
4. Neuwied, 1961; 3rd ed., 1969, "Über den Begriff der politischen Beteiligung," pp. 11–56.
5. Neuwied, 1962; 5th ed., 1971.
6. *Technik und Wissenschaft als "Ideologie"* (Frankfurt: 1968); 3rd ed., 1970, pp. 48–103. The essay itself is translated in *Toward a Rational Society* (Boston: Beacon Press, 1970).
7. "Technischer Fortschritt und soziale Lebenswelt," in *Technik und Wissenschaft als "Ideologie,"* pp. 104–119. Translation also contained in *Toward a Rational Society.*
8. "Praktische Folgen des wissenschaftlich-technischen Fortschritts," in the German edition of *Theorie und Praxis* (Frankfurt: Suhrkamp, 1971), pp. 336–359.
9. "Bedingungen für eine Revolutionierung spätkapitalistischer Gesellschaftssysteme," in *Marx und die Revolution* (Frankfurt: 1970), pp. 24–44.
10. Both in the German edition of *Theorie und Praxis.*
11. *Protestbewegung und Hochschulreform* (Frankfurt: 1971): three of these essays are included in *Toward a Rational Society,* trans. Jeremy J. Shapiro (Boston: 1970).
12. "Verwissenschaftlichte Politik und öffentliche Meinung," in *Technik und Wissenschaft als "Ideologie,"* translated in *Toward a Rational Society.*
13. *Philosophisch-politische Profile.*
14. For the political mandate of the sciences see K. O. Apel, "Wissenschaft als Emanzipation?" in *Zeitschrift für allgemeine Wissenschaftstheorie,* vol. 1, 1970, pp. 173–195; further, U. K. Preuss, *Das politische Mandat der Studentenschaft* (Frankfurt: 1969).
15. Initial attempts at developing an appropriate theoretical apparatus I have found, among others, in the work of Claus Offe.
16. In *Technik und Wissenschaft als "Ideologie."*
17. See also parallel investigations by K. O. Apel, especially the programmatic essay "Szientistik, Hermeneutik und Ideologiekritik" in the collection *Hermeneutik und Ideologiekritik* (Frankfurt: 1971), p. 7ff.
18. *Anthropologisch*—see Translator's Notes.

19. See *Erkenntnis und Interesse* (Frankfurt: 1968); 5th ed., 1971, p. 262ff. [*Knowledge and Human Interest*, trans. Jeremy J. Shapiro (Boston: 1971)]; also "Der Universalitätsanspruch der Hermeneutik," in *Hermeneutik und Ideologiekritik*, p. 120ff., and A. Lorenzer, *Sprachzerfall und Rekonstruktion* (Frankfurt: 1970).

20. Habermas–Luhmann, *Theorie der Gesellschaft oder Sozialtechnologie—Was leistet die Systemforschung?*, 2nd ed. (Frankfurt: 1971), p. 124ff.

21. *Geisteswissenschaften*—See Translator's Notes.

22. See my "Preparatory Remarks for a Theory of Communicative Competence" in Habermas–Luhmann, *Theorie der Gesellschaft*, p. 101ff.

23. This is also the only path for a general theory of semantics which offers any hope from the viewpoint of research strategy; as the efforts of Katz, Fodor, and Postal show, this theory has always foundered when attempts are made to treat meaning in terms of structural elements.

24. See K. O. Apel's introduction to the German edition which he edited of Peirce's [*Works*] *Schriften I & II* (Frankfurt: 1967 and 1970).

25. See M. Theunissen, *Gesellschaft und Geschichte, Zur Kritik der kritischen Theorie* (Berlin: 1969).

26. M. Pilot, "Jürgen Habermas' empirisch falsifizierbare Geschichtsphilosophie," in T. W. Adorno et al., *Der Positivismusstreit in der deutschen Soziologie*.

27. See K. O. Apel, "Wissenschaft als Emanzipation?"; also D. Böhler, "Das Problem des 'emanzipatorischen Interesses' und seiner gesellschaftlichen Wahrnehmung" ["The Problem of 'Emancipatory Interest' and Its Social Perception"], in *Man and World*, vol. 3, May 1970; *Metakritik der Marxschen Ideologiekritik* (Frankfurt: 1970); R. Bubner, "Was ist kritische Theorie?" in *Hermeneutik und Ideologiekritik*, p. 160ff. On the reproach of dogmatism in general, which incidentally is directed equally against Apel and me, see H. Albert, *Plädoyer für Kritischen Rationalismus* (Munich: 1971).

28. O. Negt, *Politik als Protest* (Frankfurt: 1971), pp. 87–101; quoted p. 96.

29. H. G. Gadamer, "Rhetorik, Hermeneutik und Ideologiekritik. Metakritische Erörterungen zu 'Wahrheit und Methode,'" in *Hermeneutik und Ideologiekritik*, p. 57ff.; reply by same author, ibid., p. 283ff.; H. J. Giegel, "Reflexion und Emanzipation," ibid., p. 244ff.; A. Wellmer, *Kritische Gesellschaftstheorie und Positivismus* (Frankfurt: 1969), p. 48ff.

30. Against this, see R. Bubner, "Was ist kritische Theorie?", ibid., p. 187ff.

31. T. W. Adorno, *Negative Dialektik* (Frankfurt: 1967).

32. *Mündigkeit*—see Translator's Notes.

33. *Technik und Wissenschaft als "Ideologie,"* p. 163.

34. Ibid., p. 163.

35. "Preparatory Remarks on a Theory of Communicative Competence," in Habermas–Luhmann, *Theorie der Gesellschaft*, pp. 101–141.

36. Ibid., p. 136ff.

37. See in relation to this my interpretation of Peirce and Dilthey in *Knowledge and Human Interest*, chapters 5–8.

38. Within this perspective I of course do not see that my position is characterized correctly by those who simply attribute a naturalism to my

explication of the interest of knowledge. Aside from M. Theunissen, see also
G. Rohrmoser, *Das Elend der Kritischen Theorie* ["The Misery of Critical
Theory"] (Freiburg: 1970), p. 101ff. The unavoidable circularity, in which
we become involved as soon as we approach problems which may be equivalent to the traditional one of ultimate foundations—although this can very
well be explained—may be a sign, that among other things, the concept-
pair, "contingency-necessity," is no longer to be sharply separated on this
level of argumentation. Presumably, assertions concerning contingency or
necessity of interests of knowledge are meaningless, just like those about
the contingency or necessity of the human race or the world as a whole.
Although the reproach of naturalism in the very soberly considered interpretation of Theunissen and Rohrmoser is hardly apt, neither, on the other
hand, is the somewhat less cautiously raised charge of antinaturalism by
H. Albert in *Plädoyer*, p. 53ff.

39. However, see the remark in *Hermeneutik und Ideologiekritik*,
p. 126f.

40. See *Knowledge and Human Interest*, chapters 10–12.

41. See Habermas–Luhmann, *Theorie der Gesellschaft*, pp. 171–175
(fn. 2), and p. 272ff.

42. This we can assume to be the relationship which Apel had in
mind in formulating his thesis: "Theoretical reflection and a material practical involvement are not identical, in spite of the identity of reason with
the interest of reason, but rather, on the highest stage of philosophical reflection, they diverge once more to become elements within the emancipatory interest of knowledge which are in polar opposition." ("Wissenschaft
als Emanzipation?" p. 193f.) If I may understand "theoretical reflection" to
be the procedure of rational reconstruction, then I would like to assume
for this only an indirect relation to the emancipatory interest of knowledge,
one mediated by self-reflection. For reflection I would not like to resort to
a specific involvement [*engagement*] dependent on the situation, as Apel
does, but rather assert that there is a motivation, which, if it is not tied to
the conditions of reproduction of the culture, is tied instead to the institutionalization of domination; this motivation is just as generalized as are
the other two interests of knowledge, though, to be sure, the latter are
more "deep-rooted" anthropologically.

43. Gadamer's reply in *Hermeneutik und Ideologiekritik*, p. 307f.

44. H. J. Giegel, "Reflexion und Emanzipation," in *Hermeneutik und
Ideologiekritik*, p. 278f.

45. K. Marx, *The Misery of Philosophy*, trans. H. Quelch (Chicago:
1920), p. 189.

46. G. Lukács, *History and Class Consciousness* (Cambridge, Mass.:
1971), p. 299ff.

47. Ibid., p. 300f.

48. Ibid., p. 299.

49. Ibid., p. 301.

50. Ibid., p. 304.

51. Ibid., p. 305.

52. Ibid., p. 318.

53. Ibid., p. 326.

54. Ibid., p. 327.

55. See O. Negt, *Marxismus als Legitimationswissenschaft. Zur Genese*

der stalinistischen Philosophie, Introduction to: Deborin, Bucharin, *Kontroversen über dialektischen und mechanistischen Materialismus* (Frankfurt: 1969), pp. 7–50.

56. O. Negt, *Politik als Protest,* p. 175ff., p. 214ff.

Chapter *1*

1. See W. Hennis, *Politik und praktische Philosophie* (Neuwied: 1963); also H. Maier, *Die ältere deutsche Staats- und Verwaltungslehre* (Neuwied: 1966).

2. See M. Riedel, "Aristotelestradition am Ausgang des 18. Jahrhunderts," in *Festschrift für Otto Brunner* (Göttingen: 1962), p. 278ff.; "Der Staatsbegriff der deutschen Geschichtschreibung des 19ten Jh.," in *Der Staat* 2 (1963): 41ff.; "Der Begriff der 'bürgerlichen Gesellschaft' und das Problem seines geschichtlichen Ursprungs," in *Studien zu Hegels Rechtsphilosophie* (Frankfurt: 1969), p. 135ff.

3. See Joachim Ritter, "Zur Grundlegung der praktischen Philosophie bei Aristoteles," in *Archiv für Rechts- und Sozialphilosophie* 46 (1960): 179ff.; *Naturrecht bei Aristoteles, res publica H. 6* (Stuttgart: 1961); *Metaphysik und Politik* (Frankfurt: 1969), pp. 9–179.

4. See Hannah Arendt, *Vita Activa* (Stuttgart: 1960). The study of H. Arendt's important investigation and of H. G. Gadamer's *Wahrheit und Methode* (Tübingen: 1961) have called my attention to the fundamental significance of the Aristotelian distinction between *techne* and *praxis.*

5. G. B. Vico, *The New Science,* trans. T. G. Bergin and M. H. Fisch (Ithaca, N.Y.: 1948), §§ 331, 349.

6. Summarized in H. Albert, "Probleme der Wissenschaftslogik in der Sozialforschung," in *Handbuch der empirischen Sozialforschung* (Stuttgart: 1962), vol. 1, p. 38ff.; H. Albert and E. Topitsch, eds., *Werturteilsstreit* (Darmstadt: 1971).

7. Vico, *On the Study Methods of Our Time,* trans. Elio Gianturco (Indianapolis 1965), p. 34.

8. Ibid., p. 15.

9. Consequences with respect to commitment [*dezisionistische*] are drawn, as consequences of the methodological postulate of value-freedom by K. R. Popper, *The Open Society and Its Enemies* (Princeton, N.J.: 1950). The verifiability of practical questions, which is denied not only by critical philosophers such as Popper, but above all by Positivists such as Carnap and Ayer, Empiricists such as Stevenson, and Language Analytic philosophers such as Hare, has been reasserted most recently by the so-called "good reasons approach." Here the investigation of K. Baier, *The Moral Point of View,* 2nd ed. (New York: 1965), was the pioneering work. For the logic of practical discourse, see P. Lorenzen, *Normative Logic and Ethics* (Mannheim: 1969); O. Schwemmer, *Philosophie der Praxis* (Frankfurt: 1971); F. Kanbartel, "Moralisches Argumentieren" (MS, 1971).

10. Vico, op. cit., p. 35.

11. Francis Bacon, *Novum Organum,* I, § 127.

12. See the commentaries to Vico's *Vom Wesen und Weg* by F. Schalk, op. cit., p. 165.

13. *Bürger, bürgerlich*—see Translator's Notes.

14. Thomas Aquinas, "De regime principium" ["On Kingship"], ex-cerpted in *The Political Ideas of St. Thomas Aquinas,* ed. Dino Bigongiari (New York: 1957), art. 4.

15. Thomas Aquinas, *Summa Theologica* I, Qu. 96, 4.

16. Thomas Aquinas, "De regime principium," chapter 1.

17. Thomas Aquinas, *Politics,* 1255 b.

18. H. Arendt, *Vita Activa.*

19. E. Bloch, *Naturrecht und menschliche Würde* (Frankfurt: 1961).

20. Another translation of this passage may be found in *The Discourses of Niccolo Machiavelli,* trans. Leslie J. Walker (London: 1950), Vol. I, I, 16.8, p. 255.

21. Thomas More, *Utopia,* trans. Peter K. Marshall (New York: 1965), p. 124.

22. Ibid., p. 122.

23. Ibid.

24. See N. Machiavelli, *The Prince,* Hill Thompson, trans. (New York: 1954), ch. XVIII, p. 130.

25. See Hans Fryer, *Machiavell* (Leipzig: 1938); for a critical study from the viewpoint of classical Natural Law, see L. Strauss, *Thoughts on Machiavelli* (Glencoe, Ill.: 1958); for a survey of the literature, see E. Faul, *Der moderne Machiavellismus* (Cologne: 1961).

26. See N. Machiavelli, *The Prince,* ch. VII, pp. 58ff.

27. More, *Utopia,* p. 124.

28. *Bürgerliche Privatleute*—see Translator's Notes.

29. More, *Utopia,* p. 39.

30. Ibid., p. 37.

31. "A Prince, therefore, should have no care or thought but for war and for the regulation and training it requires, and should apply himself exclusively to this as his peculiar province; for war is the sole art looked for in one who rules. . . ." See Machiavelli, *The Prince,* ch. XIV, p. 110.

32. Ibid.

33. Max Horkheimer, *Die Anfänge der bürgerlichen Geschichtsphilosophie* (Stuttgart: 1931).

34. H. Arendt, *Vita Activa,* p. 293.

35. For the concept of an interest of technical knowledge, which does not have a psychological but a transcendental significance, see my *Knowledge and Human Interest;* also, K. O. Apel, "Szientistik, Hermeneutik, Ideologiekritik," in *Wiener Jahrbuch für Philosophie,* vol. I, 1968, p. 15ff., now also in *Hermeneutik und Ideologiekritik.*

36. H. Arendt, *Vita Activa,* p. 291.

37. *Rechtskonstruktion*—see Translator's Notes.

38. See F. Borkenau, *Der Übergang vom feudalen zum bürgerlichen Weltbild* (Paris: 1934), p. 104ff.

39. J. Althusius, *Politica Methodice Digesta,* 3rd ed., ed. C. J. Friedrich (Cambridge, Mass.: 1932).

40. Hobbes, *De Homine* (Latin Works), ed. Molesworth, vol. II, ch. XIII, 9.

41. Hobbes, *De Corpore,* in *English Works,* ed. Sir William Molesworth (London: 1838), vol. I, part I, ch. 1, sec. 10; see also I, 1, 2.

42. For the anthropological construction of the state of nature see

B. Willms, *Die Antwort des Leviathan—Th. Hobbes politische Theorie* (Neuwied: 1970).

43. Hobbes, *De Cive* ("Philosophical Rudiments concerning Government and Society"), in *English Works*, vol. II, ch. I, 7.

44. Ibid.

45. See E. Topitsch, *Vom Ursprung und Ende der Metaphysik* (Vienna: 1958), p. 222ff.

46. Borkenau, *Der Übergang*, p. 476: "In the world of corruption social consciousness is not supposed to be an instinct and yet the most powerful of all motives."

47. Hobbes, *De Cive*, Epistle Dedicatory, p. vi. On this, see also Willms, *Die Antwort*, p. 111ff.

48. Ibid., ch. XIII, 4.

49. Ibid., ch. XVI, 6.

50. Ibid., ch. XIII, 16.

51. "Liberty, that we may define it, is nothing else but *an absence of lets and hindrances of motion . . .* ," Hobbes, *De Cive*, in *English Works*, ch. IX, 9.

52. "But because all the motions and actions of subjects are never circumscribed by laws, nor can be, by reason of their variety; it is necessary that there be infinite cases which are neither commanded nor prohibited, but every man may either do them or not do them as he lists himself. In these, each man is said to enjoy his liberty. . . ." Ibid., ch. XIII, 15.

53. Hobbes emphasizes "that what rights soever any man challenges to himself, he also grants the same as due to all the rest," *De Cive*, ch. 3, 14.

54. Ibid., ch. XIII, 10.

55. Ibid., ch. XIII, 3, 4.

56. Ibid.

57. This side was brought out above all by Ferdinand Tönnies (*Hobbes*, Stuttgart: 1925), while C. Schmitt emphasizes the obverse decision-theoretical (*dezisionistische*) side (*Der Leviathan in der Staatslehre des Th. Hobbes*, Hamburg: 1938). Of course, both fail to recognize the inner connection of these two aspects, which also corresponded to the objective conditions at this stage of the development of bourgeois society. See M. Horkheimer, *Die Anfänge der bürgerlichen Geschichtsphilosophie*, ch. 2, p. 37ff. On the conformity of sovereignty and the market society see the pioneering study of C. B. Macpherson, *The Political Theory of Possessive Individualism* (Oxford: 1962); furthermore, the introduction by Iring Fetscher to the German edition of *Leviathan*, trans. W. Euchner (Neuwied: 1966), p. IXff.

58. Certainly the philosopher may be permitted to construct the liberal intentions of the social contrast abstractly, in terms of Natural Law, from the political character of the state of nature, as Hobbes does, in order to measure by this the positive commands of the sovereign. However, in political praxis this claim would stand on the *same* level with all the other professed opinions about good and evil: ". . . to understand perfectly all natural and civil rights; and all manner of sciences, which, comprehended under the title of philosophy, are necessary partly to live, partly to live well; I say, the understanding of these . . . is to be learnt from reasoning; that is to say, by making necessary consequences, having first taken the beginning from experience. But men's reasonings are sometimes right, some-

times wrong; and consequently, that which is concluded and held for a truth, is sometimes truth, sometimes error." And now comes the point of this argument: "Now errors, even about these philosophical points, do sometimes public hurt, and give occasions of great seditions and injuries. It is needful therefore, as oft as any controversy ariseth in these matters contrary to the public good and common peace, that there be somebody to judge of the reasoning, that is to say, whether that which is inferred, be rightly inferred or not; . . ." (Hobbes, *De Cive,* ch. XVII, 12). And if it is not to prejudice sovereignty, this judge can only be the sovereign himself.

59. Ibid., ch. VI, 13 fn.; and ch. VII, 14.

60. Ibid., ch. VII, 3.

61. See C. Schmitt, *Der Leviathan,* p. 69: "Either the state apparatus functions or it does not function. In the first case it guarantees to me the security of my physical existence; for that it demands unconditional obedience to the laws of its functioning. All further questioning leads to a condition, "before the state is founded," of insecurity, in which, in the end, one is no longer secure in one's physical life, because the appeal to justice and truth does bring peace, but only renders war all the more bitter and malevolent."

62. Hobbes, *De Cive,* Preface, p. xxi.

63. Hobbes, *De Corpore,* in *English Works,* vol. I, part I, ch. I, 6.

64. Hobbes vacillates in his methodological determinations of the relationship of Social Philosophy and Physics (= Philosophy of Nature). He distinguishes the knowledge of effects from their generative causes—demonstrative knowledge *a priori,* which is only possible of those things which men can produce themselves—from the knowledge of the generative causes from their known effects—thus the demonstrative knowledge *a posteriori,* to which we are confined in the investigation of the things of nature, the production of which is not within our power. An example of the former is Geometry, of the latter Physics. This distinction does not do full justice to the level which the natural sciences had attained in his time; for their—tacit—criterion is the ability to reproduce the experimentally ascertained processes of nature. In Hobbes this is not so: "Because we produce the figures ourselves, Geometry is counted a demonstrative science, and can be strictly proven. On the other hand, it is not within our power to produce the things of nature" (Ch. 10, para. 5). Here Hobbes misses precisely the point of the modern method, which carries over the *verum et factum convertuntur* from Geometry, for which this had been true up till then, to the rigorous empirical sciences. However, Hobbes does accord to Social Philosophy that definition which would have done justice to Modern Physics. For Social Philosophy is to correspond to Geometry, in that it deals with relations (compacts) which men produce themselves; on the other hand, it is an empirical science like Physics, "for knowledge of the properties of a commonwealth it is necessary first to know the disposition, affections, and manners, of men . . ." (*De Corpore,* in *English Works,* vol. I, ch. I, 9). We therefore consider the formulation justified that Hobbes does Social Philosophy "with the approach" which is distinctive of Modern Physics—although his own specification of the scientific theory of Physics remains inadequate.

I see an indirect confirmation of my interpretation in the following. Vico's famous maxim for knowledge can be found in Hobbes, as far as the literal sense is concerned. Vico's statement reads: "And history cannot be more certain than when he who creates the things also describes them. Thus our science proceeds exactly as does geometry, which, while it constructs out of its elements or contemplates the world of quantity, itself creates it; but with a reality greater in proportion to that of orders having to do with human affairs, in which there are neither points, lines, surfaces, nor figures" (Vico, *New Science*, § 349). Similarly Hobbes: "As the causes of the properties which the single figure has lie in the lines which we ourselves have drawn, and as the generation of the figures depends on our own will, nothing further is required for the knowledge of any property of a figure you like than that we draw all the conclusions from the construction which we ourselves carry out in the drawing of the figure. For this reason, because we produce the figures ourselves, Geometry is counted as a demonstrative science. . . . Furthermore, politics and ethics, that is, the science of justice and injustice, fairness and unfairness, can be demonstrated *a priori*, because we ourselves create the principles by which we know the nature of justice and fairness . . . which means, the causes of justice, namely the laws and covenants." In spite of this verbal correspondence, in Hobbes nothing follows from this which would be even remotely comparable with the conclusions which Vico draws for the founding of his Scienza Nuova. If one adds to this Hobbes's dubious limitation that the construction of the state and society must be founded on a Physics of human nature, then it becomes understandable why from Hobbes's invocation of the principle *verum et factum convertuntur* follows, not a philosophy of world-history, but a mechanics of sociation: Vico seeks to defeat modern science with its own weapons, in order to renew the "ancient method of study" in such a way as to meet the requirements of the modern certainty of knowledge; Hobbes, on the other hand, seeks to revolutionize the classical doctrine of politics according to the model of modern science, thus to lay the foundation of a Social Philosophy *in the manner* of the Physics of his time.

65. Hobbes, *De Cive*, Preface, p. xiv.

66. Hobbes, *De Corpore*, part I, ch. 1, 7.

67. Ibid.

68. Hobbes, *De Cive*, Epistle Dedicatory, p. v.

69. Vico, *New Science*, p. 35f.

70. Hobbes, *De Cive*, Epistle Dedicatory, p. iv.

71. See my essay, "The Scientization of Politics and Public Opinion," in *Toward a Rational Society*, p. 62ff.

72. I. Kant, "Perpetual Peace," in *Kant's Political Writings*, ed. Hans Reiss (Cambridge, England: 1970).

73. See below, chapter 2, the interpretation of Thomas Paine.

74. The following remarks supplement the historical consideration on the topic "public opinion" in *Strukturwandel der Öffentlichkeit*, 5th ed. (Neuwied: 1971), sec. 12.

75. John Millar, *The Origin of the Distinction of Ranks*, 3rd ed. (Edinburgh: 1779), reprinted in *John Millar of Glasgow* by W. C. Lehmann (Cambridge: 1960), pp. 175–322.

76. M. Condorcet, *Sketch for a Historical Picture of the Progress of the Human Mind*, introduction by Stuart Hampshire (London: 1955).

77. The following remarks are based on an investigation by W. Hennis, *Politik und praktische Philosophie* (Neuwied: 1963).

78. E. Kapp, *Greek Foundations of Traditional Logic* (New York: 1942), especially chapter 1, p. 3ff.

79. H. G. Gadamer, "Hegel und die antike Dialektik," in *Hegelstudien* 1 (1961): 173ff.

Chapter 2

1. Hegel, *Lectures on the Philosophy of History*, trans. J. Sibtree (London: 1881), p. 465.

2. Ibid., p. 466.

3. *Naturrecht*—see Translator's Notes.

4. Edmund Burke, *Reflections on the Revolution in France*.

5. E. Rosenstock, "Revolution als politischer Begriff der Neuzeit," in *Festschrift F. Heilborn* (Breslau: 1931); K. Griewank, *Der neuzeitliche Revolutionsbegriff* (Frankfurt: 1969); R. Kosellek, *Kritik und Krise* (Freiburg: 1959), especially p. 208, fn. 97.

6. Thomas Hobbes, *De Cive*, in *English Works*, ed. Sir William Molesworth (London: 1838), vol. II, ch. XIII, 15.

7. "Qui dit un droit, dit une prérogative établie sur un devoir; point des droits sans devoirs et point de devoirs sans droit."

8. In 1786, for example, Condorcet was already occupied with the influence *de la révolution d'Amérique sur l'Europe (Oeuvres de Condorcet,* ed. A. Condorcet, O'Connor, and M. F. Arago [Paris: 1847], vol. 8).

9. "All the revolutions which till now had changed the face of empires had solely the goal of a change of dynasty or the transfer of power from one individual into the hands of many. The French Revolution is the first which is based on the doctrine of the Rights of Man and on the principles of justice." Robespierre, *Reden*, ed. Schnelle, Reclam edition, p. 371.

10. Hegel, op. cit., p. 90.

11. On this Jellinek had already based his thesis that in its understanding of itself the French Revolution remained dependent on the American model. Georg Jellinek, *Die Erklärung der Menschen- und Bürgerrechte*, 2nd ed. (Leipzig: 1904), p. 13ff.

12. A meaningful historical comparison of the French declaration of fundamental rights with its predecessor in America must therefore refer to the Declaration of Independence rather than to a version of the Bill of Rights adopted by the individual states, which are related to it in their form.

13. *The Writings of Thomas Jefferson*, 1869, vol. 8, p. 407. See C. Becker, *The Declaration of Independence* (New York: 1956), p. 24ff.

14. Jefferson, *Writings*, p. 407.

15. E. Sièyes, "Qu'est-ce que le Tiers état," ed. R. Zapperi (Geneva: 1970), p. 134.

16. Ibid., pp. 214f.

17. Ibid., p. 212.

18. Ibid., p. 216.

19. B. Güntzberg, "Die Gesellschafts- und Staatslehre der Physio-

kraten," Dissertation, Heidelberg, 1907; E. Richner, "Le Mercier de La Rivière," Dissertation, Zurich, 1931.

20. As chairman of the Commission for Popular Enlightenment, Condorcet took over this heritage of the Physiocrats in the Convention. See Güntzberg, "Physiokraten," p. 84, fn. 37.

21. B. Schickhardt, *Die Erklärung der Menschen- und Bürgerrechte in den Debatten der Nationalversammlung* (Berlin: 1931), p. 55ff.

22. Étienne Dumont, *Souvenirs sur Mirabeau et sur les deux premières assemblées législatives,* ed. Duval (Paris: 1932), p. 138.

23. Schickhardt, *Die Erklärung,* p. 56.

24. Ibid., p. 67.

25. Ibid., p. 69.

26. The interesting interpretation of E. Voegelin, "Der Sinn der Erklärung der Menschen- und Bürgerrechte," in *Zeitschrift für öffentliches Recht* 8 (1928): 82ff., fails to recognize this.

27. For the following see C. Becker, *The Declaration of Independence,* pp. 80–134.

28. *Works of James Wilson,* 1804, vol. 3, p. 99ff.

29. See Otto Vossler, "Studien zur Erklärung der Menschenrechte," in *Historische Zeitschrift* 142 (1930): 516ff.

30. O. Vossler, *Die amerikanischen Revolutionsideale in ihrem Verhältnis zu den europäischen* (Munich and Berlin: 1929), p. 26: "With that it is also clear how the Natural Law basis of the Bill of Rights of 1776 [sic], so often mentioned, is to be conceived. A comparison to its immediate predecessor, the so-called Bill of Rights of the Continental Congress, in which the appeal is still made to Natural Law and to the English Constitution and the Charters, shows that this Law of Nature of 1776 is really only a sort of residue; it is all that remains, when, due to the separation from the mother country, the appeal to the Constitution and the Charters becomes obsolete." To be sure, Vossler overlooks that it is just this residue which is revolutionary; for surreptitiously the universal principles of modern Natural Law have evolved out of classical Natural Law.

31. Actually, the essential elements of the classical doctrine of Natural Law can be found preserved in Locke's theory. The controversies in the most recent literature on Locke which have arisen over this are given a balanced presentation in W. Euchner, *Naturrecht und Politik bei John Locke* (Frankfurt: 1969). See also Euchner's introduction to Locke's Two Treatises translated into German: *Zwei Abhandlungen über die Regierung* (Frankfurt: 1967), especially p. 39ff. My interpretation refers primarily to the elements of "modern" Natural Law in Locke, neglecting his traditionalism.

32. Man already acquires property in the state of nature by the labor of his hands as he takes things out of their natural condition and appropriates them. By thus being fused with the labor power of man, nature finds its intended determination by becoming man's property. Thereby the bourgeois category of labor has liquidated the classical order of nature in which each thing evolves its essence in its own place. See John Locke, *Two Treatises of Civil Government,* II, ch. 5, 27.

33. Compare here the interpretation of Locke by Leo Strauss, *Natural Right and History* (Chicago: 1953).

34. The crucial statement reads: "The obligations of the law of

Nature cease not in society, but only in many cases are drawn closer, and have, by human laws, known penalties annexed to them to enforce their observation. Thus the law of Nature stands as an eternal rule to all men, legislators as well as others." Locke, *Two Treatises*, II, ch. 11, 135. See in detail the presentation in C. B. Macpherson, *The Political Theory of Possessive Individualism* (Oxford: 1962), chapter 5.

35. Locke, *Two Treatises*, II, ch. 11, 139.

36. Thomas Paine, *The Rights of Man*, ed. Seldon (London: 1958), p. 151.

37. Ibid., p. 161.

38. Paine, *Common Sense*, ed. Adkins (New York: 1953), p. 4f.

39. Ibid., p. 158.

40. For the following see Schickhardt, *Die Erklärung*, p. 77, also p. 63f.

41. Ibid., p. 81.

42. Leo Strauss, *Natural Right*, p. 250.

43. J. J. Rousseau, *Du Contrat Social*, II, 4.

44. Schickhardt, *Die Erklärung*, p. 45.

45. Article 21: the right to work and sustenance; Article 21: the right to public education.

46. Thomas Jefferson, in a letter to E. Carrington of January 16, 1787.

47. Iring Fetscher, *Rousseaus politische Philosophie*, 2nd ed. (Neuwied: 1965).

48. Robespierre, *Reden*, p. 358.

49. Ibid.

50. See the presentation of the New Religion and its cult in P. Bertaux, *Hölderlin und die französische Revolution* (Frankfurt: 1969).

51. Paine, *The Rights of Man*, p. 215.

52. See Vossler, *Amerikanische Revolutionsideale*, p. 149ff.

53. Robespierre, *Reden*, p. 322.

54. Paine, *The Rights of Man*, p. 175.

55. Ibid., p. 215.

56. A quite arbitrary interpretation of the relationship between the French and the American Revolutions is given by Hannah Arendt, *On Revolution* (New York: 1963). See my critique, "Die Geschichte von den zwei Revolutionen," in *Merkur* 218 (1966): 479ff.

57. Marx-Engels, *Werke*, vol. 3 (Berlin: 1959), p. 62.

58. Ibid., p. 75.

59. Ibid., p. 311ff.

60. Ibid., vol. 1 (Berlin: 1958), p. 369.

61. Ibid., p. 359.

62. Ibid., p. 366.

63. Ibid., vol. 7 (Berlin: 1969), p. 35. The *coup d'état* of Napoleon III, to which Marx devoted a special study under the title *The 18th Brumaire of Louis Napoleon*, he characterizes as follows: "Instead of society conquering itself to give itself a new content, the state appears to have gone back to its most ancient form, the simple unashamed domination by means of the sword and the monk's cowl." *Werke*, vol. 8 (Berlin: 1969).

64. See U. K. Preuss, *Zum staatsrechtlichen Begriff des Öffentlichen* (Stuttgart: 1969), especially chapter 3.

65. See my essay, "The Scientization of Politics and Public Opinion."

66. I have dealt with this in another context in my *Strukturwandel der Öffentlichkeit,* 5th ed. (Neuwied: 1971).

67. "The classical fundamental rights formulated in the liberal spirit have been transformed in their meaning under the new development of the state, even where they still bear the old form externally. To a large part they have been reformed into general legal principles, into the guarantees of legal institutions, and into organizational and corporative guarantees. Even where, according to the old form of rights, they have remained rights of freedom, they have become so permeated and circumscribed that they can only be called 'liberal' rights of freedom with reservations." E. R. Huber, "Bedeutungswandel der Grundrechte," in *Archiv des öffentlichen Rechts* 23 (1933): 79. To be sure, from this correct analysis, Huber arrives at a national constitution of a Fascist character. For he fails to recognize, that precisely in the welfare state [*Sozialstaat*] *the continuation of the tradition of the legal rights of the liberal state* requires that the function of the fundamental rights be transformed. For Huber's present position, see his study *Rechtsstaat und Sozialstaat in der modernen Industriegesellschaft* (Oldenburg: 1962).

68. For the legal discussion E. Forsthoff, ed., *Rechtsstaatlichkeit und Sozialstaatlichkeit,* Darmstadt, 1968.

69. See Habermas, *Strukturwandel der Öffentlichkeit.*

70. W. Abendroth, *Antagonistische Gesellschaft und politische Demokratie* (Neuwied: 1967).

71. R. Smend, "Integrationslehre" article in *Handwörterbuch der Sozialwissenschaften,* vol. 5 (Stuttgart: 1956), p. 299ff.

72. For example, E. Topitsch, *Sozialphilosophie zwischen Ideologie und Wissenschaft* (Neuwied: 1967).

Chapter 3

1. Joachim Ritter, *Hegel und die Französische Revolution,* Veröffentlichung der Arbeitsgemeinschaft für Forschung des Landes Nordrhein-Westfalen, H. 63 (Köln-Opladen: 1957), reprinted in J. Ritter, *Metaphysik und Politik* (Frankfurt: 1969), pp. 183–255; also J. Ritter, "Person und Eigentum," in the latter volume, pp. 256–280. See also Jean Hyppolite's contribution and that of Alfred Stern in *La Révolution de 1789 et la pensée moderne* (Paris: 1939).

2. Hegel, *Lectures on the Philosophy of History,* trans. J. Sibtree (London: 1881), p. 472.

3. Hegel, *Schriften zur Politik,* ed. Lasson, p. 157ff., now also in Hegel, *Politische Schriften* (Frankfurt: 1966), p. 140ff.

4. Hegel, *Schriften zur Politik,* p. 199.

5. See chapter 2 of this book.

6. Leo Strauss, *Natural Right and History* (Chicago: 1953), p. 120ff.

7. See the interpretation of Hobbes above, chapter 1.

8. Hegel, *The Phenomenology of Mind,* trans. J. B. Baillie (London/New York: 1966), pp. 604f. has translated the passage to which Habermas refers as follows: ". . . it divides itself into extremes equally abstract, into

cold unbending bare universality, and the hard discrete absolute rigidity and stubborn atomic singleness of actual self-consciousness . . .

"The relation, then, of these two, since they exist for themselves indivisibly and absolutely and thus cannot arrange for a common part to act as the means for connecting them, is pure negation entirely devoid of mediation, the negation, moreover, of the individual as a factor existing within the universal. The sole and only work accomplished by universal freedom is therefore *death*—a death that achieves nothing, embraces nothing within its grasp; for what is negated is the unachieved, unfulfilled punctual entity of the absolutely free self. It is thus the most cold-blooded and meaningless death of all, with no more significance than cleaving a head of cabbage or swallowing a draught of water.

9. This interpretation is criticized by A. Wildt, "Hegels Kritik des Jakobinismus," in O. Negt, ed., *Aktualität und Folgen der Philosophie Hegels* (Frankfurt: 1970), p. 256ff.

10. Edmund Burke, *Reflections on the Revolution in France.*

11. Hegel, *Philosophy of History*, trans. J. Sibtree (London: 1881), p. 466.

12. Hegel, *Philosophy of Right*, § 209ff.

13. This is analyzed by J. Ritter, *Metaphysik und Politik*, p. 35ff. See especially Georg Lukács, *Der junge Hegel* (Neuwied: 1967).

14. F. Wieacker, *Privatrechtsgeschichte der Neuzeit* (Göttingen: 1952).

15. For Hegel's incorporation of political economy, see P. Chamley, *Économie politique et philosophique chez Stewart et Hegel* (Paris: 1963); and M. Riedel, "Die Rezeption der Nationalökonomie," in *Studien zu Hegels Rechtsphilosophie* (Frankfurt: 1969), p. 75ff.

16. Hegel, *Politische Schriften*, p. 16ff.

17. K. Löwith, *Die Hegelsche Linke* (Stuttgart: 1962), Introduction.

18. Marx, *Critique of Hegel's Philosophy of Right*, trans. Annette Jolin and Joseph O'Malley (Cambridge University Press: 1970).

19. Hegel, *Politische Schriften*, p. 152.

20. Arguments against this thesis, which are worthy of note, are brought forward by H. Fulda, *Das Recht der Philosophie in Hegels Philosophie des Rechts* (Frankfurt: 1968).

21. Hegel, *Theologische Jugendschriften*, ed. Nohl, p. 284.

22. Hegel, *Jenenser Realphilosophie*, ed. Hofmeister, vol. 1, p. 239. See M. Riegel, "Hegels Bürgerliche Gesellschaft und das Problem ihres geschichtlichen Ursprungs," in *Archiv für Rechts- und Sozialphilosophie* 48 (1962): 539ff.

23. Karl Larenz, *Deutsche Rechtserneuerung und Rechtsphilosophie* (Tübingen: 1934), p. 9.

24. Larenz, *Rechts- und Staatsphilosophie der Gegenwart* (Berlin: 1935), p. 130.

25. J. Ritter, "Person und Eigentum" in *Metaphysik und Politik*, p. 278.

26. Herbert Marcuse, *Reason and Revolution*, new ed. (Boston: 1960).

27. *Hegel's Science of Logic*, trans. W. H. Johnston and L. G. Struthers (London: 1951), vol. II, pp. 460f.

28. Hegel, *Philosophy of History*, p. 23.

29. For this see the interpretation, which, however, deviates in other respects, of B. Liebruck, "Zur Theorie des Weltgeistes," in *Kantstudien* (1954–1955): 230ff.; now also in Liebruck, *Sprache und Bewusstsein,* vol. 3 (Frankfurt: 1966), p. 553ff. and p. 664ff.

30. This interpretation is opposed by M. Theunissen, who has presented an excellent report on the literature about the discussion of theory and praxis, taking its departure from Hegel, a report which also carries the discussion itself farther: M. Theunissen, *Die Verwirklichung der Vernunft,* Supplementary Issue (Beiheft) 6 of *Philosophische Rundschau* (Tübingen: 1970). For the metacritique of critical theory and the development of his own thesis on the unity of theory and praxis, see: M. Theunissen, *Gesellschaft und Geschichte* (Berlin: 1969); also, *Hegels Lehre vom absoluten Geist als theologisch-politischer Traktat* (Berlin: 1970).

31. Hegel, *Theologische Jugendschriften,* p. 224.

32. Ibid.

33. *Hegel's Science of Logic,* part 2, p. 465; see also *Rechtsphilosophie,* p. 16f.

34. Hegel, *Theologische Jugendschriften,* p. 225.

Chapter 4

1. *Das System der Sittlichkeit* is quoted from Lasson's edition of *Hegels Schriften zur Politik und Rechtsphilosophie, Sämtliche Werke,* vol. 7 (Leipzig: 1923), pp. 415–499; the two versions of the Jena *Philosophie des Geistes* were also edited by Lasson: *Jenenser Realphilosophie I, Sämtliche Werke,* vol. 19, p. 195ff., and *Jenenser Realphilosophie II, Sämtliche Werke,* vol. 20, p. 177ff.

2. G. Lukács, *Der junge Hegel* (Berlin: 1954).

3. The structure of the lectures also speaks in favor of this thesis. The categories of *language, tools,* and *family possession (Familiengut)* extend into the dimension of external existence and therefore belong, according to the later cogent divisions of the system, to the configuration (*Gestalten*) of the *objective spirit.* Still, in spite of this, they do not appear in the Jena version under the corresponding title of *real* (or *actual*) *spirit,* but instead appear in the first part of the *Philosophy of Spirit,* for which the editor has chosen the designation, within the system, of *subjective spirit.* Now according to the usage of the *Enzyklopädie,* subjective spirit consists of only those determinations which characterize the relationship of the cognitive and active subject to itself. The objectivations of language (transmitted symbols), of labor (productive forces), and of action in reciprocity (social roles) do not belong to this sphere. But in terms of them Hegel demonstrates the essence of spirit as an organization of middles (or middle ground). The Jena presentation obviously does not as yet obey the later system-structure. The "real spirit" is not set as preceding the level of subjective spirit, but represents a division which more appropriately might have borne the title "abstract spirit": in it Hegel specifies the abstract determinations of spirit in the sense of representing a unity of intelligence and will produced in fundamental connection with symbolic representation, labor, and interaction—and not in the sense of those abstractions which remain as subjective spirit when we separate from the formative process of spirit all the objectivation in which it has its external existence.

4. For another translation of this passage see *Hegel's Science of Logic*, trans. Johnston and Struthers, op. cit., vol. II, pp. 217f.

5. See D. Henrich, *Fichtes ursprüngliche Einsicht* (Frankfurt: 1967).

6. *Vorstellend*—see Translator's Notes.

7. From this viewpoint, that the process of individuation can only be conceived as socialization, and the latter in turn can only be conceived as individuation, Émile Durkheim, in his first great work *De la division du travail social* (1893), developed the basis of a sociological theory of action.

8. Hegel, *Jugendschriften*, ed. Nohl, p. 379.

9. *Realphilosophie II*, p. 201.

10. *Realphilosophie I*, p. 230.

11. In his posthumously published work *Mind, Self and Society* (1934), G. H. Mead repeats Hegel's insight—though under the naturalistic presuppositions of pragmatism—that the identity of the "I" can only constitute itself in the acquisition by practice of social roles, namely, in the complementary character of behavioral expectations on the basis of mutual recognition.

12. *Realphilosophie I*, p. 230.

13. See K. Heinrich, *Von der Schwierigkeit Nein zu sagen* (Frankfurt: 1965).

14. Kant, *Grundlegung zur Metaphysik der Sitten*, BA 98.

15. Ibid., p. 100f.

16. Hegel, *Enzyklopädie*, § 504ff.

17. Hegel, *Jugendschriften*, ed. Nohl, p. 278.

18. *Realphilosophie I*, p. 205.

19. Herder's prize essay "Über den Ursprung der Sprache" in *Sämtliche Werke*, ed. Suphan, vol. V (Berlin: 1891)—translated by Alexander Gode in *On the Origin of Language: Two Essays by Jean-Jacques Rousseau and Johann Gottfried Herder*, ed., John H. Moran and Alexander Gode (New York: 1966). [Only the first part of Herder's essay has been translated by Gode—Translator.]

20. *Realphilosophie I*, p. 211; on this see K. Löwith, "Hegel und die Sprache," in *Zur Kritik der christlichen Überlieferung*, 1966, p. 97ff.

21. *Realphilosophie I*, p. 221.

22. Hegel, *System der Sittlichkeit*, in Lasson, *Schriften zur Politik*, p. 428.

23. *Realphilosophie II*, p. 197.

24. Ibid., p. 199.

25. For this relation, which by no means corresponds to the teleology of spirit realizing itself, Hegel's *Logic* offers no appropriate category.

26. *Kant's Critique of Teleological Judgment*, trans. James Creed Meredith (Oxford: 1928), § 22 (83), p. 92.

27. "The tool as such thus wards off from man his material destruction; but in this it still remains . . . his activity. . . . In the machine man abolishes [sublates] even this formal activity of his, and lets the machine do all the work for him. But this deception which he carries out against nature . . . is avenged on him; by what he gains from nature, and the more he subjugates her, the lower he becomes himself. By letting a variety of machines work on nature, he does not abolish the necessity of his own working, but only defers it, makes it remote from nature, and is no longer oriented as a living being toward it as living nature [*richtet sich nicht*

lebendig auf sie als eine lebendige]; instead this negative living character takes flight, and the labor that remains for man itself becomes more machine-like" (*Realphilosophie I*, p. 237). Meanwhile, technical progress has gone far beyond that primitive stage represented by the mechanical loom; the stage which confronts us is characterized by the self-regulating control over system of goal-directed rational action; and it is uncertain whether the cunning consciousness of machines which simulate the achievements of consciousness will not one day be itself outwitted [*überlistet*], even if the worker then would no longer—because control has slipped from his hands— have to pay the price for the growing power of technological control which he has had to pay up to now in the currency of alienated labor—for then labor itself would become obsolete.

28. *Realphilosophie I*, p. 235.
29. *Realphilosophie II*, p. 221.
30. Ibid., p. 218.
31. Ibid., p. 219.
32. *System der Sittlichkeit*, p. 442.
33. Hegel, *Enzyklopädie*, § 433ff.
34. Ibid., § 384.
35. *Über die wissenschaftlichen Behandlungsarten des Naturrechts*, Jubiläumsausgabe, vol. 1, p. 500.
36. Ibid.
37. See chapters 3 and 5 of this volume.
38. K. Löwith, *Von Hegel zu Nietsche*, 1961; see also Löwith's introduction to the collection of texts *Die Hegelsche Linke* (Stuttgart: 1962).
39. See my *Knowledge and Human Interest* (Boston: 1971), especially chapter 3.

Chapter 5

1. W. R. Beyer, *Zwischen Phänomenologie und Logik: Hegel als Redakteur der Bamberger Zeitung* (Frankfurt: 1955).
2. H. Fulda, *Das Problem einer Einleitung in Hegels Wissenschaft der Logik* (Frankfurt: 1965).
3. The writings mentioned in the following are contained in Hegel, *Politische Schriften* (Frankfurt: 1966).
4. H. Falkenheim, "Eine unbekannte politische Druckschrift Hegels," in *Preussische Jahrbücher* 138 (1909).
5. See F. Rosenzweig, *Hegel und der Staat* (München-Berlin: 1920), p. 47ff.
6. K. Hoffmeister, *Dokumente zu Hegels Entwicklung* (Stuttgart: 1936), p. 248ff. and p. 549ff.
7. Rudolf Haym, *Hegel und seine Zeit* (1857; Darmstadt: 1962). [Haym was a biographer of strong liberal sentiments in the latter half of the nineteenth century. Aside from his biography of Hegel he also wrote lives of Wilhelm von Humboldt, Kant, and what is perhaps still the best biography of Herder.—Translator.]
8. Ibid.
9. K. Rosenkranz, *Apologie Hegels gegen Dr. R. Haym* (Berlin: 1958).
10. F. Rosenzweig, *Hegel*, p. 61ff.

11. Ibid., p. 88; K. Hoffmeister, *Dokumente*, p. 468ff.

12. W. R. Beyer, "Hegels Mitarbeit am 'Württembergischen Volksfreund,'" in *Zeitschrift für Philosophie*, vol. 14 14 (1966): 709ff.

13. F. Rosenzweig, Hegel, p. 48ff.

14. Hegel, *Lectures on the Philosophy of History*, trans. J. Sibtree (London: 1881), p. 472.

15. *Hegel's Science of Logic*, trans. W. H. Johnston and L. G. Struthers (London: 1951), vol. II, p. 460f.

16. Ibid., p. 465.

17. Ibid., p. 464.

18. See a differing interpretation in H. Fulda, *Das Recht der Philosophie in Hegels Philosophie des Rechts* (Frankfurt: 1968).

19. Hegel, *Theologische Jugendschriften*, pp. 267–293.

20. G. Rohrmoser, *Subjektivität und Verdinglichung* (Gütersloh: 1961); also, *Emanzipation und Freiheit* (Munich: 1970), especially chapter 4, "Theologie und Gesellschaft."

21. M. Riedel, "Tradition und Revolution in Hegels 'Philosophie des Rechts,'" in *Studien zu Hegels Rechtsphilosophie*, p. 100ff.

22. Hegel, "Wissenschaftliche Behandlungsarten des Naturrechts," *Sämtliche Werke*, ed. Glockner, vol. 1, p. 500ff. For this see M. Riedel, "Hegels Kritik des Naturrechts," in *Studien zu Hegels Rechtsphilosophie*, p. 42ff.

23. K. Hoffmeister, *Dokumente*, p. 352.

24. Hegel, *Theologische Jugendschriften*, pp. 219–229.

25. Hegel, *Sämtliche Werke*, vol. 1, p. 497f.

26. Ibid.

27. Hegel, *Jenenser Realphilosophie*, *Sämtliche Werke*, vol. 19, pp. 218–241; vol. 20, pp. 194–225.

28. G. Lukács, *Der junge Hegel* (Neuwied: 1967); see also Chapter 4 above.

29. Hegel, *Sämtliche Werke*, vol. 16, p. 351f.

30. Ibid., p. 355.

31. Ibid., p. 356.

32. Marx/Engels, *Werke*, vol. I (Berlin: 1958), p. 285.

33. E. Topitsch, *Die Sozialphilosophie Hegels als Heilslehre und Herrschaftsideologie* (Neuwied: 1967), especially p. 63ff.; a more appropriate judgment by H. R. Rotleuthner, "Die Substantialisierung des Formalrechts," in O. Negt, ed., *Aktualität und Folgen der Philosophie Hegels* (Frankfurt: 1970), p. 215ff.

34. K. R. Popper, *The Open Society and Its Enemies* (Princeton, N.J.: 1950).

35. E. Fleischmann, *La Philosophie politique de Hegel* (Paris: 1964).

36. Against this thesis, which in my view cannot be considered a reproach, the defense of Hegel is taken up by those, who, departing from the theological tradition, have undertaken to salvage Hegel's doctrine of absolute spirit. To be mentioned here, besides theologians like Küng and Pannenberg, are, on the one side, B. Liebruck, in *Sprache und Bewusstsein* (Frankfurt: 1964) and subsequently (in 5 volumes), and on the other, M. Theunissen, in *Hegels Lehre vom absoluten Geist als theologisch-politischer Traktat* (Berlin: 1970)—though in other respects they hold contrary positions.

37. On the critical reception of Hegel see O. Negt, *Aktualität und Folgen der Philosophie Hegels.*

Chapter 6

1. A. Shonfield, *Modern Capitalism* (London and New York: 1969).
2. Herbert Marcuse, *Eros and Civilization* (Boston: 1955).
3. See H. Arendt, *Konzentration in der westdeutschen Wirtschaft* (Pfullingen: 1966); J. Huffschmid, *Die Politik des Kapitals: Konzentration und Wirtschaftspolitik in der BRD* (Frankfurt: 1969); Gabriel Kolko, *Wealth and Power in America* (New York: 1962).
4. Popitz, Bahrdt, Kesting, Jüres, *Das Gesellschaftsbild des Arbeiters* (Tübingen: 1957); now also, F. Kern and M. Schuman, *Industriearbeit und Arbeiterbewusstsein* (Frankfurt: 1970).
5. See the Marxist critique of these theories in the *Monthly Review* 11 (1959); also *Periodikum* 12; recently, Paul A. Baran and Paul M. Sweezy, *Monopoly Capitalism* (New York: 1966).
6. Herbert Marcuse, *Soviet Marxism* (New York: 1958).
7. Of course, this perspective has changed considerably since 1960, due to, above all, China's political role and the movements for national liberation in the Third World.
8. To be sure, it was only the war in Vietnam which again awakened a theoretical interest in the problem of imperialism and the international division of labor.
9. For Poland see the recent excellent Marxist investigation of J. Kuron and K. Modzelewski, *Monopolkapitalismus* (Hamburg: 1969).
10. *Marxismusstudien des evangelischen Studiengemeinschaft*, Tübingen, vol. 1, 1954; vol. 2, 1957; vol. 3, 1960; vol. 4, 1962.
11. An argument against Landgrebe's position is contained in A. Wellmer, *Kritische Gesellschaftstheorie und Positivismus* (Frankfurt: 1969), chapter 2.
12. For this, see G. Hillmann, *Marx und Hegel* (Frankfurt: 1966).
13. T. W. Adorno, *Zur Metakritik der Erkenntnistheorie* (Stuttgart: 1956), especially the Introduction, p. 12ff.
14. Note, however, that there is a renaissance of study concerning the systematic problems of political economy:
On Marx's economic writings: R. Rodolski, *Zur Entstehungsgeschichte des Marxschen 'Kapitals'* (Frankfurt: 1969); Ernest Mandel, *The Formation of the Economic Thought of Karl Marx* (New York: 1971); H. Reichelt, *Zur logischen Struktur des Kapitalbegriffs bei Marx* (Frankfurt: 1970).
Contributions to the renewal of Marxist economic theory: Above all, Paul Sweezy, *The Theory of Capitalist Development* (New York: 1942), *The Present as History* (New York: 1953); P. A. Baran, *The Political Economy of Growth* (New York: 1967); P. A. Baran and Paul M. Sweezy, *Monopoly Capitalism* (New York: 1966); M. Dobb, *Studies in the Development of Capitalism* (London: 1963), *Welfare Economics and the Economics of Socialism* (London: 1969); C. H. Feinstein, ed., *Socialism, Capitalism, and Economic Growth* (Cambridge: 1967); E. Mandel, *Marxist Economic Theory* (New York: 1969); E. Varga, *The Great Crisis and Its Political Consequences* (London: 1935); J. M. Gillman, *Prosperity in Crisis* (New York: 1965); Paul

Mattick, *Marx und Keynes* (Frankfurt: 1970); E. Altvater, *Gesellschaftliche Produktion und ökonomische Rationalität* (Frankfurt: 1968); H. Hemberger, L. Maier, H. Petrak, O. Reinhold, and K. H. Schwank (Institut für Gesellschaftswissenschaften beim ZK der SED [Central Committee of the (East German) Socialist Unity Party]), *Imperialismus heute: Der staatmonopolistische Kapitalismus in Westdeutschland* (Berlin: 1966).

On the relationship of Marxist and bourgeois economics: D. Horowitz, ed., *Marx and Modern Economics* (New York: 1968); O. Lange, *Politische Ökonomie* (Frankfurt: 1968); J. Robinson, *Collected Economic Papers* (New York: 1957), *Economics, an Awkward Corner* (London: 1966); A. Löwe, *Politische Ökonomie* (Frankfurt: 1968); for more recent analyses of advanced capitalism, J. K. Galbraith, *The New Industrial State* (Boston: 1967); R. L. Heilbronner, *The Limits of American Capitalism* (New York: 1966; A. Shonfield, *Modern Capitalism* (London and New York: 1969); E. Varga, *Die Krise des Kapitalismus und ihre politischen Folgen* (Frankfurt: 1969); M. Kidron, *Western Capitalism Since the War* (London: 1970).

[The above is a somewhat condensed list compiled from the bibliographical note appended to this chapter in the German edition of 1971.— Translator.]

15. Max Horkheimer and T. W. Adorno, *Die Dialektik der Aufklärung* (Amsterdam: 1947); H. M. Enzensberger, "Bewusstseinsindustrie," in *Einzelheiten* (Frankfurt: 1962).

16. See note 14 above.

17. R. Bendix and S. M. Lipset, eds., *Class, Status, Power* (New York: 1966).

18. J. Schumpeter, *Kapitalismus, Sozialismus und Demokratie* (Bern: 1950), p. 17ff.

19. For this and the following compare my changed conception in *Zur Logik der Sozialwissenschaften* (Frankfurt: 1970), and *Knowledge and Human Interest* (Boston: 1971); also in the Introduction to this volume.

20. For a revision of the conventional theory of social roles, which to a large extent obviates these doubts, see L. Krappmann, *Soziologische Dimensionen der Identität* (Stuttgart: 1971); also H. Popitz, *Der Begriff der sozialen Rolle* (Tübingen: 1967); H. P. Dreitzel, *Die gesellschaftlichen Leiden und das Leiden an der Gesellschaft* (Stuttgart: 1968).

21. R. Dahrendorf, "Homo Sociologicus," in *Kölner Zeitschrift für Soziologie und Sozialpsychologie* 10 (1958); "Sozialwissenschaft und Werturteil" in *Gesellschaft und Freiheit* (1961), p. 27ff.

22. Kant, *Critique of Pure Reason,* trans. N. K. Smith (New York: 1928), A651, pp. 537f.

23. Max Horkheimer, "Traditionelle und kritische Theorie," in *Zeitschrift für Sozialforschung* (1937): 253, 264; now also in *Kritische Theorie* (Frankfurt: 1968), vol. 2.

24. See for example, E. Topitsch, *Sozialphilosophie zwischen Ideologie und Wissenschaft* (Neuwied: 1962).

25. See my inaugural lecture "Erkenntnis und Interesse" in *Technik und Wissenschaft als "Ideologie"* (Frankfurt: 1968).

26. This is based on studies concerning the history of ideas in R. Koselleck, *Kritik und Krise* (Freiburg: 1959), p. 189ff.

27. For the relationship, in the history of ideas, between the dialectic and mysticism, see most recently E. Topitsch, "Marxismus und

Gnosis," in *Sozialphilosophie zwischen Ideologie und Wissenschaft* (Neuwied: 1962), p. 235ff.

28. Marx, *Frühschriften*, p. 17.

29. Hegel, *Heidelberger Enzyklopädie*, ed. Glockner, § 391.

30. A. Schmidt, in the introduction to L. Feuerbach, *Anthropologischer Materialismus*, vol. I (Frankfurt: 1967), pp. 5–56.

31. Marx, *Capital*, trans. Eden and Cedar Paul, vol. 1 (New York: 1928), p. 45; on this recently, H. Reichelt, *Zur logischen Struktur des Kapitalbegriffs bei Marx* (1970).

32. Marx, *Capital*, vol. 1, p. 49. Bracketed material is found in the English translation but is not quoted by the author.

33. Ibid., p. 154.

34. Marx, *Capital*, vol. 3 (Moscow: 1962), p. 245.

35. See M. Gillmann, *Das Gesetz des tendenziellen Falls der Profitrate* (Frankfurt: 1969).

36. Marx, *Capital*, vol. 3, p. 209.

37. R. Rosdolsky, "Zur neueren Kritik des Marxschen Gesetzes der fallenden Profitrate," in *Kyklos* 9 (1956): 208ff.

38. Thus N. Moszkowska, *Das Marxsche System* (Berlin: 1929), p. 118.

39. R. Rosdolsky, "Zur neueren Kritik," p. 219, fn. 23, 24.

40. J. Robinson, *An Essay on Marxian Economics;* see also her *Collected Economic Papers* and *Essays on the Theory of Economic Growth* (New York: 1962).

41. Marx, *Grundrisse der Kritik der Politischen Ökonomie* (Berlin: 1953), p. 592. See *The Grundrisse—Karl Marx,* ed. and trans. by David McLellan (New York: 1971), p. 141. Only extensive excerpts from the *Grundrisse* are included in this volume.

42. See the recent work of R. Rosdolsky, *Zur Entstehungsgeschichte des Kapitals* (Frankfurt: 1968).

43. Marx, *Grundrisse*, pp. 243, 246. This passage is not included in McLellan, *op. cit.*

44. Ibid., p. 592f. See also McLellan, *op. cit.*, p. 142.

45. In this way the legitimate objection raised by various Keynesians could be met, that "the Ricardian-Marxian use of man-hours of socially necessary labor time as the unit of calculation led to an almost exclusive concentration upon the distribution of the national product among the different social classes" (John Strachey, *Contemporary Capitalism* [New York: 1956], p. 143f). Only with the help of modern statistical methods could a determination of the social product in its volume also be attained: "The problem of finding a measure of real output . . . is not solved by reckoning in terms of value, for the rate of exchange between value and output is constantly altering" (J. Robinson, *Marxian Economics*, p. 19f.). Actually the "real output" can only appear in the computation of value, when the index of productivity is taken into consideration in the law of value.

46. Marx, *Capital*, vol. 1, p. 158.

47. For a critique of my considerations here, see M. Müller, "Habermas und die Anwendbarkeit der Arbeitswertstheorie," in *Zeitschrift Sozialistische Politik* (April 1969): 39–53; also K. Hartmann, *Die Marxsche Theorie* (Berlin: 1970), p. 382ff., p. 471f.

48. Marx, *Capital*, vol. 3, p. 239f.

49. Ibid., p. 252. [The English translation reads here: ". . . a law which, being understood and hence controlled by their common mind, brings the productive process under their joint control."—Translator.]

50. J. Strachey, *Contemporary Capitalism,* pp. 182, 185; see also J. Robinson, *Marxian Economics.*

51. On the theory of state intervention under advanced capitalism, see: J. K. Galbraith, *The Affluent Society;* M. Kidron, *Western Capitalism Since the War;* A. Shonfield, *Modern Capitalism.*

52. Marx, *Capital,* vol. 3, p. 253.

53. Against this, F. Tomberg, *Basis und Überbau* (Neuwied: 1969); W. Müller and Ch. Neusüss, "Die Sozialstaatsillusion und der Widerspruch von Lohnarbeit und Kapital," in *Zeitschrift Sozialistische Politik* (October 1970): 4ff.; a promising beginning for an analysis of the changed relationship between the political and the economic system is developed by C. Offe, "Politische Herrschaft und Klassenstrukturen," in Kress and Senghaas, eds., *Politikwissenschaft* (Frankfurt: 1969), p. 155ff.; also, J. Hirsch, *Wissenschaftlich-technischer Fortschritt und politisches System* (Frankfurt: 1970).

54. Strachey, *Contemporary Capitalism,* p. 181; see also the studies mentioned above of Galbraith, Kidron, Offe, and Shonfield.

55. See my interpretation of Marx in *Knowledge and Human Interest,* p. 25ff.

56. See the recent textbook brought out by A. Kosing, *Marxistische Philosophie.* For the relationship of Marxism in its original form to the distorted form of "Diamat," see G. Lichtheim, *Marxism: A Historical and Critical Study* (London: 1961), *A Short History of Socialism* (London: 1970); I. Fetscher, *Karl Marx und der Marxismus: Von der Philosophie des Proletariats zur politischen Weltanschauung* (Munich: 1967).

57. Marx, *The German Ideology,* Fourth Thesis on Feuerbach, Parts I and II, edited by R. Pascal (New York: 1947), pp. 197f.

58. E. Bloch, *Das Prinzip Hoffnung* (Frankfurt: 1959), *Tübinger Einleitung in die Philosophie,* expanded ed. (Frankfurt: 1970).

59. See the posthumous publication of T. W. Adorno's *Ästhetische Theorie* (Frankfurt: 1970).

60. See my study of Adorno, "Vorgeschichte der Subjektivität und verwilderte Selbstbehauptung," in *Philosophisch-politische Profile* (Frankfurt: 1971), pp. 184–199.

61. See A. Wellmer, *Kritische Gesellschaftstheorie und Positivismus* (Frankfurt: 1969), p. 69ff.

62. Vico, *The New Science,* trans. T. G. Bergin and M. H. Fisch (Ithaca, N.Y.: 1948), book 1, § 349.

63. Löwith's remark is correct insofar as Vico's is no longer in conformity with his own principle, when, toward the end of his work, he speculates on a completion of world-history. See K. Löwith, *Weltgeschichte und Heilsgeschehen* (Stuttgart: 1953), p. 124.

64. See my study on the relation of politics and morality in *Das Problem der Ordnung,* ed. Kuhn and Wiedmann (Meisenheim: 1962), p. 94ff.

65. Horkheimer treats the problem of prediction in the social sciences in this sense in *Zeitschrift für Sozialforschung* 2 (1933): 407ff.

66. Against this, see H. Kesting, *Geschichtsphilosophie und Weltbürgerkrieg* (Heidelberg: 1959).

67. I myself have often made uncritical use of the idea of a human

species which constitutes itself as the subject of world-history in this book as well as in subsequent writings. It was not until I began my preliminary work on a communication theory of society that the import and implications of the hypostatizing generation of subjectivity on the higher levels became clear to me. See Habermas and Luhmann, *Theorie der Gesellschaft oder Sozialtechnologie* (Frankfurt: 1971), pp. 172–181, and also the Introduction to this book.

Chapter 7

1. I have treated this since in *Knowledge and Human Interest* (Boston: 1971).

2. See my investigation, *Technik und Wissenschaft als "Ideologie"* (Frankfurt: 1968). The essay of that title appears as "Technology and Science as Ideology" in *Toward a Rational Society* (Boston: 1970).

3. Paul Thiry d'Holbach, *Nature and Her Laws by Mirabaud* (London: 1816), p. 1. See on this G. Mensching, *Totalität und Autonomie: Untersuchungen zur philosophischen Gesellschaftstheorie des französischen Materialismus* (Frankfurt: 1971).

4. Holbach, pp. 5f. The 1816 English version has a slightly different translation.

5. Ibid., p. 5.

6. Johann G. Fichte, *Werke,* ed. Medicus (Darmstatt: 1962), vol. 3, p. 17.

7. Ibid.

8. Schelling, *Werke,* Münchner Jubiläumsausgabe, vol. I, p. 236.

9. Ibid., p. 229.

10. On Fichte, see W. Schulz, *J. G. Fichte, Vernunft und Freiheit* (Pfullingen: 1962); W. Weischedel, *Der Zwiespalt im Denken Fichtes* (Berlin: 1962).

11. Fichte, *Werke,* vol. 3, p. 17.

12. An insight which Horkheimer and Adorno developed in their *Dialektik der Aufklärung.* See my study on Adorno's philosophy in *Philosophisch-politische Profile* (Frankfurt: 1971), pp. 176–199.

13. See Habermas, *Knowledge and Human Interest.*

14. On the Semiotics of Charles Morris, see K. O. Apel, "Sprache und Wahrheit," in *Philosophische Rundschau* 7 (1959): 161ff.; "Szientismus oder transzendentale Hermeneutik?" in R. Bubner (et al.), *Hermeneutik und Dialektik,* vol. 1 (Tübingen: 1970), pp. 105–144.

15. With the exception of the values immanent to science which are specified by the logical and methodological rules.

16. Ontological doctrines fall under this as well as dialectical ones, classical Natural Law as well as modern philosophies of history. It is not accidental that Popper places Plato in the ranks of the great dogmatists next to Hegel and Marx—as so-called Historicists.

17. E. Topitsch, *Sozialphilosophie zwischen Ideologie und Wissenschaft* (Neuwied: 1962), p. 279.

18. See G. Gäfgen, *Theorie der wissenschaftlichen Entscheidung* (Tübingen: 1963).

19. Ibid., p. 26f. "The result of the decision must by no means appear as 'reasonable' in the ordinary sense, as the actor may have a value system,

which though it is coherent in itself, may appear absurd in comparison to that of other actors. Such absurdity can only be defined by comparison to a standard of normality of values and goals. . . . This kind of irrationality refers to the content and not to the form of the decisions."

20. Ibid., p. 99.

21. Ibid., p. 176ff.

22. John Dewey, *The Quest for Certainty* (New York: 1960), p. 43.

23. H. Rittel, "Überlegungen zur wissenschaftlichen und politischen Bedeutung der Entscheidungstheorien," Studiengruppe für Systemforschung, Heidelberg, MS, p. 29f.; "Instrumentelles Wissen in der Politik," in H. Krauch, ed., *Wissenschaft ohne Politik* (Heidelberg: 1966), pp. 183–209.

24. See N. Luhmann, *Zweckbegriff und Systemrationalität* (Tübingen: 1968).

25. K. R. Popper, *The Open Society and Its Enemies* (Princeton, N.J.: 1950).

26. D. Pole, *Conditions of Rational Inquiry* (London: 1961), p. 30ff.

27. See the concluding chapter of G. Radnitsky, *Contemporary Schools of Metascience*, vol. 2, 2nd ed. (Göteborg: 1970).

28. H. Albert, "Ethik und Metaethik," in *Archiv für Philosophie*, vol. 2, 1961, p. 59f.; *Traktat über kritische Vernunft* (Tübingen: 1968), especially chapter 3.

29. See *Toward a Rational Society*, pp. 50f.

Index